The Challenge for Government

THE CHALLENGE FOR GOVERNMENT

Priorities for the Next Five Years

Edited by

Joe Mulholland

The Liffey Press

Published by
The Liffey Press
Ashbrook House
10 Main Street
Raheny, Dublin 5, Ireland
www.theliffeypress.com

A catalogue record of this book is
available from the British Library.

ISBN 978-1-905785-38-4

Photographs by Michael O'Donnell
Additional Photos by Mary Ita Boyle

Printed in Ireland by Colour Books.

Contents

Contents

Contents

Contents

12. Reinforcing the European Union

Acknowledgements

This book would not have appeared without the generous help given to us again by Mr. Paddy Kelly of Redquartz Developments, Dr. Martin Naughton of Glen Dimplex, Mr. Tony Sheridan of CampusIT and Mr. Maurice Regan and we are very grateful to them for their invaluable support and encouragement.

We are, of course, grateful also to this year's contributors to the MacGill School who provided for the most part the contents of the book and who gave unstintingly of their time to write papers and travel to Donegal in July. I feel especially indebted to those government ministers and opposition spokespersons who, so soon after what was a hard fought and demanding election campaign, agreed to take time out of their schedules to talk at MacGill about the priorities for government for the next five years.

This is the second of our volumes to be published by The Liffey Press and I thank them, and especially their MD, Mr. David Givens, for their help, courtesy and unfailing professionalism.

The MacGill Summer School itself would not have become the institution it now is without the generous support of a few friends and benefactors. We take this opportunity of thanking in particular Donegal Co. Council, RTE, Donegal Local Development Co. and the EU Commission Representative's office in Dublin.

The help and advice of Mr. Charles Byrne who brings, with many other qualities, his technical expertise, Ms. Nuala Naughton, and RTE journalists Mr. Tommie Gorman, Mr. Joe Little, Mr. George Lee and Mr. Paul Cunningham are of such importance to us and are deeply valued and appreciated.

Also important and invaluable are the help and support of Mr Michael Norris and his son Karl, and we thank them.

We would also like to thank our Committee in Glenties and, in particular, the Chairman, Mr. Michael Gallagher and the Secretary, Ms. Mary Claire O'Donnell, who has been a stalwart of the School over the past twenty-seven years.

And, of course, there is the much valued Highlands Hotel with its kind owners, the Boyle family, and its wonderful staff who, year after year, provide an oasis of welcome and hospitality to the participants and guests of MacGill and we wish to thank them here publicly for their help and kindness.

Joe Mulholland
October 2007

Joe Mulholland

Director of the MacGill Summer School & Arts Week

Born in Donegal and educated at Stranorlar Boys' N.S., the Finn College, Ballybofey, De La Salle Teachers' Training College Manchester, University of Nancy, France (L.ès.L., Doctorat ès L.) and University of London (BA Hons.). Held several executive positions in RTÉ and is an award-winning documentary producer. With a local committee in Glenties, founded the MacGill Summer School in 1981 and, with the exception of a few years, has been the school's Director since then. Has chaired the News Group of the European Broadcasting Union 1992-6 and has contributed to the French media including the newpaper, Le Monde. He is currently chairman of the Board of the National College of Art & Design (NCAD). Received a Donegal Person of the Year award in 2002.

Foreword

It is hard to believe that the MacGill Summer School is now in its twenty-seventh year and that it has been witness to such momentous change in Northern Ireland as well as in the Republic. Even as recently as last year, the session on Northern Ireland on the last evening of the School, with some of the contributors so divided and apparently so entrenched, many members of the large audience went out into the July night wondering if there would ever be real progress made in the North and if trust could ever be established. This year, our sessions on Northern Ireland were, whilst not forgetting the hurt and sadness that still endure and the problems to be overcome, about looking forward in Northern Ireland, about planning its economic and social future and about building trust and confidence between the communities. The euphoria felt by all on May 8th of this year endures and was certainly to be experienced in Glenties in July and is reflected in the pages of this volume.

Regarding the other part of the island of Ireland, in the tradition of the MacGill school we also looked to the future and discussed the priorities which our new coalition government, brought to office after a hard-fought campaign, must now deal with. As we approach the end of the first decade of the new century, we live in uncertain times and nothing can be taken for granted. Our economy and its state of health is obviously the main priority but by no means the only one. It is true that the Irish economy continues to perform well with a growth rate that is the envy of Europe but there are worrying signs that need to be heeded and acted upon, particularly in the areas of our productivity and competitiveness, and we have here the views of An Tanaiste and Minister of Finance Brian Cowen TD as well as of Joan Burton TD and of Jim O'Hara and Brian O'Connell who are at the coalface of our industrial life. Their views on the future shape and physiognomy of what has become known as the Celtic Tiger are certainly worthy of everyone's attention.

There are of course other priorities that have to be faced up to and, in fact, have a direct bearing on the future performance of the economy and consequently on the future well-being of all our citizens. None is more pressing than the future sources of our energy which is now the responsibility of one of the first Green ministers in the history of the state, Eamon Ryan TD. As the price of oil continues to rise with some producing countries remaining very unstable and oil reserves now becoming dangerously depleted, the industrial nations of the world and in particular Ireland, with its over-dependency on imported oil, are vulnerable.

And, in any case, there is the problem of climate change which, as the other Green minister, John Gormley, points out, is now the greatest threat to our planet and to mankind. There is obviously an urgent need for all countries, including Ireland, with an excess of greenhouse gas emissions to play their full part in replacing fossil fuels by renewable energy and implementing energy-saving measures as well as perhaps, as argued by Dr. Ed Walsh in his paper, taking seriously on board the nuclear energy option. A crucially important question asked here is how can Ireland meet its obligations and play its part in the battle against climate change whilst at the same time continue to build its economy. In any case, these chapters are required reading not only for environmentalists, and most of us at this stage belong to that group, but for anyone who wishes to be informed by the most up to date data and research available.

And again allied to the future of the economy and its capacity to compete in the world marketplace is our system of education and the level of our investment in it. Everyone agrees that the fact that Ireland had a well-educated young population was one of the factors which contributed substantially to our economic miracle. There are, though, increasing worries that we are not keeping up with the demand for research and development-based industries and that we are not taking sufficient measures to ensure that we are near the top of the world league in education at all levels. As is evident from the papers on the economy and on education, how we invest in education and what policy decisions we take regarding it are as important as the state of our infrastructure or the price and sources of energy and labour.

The state of our public service and the need to reform it has also a direct bearing on our economy. It is now generally recognised that without an efficient public service that gives value for the taxpayers' money spent, recognises and promotes talent and effort and in which every measure of productivity does not have to be accompanied by special pay awards, the economic life of the country will be put in jeopardy by constantly rising costs and our competitiveness, already under pressure, further endangered. Reading this chapter must lead to the conclusion that this is one of the government's most pressing priorities and one of its most difficult challenges.

Other challenges facing our new government include some that have been the subject of analysis and debate in Glenties in the past. The state of our health service remains one of the most difficult. In spite of considerable amounts of taxpayers' money having been, and continuing to be, spent on it, this crucially important area of the public services remains in a perilous and unsatisfactory state. As our contributors to this chapter make clear, it is not only a question of money or private versus public (and this debate is present in these pages) but the problem is multi-faceted. Disease prevention, for example, and emphasis on a healthy lifestyle would go a long way towards contributing to a health service capable of responding more speedily to those in genuine and dire need of treatment and care. Usually, not enough emphasis is placed on this side of the argument in the debate which is apparently set to continue over the next five years.

All in all, the small and pleasing town of Glenties was once more a hive of thought, argument and debate in mid-July as our eminent contributors and their incredibly attentive audiences focused on some of the principal issues facing the new administrations in Dublin and Belfast. The fruits of their deliberations, reproduced here, are essential reading for all those interested in Ireland and its future welfare and development.

Mark Hennessy, Political Correspondent, *The Irish Times*

Introduction

The Next Five Years May Well Be More Testing

MARK HENNESSY
Political Correspondent, *The Irish Times*

Mark Hennessy

Political Correspondent, *The Irish Times*

Born in London and brought up in Co. Cork. Educated at Mitchelstown CBS. Previously held several positions with The Cork Examiner (now The Irish Examiner) including news editor, Europe editor and political correspondent. Young Journalist of the Year in 1988, European Journalist of the Year in 2000 and Political Journalist of the Year in 2002.

The Next Five Years May Well Be More Testing

Sometimes, historic change can seem very ordinary. Indeed, the true measure of momentous events is often the very ordinariness of life that they allow to spring forth. For nearly 30 years, people have gathered in Glenties for the Patrick MacGill Summer School during the darkest days of the Troubles that blighted both sides of the Border. There were times, as Joe Mulholland said in his concluding remarks at this year's school, when many in the hall were in despair, bereft of hope, full of dread for the future.

Through it all, the MacGill Summer School gave a platform to many, often conflicting, voices; and helped, perhaps, to grow relationships that later became important. This year, however, all had changed. Instead of tribal loyalties, key players in Northern Ireland came to speak about Northern Ireland's economy, its need for better infrastructure. The talk was of reform in the public services, not revolution; an end to poverty, rather than an end to the union; the delivery of better health services, not a united Ireland.

A summer school first-timer, the Democratic Unionist Party's Ian Paisley Junior, spoke of the lasting settlement and political stability that had been achieved. Indeed, significant parts of his speech could have been swapped with that of Sinn Fein's Martin McGuinness, such was the degree of unity of purpose between the two.

For now, Northern politicians are understandably basking in the pleasures of office. However, such pleasures are not guaranteed, and do not last.

For now, Northern politicians are understandably basking in the pleasures of office. However, such pleasures are not guaranteed, and do not last. The Northern public had for the most part switched off politics before 2007's extraordinary events when NI hurtled towards a settlement on roads where it had previously dallied. The speed of the deal surprised many and left some doubters; yet there is little doubt but that politicians must soon make significant differences to the lives of the ordinary people. But the scale of the challenge ahead is daunting, as pointed out by Northern Ireland business leader, Stephen Kingon, who highlighted the North's dependency on public jobs.

Internationally, the appearance of Republican, Nationalist and Unionist leaders speaking with one voice will be a major selling point as Northern Ireland seeks foreign investment. But the gloss offered by such unity is not indefinite. Many of those directly involved know only too well that Northern Ireland must strike quickly.

For years, the Democratic Unionist Party displayed a bombastic confidence which rather poorly concealed the underlying resentment, fear and, sometimes, sense of inferiority of many of its members. Today, though, the DUP is more genuinely confident in itself and confident that its enemies on its own side of the divide are in retreat, can be brought into a closer alliance, or unsure of what to do next. "The pressure on us was not to do things quickly, but to do them right. The patient approach has transformed the political situation in Northern Ireland," said Paisley.

The fact that Paisley was there at all was in itself interesting. The fact that McGuinness felt that he could quietly have fun at his expense about how he got there by helicopter was even more so. McGuinness is such a regular at the MacGill school that he has begun to perform by rote, as he once more showed with tales of visiting Ardara native, now in her nineties, Molly Gallagher. Annually, she receives a bottle of whiskey from the Derryman on his way to Glenties. Annually, McGuinness tells MacGill all about her.

In the Republic, the exhaustion left by the general election had not yet faded before senior politicians began to make the annual pilgrimage to Glenties – this time to debate the priorities that should be set for the five years.

Fine Gael leader Enda Kenny opened the summer school though, to be frank, the speech was somewhat tame, lacking fresh ideas; the work, perhaps, of people who wanted to be on holidays. And he pulled some of his punches. In his prepared speech, he had accused Fianna Fáil of running an election campaign based on "fear and scaremongering" and dishonest attacks. Speaking in the Highlands Hotel, faced with some Fianna Fáil supporters in the hall, he dropped the dishonesty charge. The year had been too long for a needless row now, perhaps.

In his speech, Finance Minister Brian Cowen offered some blunt thoughts on Ireland's future, warning that, while costs must be controlled, this alone, even if it could be brought about, would not be enough to safeguard the country's future. "Countries cannot compete on the back of low costs alone. I for one do not want to live in a low-cost, low-wage economy. I do want Ireland to be a country that competes not on the back of endless rounds of cost reductions, but rather on the back of the stronger grounds of profitability and value creation," he declared.

In his speech, Finance Minister Brian Cowen offered some blunt thoughts on Ireland's future, warning that, while costs must be controlled, this alone, even if it could be brought about, would not be enough to safeguard the country's future.

So often, Cowen, bright, articulate, stands just one step away from offering a real political vision, but he may soon have greater opportunities to show his mettle since Exchequer figures, while still good, will be tighter in 2007 than they have been for some years. In a shot across the bow of the trade unions, the Government, he said, would not concede benchmarking pay increases to State employees without real productivity gains, but history does not inspire confidence. The first round of benchmarking, which now costs the taxpayer €1 billion a year was a farrago of half-truths, buttressed by analysis never since revealed. Too often, the reality on the ground falls short of the rhetoric.

In a shot across the bow of the trade unions, the Government, he said, would not concede benchmarking pay increases to State employees without real productivity gains, but history does not inspire confidence.

If proof were needed that benchmarking has failed to live up to any of its promises, it most certainly came from IMPACT general secretary and former Irish Congress of Trade Unions' President, Peter McLoone. According to McLoone, the jury is still out on whether benchmarking pay awards to State workers, now costing €1.3 billion annually, helped to improve public services; and it was clear that the public did not believe it had delivered much. He warned that public sector workers are now increasingly under a critical spotlight. The choice for unions – particularly public service unions – is to let those who care more for private profit than for public service to set the agenda, or to boldly set it ourselves.

"Campaigns to defend public services must start from the premise that our strongest allies are the people we serve," he told a debate on the need for public service reform. Continuing, he asserted that "There remains a strong culture of support for public provision throughout this island, where ordinary people have no stomach for the unfettered free market approach," However, he proceeded to inform the audience that he doesn't "think that that will remain unless the consumer out there can see a vast improvement in some areas."

He also warned that "Unions have a responsibility to genuinely engage with debates about the quality, more responsiveness and increased flexibility in service provision if we are to retain public belief in our own bona fides. That means our campaigns must go beyond protecting the status quo and restating what we are against". However, it remains to be seen if civil and public servants will follow Mr McLoone's line when it comes to the negotiation of a second round of benchmarking, even if the Government will not be so keen, or in a position to buy industrial peace.

Freed from the constraints of working within the State system, the usually outspoken Cormac Lucey, the former special adviser to the Progressive Democrat Tánaiste and Minister for Justice, Michael McDowell, was even more outspoken than ever. Public officials, he said, should be put under the microscope just as often, if not more so, than politicians. For too long, the Irish civil and public service has hidden behind an anonymity, helpful when responsibility is to be avoided.

"There are outstanding civil servants. But there are weak, venal and lazy public servants who are shielded by the reluctance of the trade union movement to have transparent accountability of such people…. The trade unions' championing of strong public servants is weakened by its reluctance to allow fair and just treatment of those who are weak, who come into work at 11.00 am and who might leave at 2.30 pm," said Lucey.

This reality gap between the State's performance and what it says it wants was graphically illustrated by Minister for Community, Rural and Gaeltacht Affairs, Eamon Ó Cuív, during his passionate promotion to the summer school of the value of rural life. Sharply attacking his own local authority, Galway County Council, in the question and answer session for its policy of insisting on roadside construction near to services, he said, rightly, that it has led to the destruction of much of the landscape in the countryside.

"Planners", he said, "should heed the Government's edict and allow more rural houses; but hide them away down lanes and valleys" "I had endless, endless rows with Galway County Council. They have destroyed, and this is the irony of it, the landscape of rural Ireland and at the same time resisted allowing people live in rural Ireland. "How they have done it is by their absolute insistence on road frontage, and the dragging of people down on to the main roads, on to the tourist roads, instead of 'losing' our houses in the folds and the hollows, the hills of Ireland, where you could have lost twice as many houses, preserved our landscape and at the same time preserved our rural population," said Mr Ó Cuív.

In reality, Mr Ó Cuív's suggestion would do something to halt the spread of unsightly ribbon development on every minor road in the country, but it will do little to deal with the water, transport and sewage issues provoked by such planning. And it is the job of the government of the day to set national guidelines, and to ensure that they are honoured by the local authorities. Too often, the Government acts as if it is an interested bystander, left to pick up the mistakes of others. It is not, and it should not be. Land should not be zoned without full provision being made for schools and other necessary social services. The Lotto-like winnings enjoyed by landowners over the last decade have been at the expense of society at large.

For the last five years, politicians have had to make few enough hard choices as the resources were there to cover most, though not all, requirements. The next five years may well be more testing. Vision will be required; and it is something of which we have too little in Irish politics.

And it is the job of the government of the day to set national guidelines, and to ensure that they are honoured by the local authorities. Too often, the Government acts as if it is an interested bystander, left to pick up the mistakes of others.

Fr Alec Reid, C.Ss.R
Peace Activist

Rev Harold Good OBE
Former Moderator of the Methodist
Church in Ireland

Nuala O'Loan
Police Ombudsman for Northern Ireland

Ian Paisley, Jnr, MLA
Junior Minister in the Offices of the First
and Deputy First Ministers, NI Executive

Martin McGuinness MP, MLA
Deputy First Minister, NI Excecutive

Chapter 1

The Future of Northern Ireland

Dialogue is the Most Important Dynamic in Conflict Resolution
Fr ALEC REID C.Ss.R.
Peace Activist

Building a Society from which No One Will Feel Excluded
REV HAROLD GOOD OBE
Former Moderator of the Methodist Church in Ireland

Leaving Behind the Bitterness of Sectarianism
NUALA O'LOAN
Police Ombudsman for Northern Ireland

A Great Opportunity to Shape the Future
IAN PAISLEY, JNR MLA
Junior Minister in the Offices of the First and Deputy First Ministers, NI Executive

We Have Begun to Script a New History
MARTIN McGUINNESS MP, MLA
Deputy First Minister, NI Executive

Fr. Alec Reid C.Ss.R

Peace Activist

Born in Dublin, he joined the Redemptorists in 1949 and after his religious profession in 1950 he studied for the priesthood at NUI Galway and the Redemptorist Seminary, Cluain Mhuire Galway. In 1959 he began his life as a Redemptorist preacher and missionary. In 1962, he was appointed to Clonard Monastery and was based there for about 40 years. During "the troubles", he was involved in the conflict, trying to promote understanding and reconciliation between the Nationalist and Loyalist communities. From the early 1980s on, Fr. Reid, together with colleagues, was secretely exploring ways to bring about a peaceful settlement in the North including having regular talks with the President of Sinn Féin, Gerry Adams. This process eventually led to the declaration of the IRA ceasefire in 1994. In 2005, Fr. Reid, together with the Rev. Harold Good, acted as an independent observer to verify the decommissioning of IRA weaponry. He is currently engaged in the peace process in the Basque Country.

Dialogue is the Most Important Dynamic in Conflict Resolution

I believe that, before we consider the priorities for Government for the next five years, we should look at the lessons of the Irish peace process to date. I say this because, in my view, we need to keep them in mind as we consider those priorities. Otherwise, we shall not be as informed as we could and we need to be, if we are to deal with them in a successful way. I call them "Lessons from the Street" because they were learnt in and through the experience of peacemaking at the coalface of the Irish conflict over a period of 35 years or so.

The First Lesson

The first of these lessons has to do with human dignity because it tells us that the dignity of the human person is the supreme moral value in all human affairs. This means that it is the criterion which determines whether any particular law, custom or institution is just or unjust and whether any given form of personal, social or political behaviour is moral or immoral.

It follows, therefore, that respect for the dignity of the human person is the first of the moral virtues in the sense that all the other virtues that characterise human morality flow from it. It also follows that that dignity is the source of every human right that any indi-

> ... respect for the dignity of the human person is the first of the moral virtues in the sense that all the other virtues that characterise human morality flow from it.

vidual, community or nation can truly claim to own as a natural God-given endowment. The fact that every human right is rooted in the dignity of the human person means that this dignity is the foundation of justice in every human society. This in turn means that real and permanent peace, within and between every human society, has to be based at all times on the practice of due respect for human dignity.

The Second Lesson

The second lesson flows naturally from the first because it has to do with the spirit that should inspire all person to person communication if that communication is to be in keeping with the respect that is due to human dignity. It would not be possible here to discuss the full significance of dialogue as the dynamic which must energise all interpersonal relationships if these relationships are to be truly human. For that reason, I shall confine my comments to the role of dialogue in peacemaking. The second lesson from the streets tells us that dialogue is the most powerful and, at the end of the day, the only effective dynamic of peaceful and democratic conflict resolution.

The second lesson from the streets tells us that dialogue is the most powerful and, at the end of the day, the only effective dynamic of peaceful and democratic conflict resolution.

It is vital, therefore, to understand what it means and how to go about it in practice. Dialogue may be described as a form of interpersonal or inter-communal communication which is characterised by a spirit of profound respect for the dignity of the human person and the rights that, under God, naturally belong to it. In the context of peacemaking, it sets up direct, face to face communication between people who are in conflict with each other for reasons that have to do with historical, political or cultural differences that are causing death and destruction on the streets.

The object of such dialogue is always the same – to resolve the conflict in question through an agreement which would respect the rights of all the participants and, at the same time, allow each one of them to remain faithful to the spirit of their own principles. In its pure state, therefore, dialogue is a very sensitive form of communication during which those who take part in it engage with one another in a spirit of mutual respect for the dignity and the rights of all the people concerned with a view to searching for the kind of agreement I have just described.

The dialogue then becomes a search for the common ground that would form the basis for such an agreement. That is why listening is the first and most important activity of dialogue; listening with the head but also, and indeed more so, with the heart to the other parties as they explain their own positions on the conflict at issue. The purpose of this listening is to uncover the common ground that will enable the parties concerned to build the kind of agreement which will resolve their conflict.

This listening approach is based on the fact, long proven by the experience of peacemaking in Ireland, that when any of the parties to a political conflict that is breaking out on the streets are explaining their understanding of its nature and its causes, they are bound to say things with which the other parties can agree. Then, as the communication between them deepens more and more under the enabling influence of the dialogue approach to it, more and more areas of agreement are revealed and, with them, more and more areas of corresponding common ground until, at the end of the day so to speak, the common ground will have grown to a point where it can form the basis for the next stage of the dialogue, namely, the negotiation through which the parties concerned will be able to reach an agreeement that accommodates the rights of all concerned without asking any of them to be unfaithful to the principles that define their own historical, political or cultural identies.

The Third Lesson

The third lesson from the streets points to the dynamic that comes into operation when what I shall call the two fundamental principles of human achievement, namely, the female principle and the male principle, blend together in spirit to form a new, unitary principle.

The significance of this dynamic for the common good of society emerged from the experience of peacemaking in Ireland over many years. It is based on the fact that the female and male principles, while separate, are, at the same time, complementary to each other.

I can spell out the implications of this fact by saying that the female principle represents the other half of the male principle and, in a corresponding way, that the male principle represents the other half of the female principle. This means that each has a natural capacity to combine with the other in a way that creates a third entity that is neither male nor female but a synergetic bending of the spiritual, intellectual and emotional characteristics of both.

I can explain this further by saying that the attributes of heart, mind and spirit that characterise the nature of the female principle complement or, if you like, are "the other half" of the attributes of mind, heart and spirit that characterise the nature of the male principle. To create the female-male dynamic under consideration here, these two sets of spiritual, intellectual and emotional attributes must be activated by a female-male dialogue on an issue that, for example, affects the common good of society. The purpose of this dialogue will be to develop a female-male consensus on how to manage the issue.

To create the female-male dynamic under consideration here, these two sets of spiritual, intellectual and emotional attributes must be activated by a female-male dialogue on an issue that, for example, affects the common good of society.

The female-male dynamic will come into play during the dialogue, the formation of the consensus and, then, in the actions that will be subsequently taken to settle the issue.

Here it is crucial to note that to achieve the female-male dialogue, the female-male consensus and the female-male dynamic of the kinds in question, the group concerned must be balanced in terms of gender composition. Experience shows that to ensure the necessary balance, the ratio of men to women or women to men should not be below 40 to 60 per cent.

It goes without saying that the members of any group of men and women who wish to conduct their business on the basis of a female-male dialogue and a female-male consensus would have to have the abilities and the skills that would enable them to manage that business in a successful way. It also goes without saying that a process of female-male dialogue would need a competent moderator to organise and facilitate it. It would be the responsibility of the leadership of the group to provide that facility. It would also be their responsibility to decide, in consultation with the members of the group, if and when a female-male consensus had emerged from the dialogue. What I am speaking of then is a female-male consensus about how to deal with an issue that would affect the common good of society; a consensus that would have emerged from a female-male dialogue on the same issue.

I am stressing this point because, in the past, when I spoke about the need for a female-male dynamic, some people thought I was suggesting that the world would be a much better place if women were to take over the positions of political and economic power that have been, and to a very large extent still are, occupied by men. I would like to emphasise, therefore, that I am not suggesting or implying this in any way. The evidence of history shows that women who occupy positions of power and authority in society make as many mistakes as men in similar positions. The mistakes of the women will be different from the mistakes of the men but, in terms of their frequency and the damage they could do to the common good, their effects on society will be equally negative.

The third lesson of the Irish peace process has a special significance for the cause of peace and justice throughout the world because of what it implies about the relationship between that cause and the female-male dynamic I have described above. I would like, therefore, to explain that relationship as I see it. I shall do so by looking at some of the disasters that have afflicted society over the past century or so and which, in one way or another, continue to afflict it to the present day. Here, for example, I am thinking of the two world wars of the twentieth century, the atrocities of the Nazi regime, local conflicts

What I am speaking of then is a female-male consensus about how to deal with an issue that would affect the common good of society; a consensus that would have emerged from a female-male dialogue on the same issue.

like those of Korea and Vietnam, the conflict in the Middle East, the attack on the World Trade Towers in New York, the Taliban regime and, not least, the conflict in Northern Ireland. I am also thinking of the widespread abuse of human rights and the poverty and disease that afflict so many.

This brings me to the main point I wish to make here. It has to do with the relationship between the disasters listed above and the message of the third lesson of the Irish peace process. The message is one of hope because it indicates that those disasters either would not have happened or, if they had, their evil consequences would have been minimised and the time it took to resolve them lessened to a very significant degree if the political and economic institutions that organise societies throughout the world had been governed on the basis of the female-male consensus.

Here, I would like to stress that, in giving this explanation of the third lesson of the Irish peace process, I am not in any way suggesting what the lesson itself does not suggest, namely, that the men who were responsible for the exercise of political and economic power over the last century or so were to blame for the disasters that bedevilled it because of some innate defect in the male side of the gender equation, that is, in the qualities that characterise maleness as such.

The third lesson of the Irish peace process points, therefore, to the conclusion that neither men on their own nor women on their own, that is, on the basis alone of their maleness or femaleness , are able to cope in a consistently successful way with the responsibilities of caring for the common good of society. Given the truth of this conclusion, it follows that a female-male approach to the care of the common good would be far better than an approach which would be mainly male or mainly female in character. This in turn leads to the conclusion that a society governed by a female-male consensus will avoid, or at least significantly reduce, the tragedies, big and small, that would otherwise descend upon it.

This lesson has other implications for the development of justice and peace in society but it would not be feasible to deal with them here. I shall, therefore, finish these comments by saying that, given all its implications, it should be regarded as one of the most important lessons of the Irish peace process.

The Fourth Lesson

The fourth lesson from the streets has to do with the rights of a community that can truly claim an historical, political and cultural identity of its own. It tells us that these rights are based on the dignity of the human person and the respect that is due in justice to it. This

This in turn leads to the conclusion that a society governed by a female-male consensus will avoid, or at least significantly reduce, the tragedies, big and small, that would otherwise descend upon it.

means that the rights of such a community are human rights. It is important to note this statement because, as the fourth lesson from the streets also tells us, it articulates one of the fundamental principles of peaceful and democratic conflict resolution. As such, it applies to every conflict of the kind under consideration here because, in the final analysis, all these conflicts are about human rights.

This is particularly true of every political conflict that tends, again and again, to break out in violence on the streets because, as the evidence of history shows, the fact that it does so is a sure sign that the issues at stake in it have to do with the human rights of all the parties concerned. The Irish conflict is a classical example of this because the issue at the heart of it was related to the human rights of the Nationalist and Unionist communites in Ireland.

That is why the settlement, represented by the Good Friday Agreement in 1998, is based on the recognition and the accomodation of the rights of both communities. The right to claim a historical, political and cultural identity of one's own belongs to each and every person who wishes to do so by virtue of his or her dignity and the rights that, under God, naturally belong to it. The right to form or join such a community also belongs to each and every person who wishes to do so by virtue of the same dignity and the same rights.

> **The right to claim a historical, political and cultural identity of one's own belongs to each and every person who wishes to do so by virtue of his or her dignity and the rights that, under God, naturally belong to it.**

The Rev Harold Good, OBE

Former Moderator of the Methodist Church in Ireland

Born in Derry and educated at Strandtown Primary School, Methodist College, Belfast, Edgehill Theological College, Belfast and Christian Theological Seminary, Indianapolis. Ministered in the Republic of Ireland and in the US before returning to Northern Ireland. Appointed to the Shankill area of Belfast and also served part-time as chaplain to Crumlin Road Prison. In 1973, appointed Director of the Corrymeela Community Centre for Reconciliation. He returned to pastoral ministry in 1978 and also part-time chaplain at Belfast City Hospital. In 2001 he was elected to serve as President of the Methodist Church in Ireland. He has held a number of public appointments including: chair of the N.I. Council of Social Service, chair of the Personal Social Services Committee, member of the N.I. Human Rights Commission and is currently chairperson of the N.I. Advice Services Alliance. He is a founder member of the "Healing through Remembering" organisation. Together with Fr. Alec Reid he acted in 2005 as an independent observer to verify decommissioning of IRA weaponry which paved the way to a political settlement in N. Ireland. With Fr. Reid he has also been involved in the Basque Country peace process.

Building a Society from which No One Will Feel Excluded

... it has been important to begin by remembering how we have come to where we now are. In doing so, we take this opportunity to acknowledge the courageous leadership of all those who "on-stage" and "off", past as well as present, from this island and elsewhere, have enabled this to happen.

In addressing "Priorities for Government" this school will focus on a promising future rather than a bleak past. However, in setting the scene for this debate it has been important to begin by remembering how we have come to where we now are. In doing so, we take this opportunity to acknowledge the courageous leadership of all those who "on-stage" and "off", past as well as present, from this island and elsewhere, have enabled this to happen. And none has played a more crucial role on this journey than John Hume. So thank you for the honour of being associated with this, the Annual Lecture which bears his name.

On the day that the parties finally agreed the deal brokered at St. Andrews, my wife and I celebrated with a night out. We chose the film, *Amazing Grace*, which was an inspired choice. Without under-estimating the unrelenting contribution of good human beings from every side and quarter, there was something else at work within this process which can only be described as a work of "Grace". Others may prefer a more "secular" word but, however we describe it, 'tis a wonder to behold!

However, to assume that we have "arrived" and that there is little more we need do would be to ignore the stark lessons of history, reminding us that the cause of most wars can be traced back to unresolved issues from a past conflict – a costly lesson which was ignored in 1918, following what was thought to be the end of the "war which was to end all wars"!

When visiting Mumbai, we toured old churches which had been left behind by the British Raj. "This", said our host, "is the Afghanistan Church". Rather puzzled, I read the inscription:

"This church is dedicated
> to the memory
> of the officers and men,
> too many to name,
> who gave their lives in the
> Afghanistan War of 1847 - 1853"

And where are we now! Too often, the assumed settlement of a conflict has merely been the sowing of the seeds of the next. Hence the importance of the theme for this week, "Priorities for Government …"

While primary responsibility for the governance of Northern Ireland must rest with the newly devolved administration at Stormont we are mindful of neighbouring centres of government with which, to borrow a once familiar phrase, we are "inextricably linked". I suggest, therefore, that these priorities are no less relevant for them.

To help me prepare this paper, I asked some folk to tell me of their priorities for this new administration. Like all of us, they had very personal "wish lists". Not surprisingly, there was more than one reference to rates and water charges! Others provided lists of what I describe as functional priorities including issues such as:

- roads and transport
- affordable housing
- health and education
- infrastructure and investment
- urgent environmental issues

to mention but a few.

It is encouraging to note that in "Making a Difference", published by the First and Deputy First Ministers, they also list these among priorities which they will " be urgently tackled … in an open, transparent and accountable way".

I have noted that throughout this week these issues will be addressed in depth and in detail by others much more competent than I. So this evening, I will focus on what I describe as "aspirational" as distinct from "functional" priorities.

However, to assume that we have "arrived" and that there is little more we need do would be to ignore the stark lessons of history, reminding us that the cause of most wars can be traced back to unresolved issues from a past conflict …

In identifying common themes from my respondents, I offer three priorities for government as a "backdrop" to your more detailed deliberations. Here is the first.

An Unequivocal Commitment to a Shared Vision

Over 30 years ago, I organised a weekend conference at Corrymeela entitled "When Peace Breaks Out". Clearly, at that bloodiest period of our history we could easily have settled for a definition of peace as merely the cessation of violence and the establishment of any form of government acceptable to the people of these islands. However, out of that debate we accepted two realities: firstly, that there is much more to "peace" than the ending of physical conflict, and secondly, that it is only when violence has ceased could the building of a lasting peace begin.

However, out of that debate we accepted two realities: firstly, that there is much more to "peace" than the ending of physical conflict, and secondly, that it is only when violence has ceased could the building of a lasting peace begin.

It was the Hebrew people who understood this more than most. For them, the peace of which we speak is embodied in that distinctive Biblical word *shalom*. In going well beyond "the absence of violence", *shalom* paints the vision of a just society in which each and all are truly valued and from which none are excluded. In more earthy prose, our modern-day prophet, Michael Longley, puts it another way:

> Who was it who suggested that the opposite of war
> Is not so much peace as civilisation ?

Longley goes on to speak of the murdered Catholic greengrocer who died in the arms of his Methodist minister neighbour, of ice cream vendors, cobblers, butchers and corner shop keepers, all of whom know what it is to care and to be cared for by one another.

> . . . who can bring peace to people who are not civilised?
> All of these people, alive or dead, are civilised.

This is Longley's interpretation of *shalom*!

In March 2005, the Offices of First and Deputy First Minister published a strategic framework document entitled "A Shared Future". In the foreword, the then Secretary of State, Paul Murphy, wrote:

> Government's vision … is for a peaceful, inclusive, prosperous, stable and fair society firmly founded on the achievement of reconciliation, tolerance, mutual trust and the protection and vindication of human rights for all. It will be founded on partnership, equality and mutual respect …

This is *shalom*, a society from which none will feel excluded and none will be left behind.

But how does a Government incarnate the vision? How does the lofty ideal "trickle down" to the street where Joe Public and Bridget and their children must live out their daily lives? And how do they confound the sceptics, particularly those who seem intent on undermining the process? This leads me to my second priority for our politicians.

To Build Confidence within and between Themselves

From public and private appearances, there are encouraging signs that this is already happening.

For me, it began on May 8th. It was not only in what was being said in the Chamber and on the steps of the Great Hall, but in what I was privileged to hear and see in the wings. For me, the most memorable image of the day was that of Ian Paisley and Martin McGuinness entering Parliament Buildings through that revolving door – the door made famous by the infamous Michael Stone! Remember … the hand of one gently navigating the other. The offering of respect and safe passage by one and acceptance by the other. In another context this would be considered a trivial incident, but for me this was the "hand of history" – worth more than a thousand contrived handshakes!

Whatever about swords and ploughshares, we have seen snowballs melt into broad grins as historic and bitter enemies become increasingly confident as well as comfortable in their dealings with one another. If sustained, this will create a new culture of respect and acceptance, not only within government but, as we are already seeing, in the way that citizens relate to one another. For example, look at the more responsible way in which communities are attempting to resolve contentious issues such as parades.

"Work-in" or "love-in", call it what you like, but every sign and symbol of confidence between the players in London, Belfast and Dublin will give hope to a still deeply divided community. Only when the walls come down between our politicians can we begin to talk about dismantling grotesque "peace walls" which are a blight upon any landscape. As Gandhi once said, "Be the change you wish to make".

I heard F.W. de Clerk speak of his part in the ending of apartheid. He confessed that it was for purely pragmatic reasons that he and others embarked upon that journey. The economy was "going down the tubes". South Africa was the pariah of the civilised world and was on the verge of the bloodiest civil war. Then, he said, "I remember the day when I realised what we were doing was *morally* right".

In Bilbao, Father Alec and I shared a platform with Rolf Meyer, de Clerk's former Minister of Security and Intelligence in the apartheid government. In his "Ten Steps to Peace", number ten was "a

> Only when the walls come down between our politicians can we begin to talk about dismantling grotesque "peace walls" which are a blight upon any landscape. As Gandhi once said, "Be the change you wish to make".

change of heart", without which the process could not be complete. It was this which freed Afrikaner and ANC to form new alliances based on confidence in themselves and in one another.

My third priority for government is an extension of the second.

To Win the Confidence of the People

After the wasted years, it is not surprising that there is much scepticism and a loss of confidence in political institutions. "Is it for real?" I am regularly asked. In reply, I say that I have been preaching about conversion for over 40 years and I'm not giving up now! However, as every zealous convert to any creed or cause will discover, one is not automatic and accepted, even by those who want to believe. There will be lingering doubts as to how genuine is the change, as well as fears about motives yet to be revealed!

Thus, as perceptive political leaders have discovered, however genuine the transformation of their policies and practice, the confidence of the people cannot be assumed.

In middle class drawing rooms, which have suffered the least, there is general support for a plague on all political houses. Those in economically and socially-excluded communities expect little more than a string of broken promises. Younger voters are largely disenchanted and disengaged with politics of any hue.

So, as in other areas of life, political confidence must be earned through delivery of product. This is why the functional priorities to be discussed throughout this week are so important. Whether it be bins or buses, pensions or pavements, the confidence of the electorate will be determined by "deeds not words".

Some would say that there must be a change of culture and context before government can succeed with any practical priority. It is my friend George Quigley who reminds us that in the business world a change of company culture is the end product of all that has to happen, not its pre-condition. Therefore, politicians working together on common tasks, however mundane and predictable they may appear, will offer the best chance of earning confidence and creating the social capital we so badly need. Sir George quotes an old Spanish proverb reminding us that "roads are made by walking".

A priority for government in any society that seeks to move forward is to ensure that no one group or individual gets left behind. Given our sad history of "exclusion" there can be no greater priority for us. Never again, must any section of our society be given reason to believe that they must resort to the language of violence in order to be heard or valued. This is the message of the Good Friday Agreement, and therefore a priority for government. As John Hume would

There will be lingering doubts as to how genuine is the change, as well as fears about motives yet to be revealed!

remind us, whatever our legitimate political aspirations "our immediate priority is to unite people, rather than territory".

In spite of the "hype" around the restoration of a devolved government, there are many who still do not feel included and do not share the spirit of optimism of which we speak here. Those who have suffered the grievous loss of a loved one or suffer from enduring injuries will wonder why it has taken so long and at such cost to them as well as others. They in particular have a right to an honest acknowledgement of their pain and an assurance that they will not be forgotten within the current "euphoria". In-depth studies of truth and reconciliation processes, carried out by our "Healing through Remembering" project, have long ago confirmed for us the rightness of some such process on our island, but only when the conditions are right. We believe that time has now come.

In suggesting how we might begin to deal with this issue, dare I make a simple suggestion which many will dismiss as naïve and unrealistic: why not a simultaneous opportunity for all, from every institution and sector of society, to put up our hands in unreserved acknowledgement of what we have done to one another, asking forgiveness for our sins of silence and omission as well as of commission? I would argue that we in the churches should be the first but would be happy to share that space with our politicians.

Space must be found for the contribution of those who have played their part in the political and civic life of our community throughout the bleak years who now, like the elder brother, feel sidelined and for those who mistakenly resorted to totally unacceptable means to promote their political causes, but who are now committed to making a constructive contribution to their communities – a contribution which they are uniquely placed to make.

If the ultimate test for good government is how it cares for the most vulnerable and marginalised members of society, there are clear priorities for our politicians, amongst them:

- People of all ages in obvious need of better health and social care.
- Teenagers at risk of suicide. Last year, of 291 suicides in Northern Ireland, the majority were fine young people who felt so excluded that they could see no future. This is unacceptable.
- Families living in poverty. Very recent research by Save the Children Fund reveals that 24 per cent of our children in Northern Ireland now live under the poverty line! This is unacceptable.
- Low achievers in our schools, an issue linked to poverty-with an unacceptable percentage leaving school without any academic qualification, particularly in traditional Protestant/Loyalist areas. An obvious priority is to find a way of selecting who is "in", rather than selecting who is "out".

Very recent research by Save the Children Fund reveals that 24 per cent of our children in Northern Ireland now live under the poverty line! This is unacceptable.

In seeking to build confidence, a wise government will give priority to the building of strategic alliances. It will seek serious engagement with civil society.

In seeking to build confidence, a wise government will give priority to the building of strategic alliances. It will seek serious engagement with civil society. It will value and realistically resource the voluntary sector, not reluctantly as one might treat a nuisance partner, but as a crucial player in the task of confidence building and social cohesion.

Ultimately, however lofty and well-presented, any priority must be matched by "will". St John records the story of a man with a physical paralysis who for 38 years lay beside the healing waters at the Pool of Bethesda. One day the Lord passed by and asked a foolish if not insulting question, "Do you want to be healed?" Was not this his priority for all of these 38 years?

Thirty-eight years! Coincidentally, this is exactly how long we have been suffering from our political paralysis! After all of these wasted years, it is not as unreasonable as it might sound for us to ask of government what it is entitled to ask of us, "do we really want to be healed?"

I end with the story of a little girl, now an adult and most likely to have children of her own. In the very violent seventies, the *Belfast Telegraph* invited children to tell us of their hopes for peace and what sort of Northern Ireland they wanted to grow up in. I still have the faded copy of what one little girl wrote:

> I want to grow up in a Northern Ireland where you can look at
> a sunset without wondering what they're bombing tonight.

I wonder if she remembered that when she saw the cover design for the Good Friday Agreement. Let us determine that our priorities will ensure that this child's vision and our expectations will be fully realised. As it says on that cover: "The decision is ours!"

Nuala O'Loan

Police Ombudsman for Northern Ireland

Born in Bishop's Stortford, England and educated at Convent of the Holy Child, Harrogate, College of Law, London, King's College, London. A solicitor, lecturer in law, Ulster Polytechnic 1976-80, lecturer in law University of Ulster 1984-92, Jean Monnet Chair in European law 1992-99, Senior lecturer 1992-2000. Appointed first Police Ombudsman for Northern Ireland in 2000. Had been a member of Police Authority 1997-9 and lay visitor to RUC stations 1991-7. Was chairperson NI Consumer Council for Electricity 1997-2000. Was also member of the General Consumer Council and legal expert member of the EU Commission's Consumer Consultative Council. Has written extensively on law, policing, faith and other issues. Awarded a Peace Person of the Year Award by PEACE in 2003.

Leaving Behind the Bitterness of Sectarianism

I want to refer to three issues: trust, interfaces and the legacy of the Troubles.

Trust

I will start with trust, because trust is key to all our relationships and our relationships are key to our future. What is the essence or basis upon which trust will develop? I think that the answer is to be found within some words which will be familiar to many here, which would, I think, be accepted by men and women of all faiths and none, because of the simplicity of the message. Those words are:

> Love is patient; love is kind
> and envies no one.
> Love is never boastful, nor conceited, nor rude;
> never selfish, not quick to take offence.
> There is nothing love cannot face;
> there is no limit to its faith,
> its hope, and endurance.
> In a word, there are three things
> that last forever: faith, hope, and love;
> but the greatest of them all is love.

I will start with trust, because trust is key to all our relationships and our relationships are key to our future.

It is not difficult to translate this into the current situation in Northern Ireland. Never again must we see divisive, distrustful and contemptuous behaviour towards our fellow citizens. Our civic responsibilities are clear, and we are now seeing a new modus operandi between our elected politicians. The distinction between what is and what went before is very stark and it has left commentators questioning whether it is real. We need certainty that those responsible for governance in all its forms will act with integrity for the future. Then that integrity will be the model for society. Thus, we will really be able to move forward, leaving behind the hatreds and bitterness of sectarianism and division.

Interfaces

Symbolic of the breakdown in trust in our community are our interfaces. The city of Belfast is scarred by high walls, topped with barbed wire, put there to prevent the two sides of the community (disregarding all our other constituent parts) from attacking and even killing each other. There are, to my understanding, 58 interfaces. The NIO have identified 41 in Belfast alone. As Duncan Morrow said in a powerful speech at the CRC Interface Project Conference last November, "above all, interfaces tell us where we are unsafe and safe, telling us more about the obstacles to reconciliation than many long speeches. And for people who live near to the boundary, they create a target zone, in which people are 'legitimate targets' because of who they belong to, no matter what they do."

There can be no doubt that these interfaces, and their attendant "peace walls", have seriously disrupted the normal flow of life in our capital city, and in the other areas in which they are to be found. They are but a symptom of the dysfunctionality which prevails, and they have a significant impact on the lives of those who live or work in the relevant areas. They mean that people cannot walk from one street to another, that they cannot access shops, health services, leisure centres and other facilities without taking diversions which can be very lengthy and can require an individual to walk through the territory of the other to get to the place they need to be. This in turn leaves them vulnerable to attack. My own son was critically injured in such an attack over a year ago. He is still receiving medical care and is in a lot of pain. He is only one of a huge number of people whose lives have been blighted by vicious sectarian attacks. There is clearly an urgent and very complex need to be addressed here.

There are various projects which are attempting to address these issues. The normalisation of these areas is key to our future. The existence of the walls does mean protection in the short term, but it also

> ... above all, interfaces tell us where we are unsafe and safe, telling us more about the obstacles to reconciliation than many long speeches.

creates a dynamic within which communities cannot integrate.

It is important to emphasise that I am not suggesting that we should take any peace wall down until the people of the area want this to happen. I know that in some areas people do want to find ways to resolve the differences which necessitate the peace walls, and hence to be able to come eventually to a time when they can be deconstructed, like the Berlin Wall, and the divided communities can live at peace.

For this to happen, there will of course have to be community will accompanied by inter-agency support to enable the necessary structural work and developments. My hope would be that the Assembly will take a very proactive role in leading and facilitating the reconstruction of our land without these symbolic and very real walls of division.

My final issue relates to what we have taken to calling the Legacy of the Past. As Maya Angelou said, "History, with all its wrenching pain, cannot be unlived. If faced with courage it need not be lived again."

The Legacy of the Past

That, too, is a very significant challenge. We have seen peace break out and break down again in places like the Spanish Basque Country, where ETA are now again planting bombs etc., Sri Lanka, where the Tamil Tigers seem once again to be in dispute and the Middle East which has seen centuries of violence. We must ensure that we leave no unresolved legacy of the Troubles, which may enable people to attempt to justify any return to violence.

Our conflict left thousands dead and tens of thousands injured. It left, probably hundreds of thousand touched in some way by the consequences of what happened. As a people we are now showing signs that we think we are ready to "move on". Senior public figures are saying that we need to face forward and not to be looking backwards, that we must not allow the past to hinder future developments; that it is time to forget; that there is nothing to be learned from "picking over old sores".

Government has established a Review, led by Archbishop Eames and Dennis Bradley, which seems to have an 18-month remit to try and identify how, as a people, we want to deal with the past. If justice and policing are devolved, as anticipated within that 18-month period, Eames and Bradley will probably report ultimately to the Assembly. Neither I, nor anybody else, can foretell what that review will suggest.

What I would like to do now is to articulate some facts:

As a people we are now showing signs that we think we are ready to "move on". Senior public figures are saying that we need to face forward and not to be looking backwards, that we must not allow the past to hinder future developments; that it is time to forget; that there is nothing to be learned from "picking over old sores".

1. We all have rights under European and domestic law. These rights are widely talked about but, I sometimes think, not widely understood. However, there can be no doubt that under our law police are under a statutory duty to protect life and property, to preserve order, to prevent the commission of offences and to take measures to bring offenders to justice.

That statutory duty is not qualified. Police officers across the world have a duty to bring offenders to justice. Sometimes they do so after decades. Investigative techniques develop, enabling offenders to be identified years after the crime was committed. This is normal. Officers will always tell you that unsolved murder crime investigations remain open. That is what the law requires.

My office is regarded internationally as a model for independent police accountability. We have secured very high confidence levels with both the public and police officers who have been investigated. A total of 83 per cent of the public and 84 per cent of police officers who have been investigated think that we are fair; 78 per cent of the general population believe that we are impartial; and 92 per cent of officers who have been investigated say that they were treated impartially. My staff have worked very hard to achieve this.

In my case, I have a statutory duty to investigate any case in which the conduct of a police officer may have resulted in a death. I do not have any discretion in the matter. The Chief Constable cannot deal with these cases. Parliament has decreed that the Police Ombudsman must do this work and so at the present time, the PSNI HET and MIT are reviewing all the deaths of the Troubles to determine whether investigation is possible. We are dealing with multiple cases referred to us by Government or the PSNI which we must investigate. They involve the deaths of ordinary people from both sides of the community, including police officers, soldiers, prison officers. They resulted in broken lives, trauma, terror, grief which endures over decades. As a people, we have wept bitter tears – *sunt lachrimae rerum at mentem mortalia tangunt.*

> Our society was characterised by a level of fear which did not exist here in the Republic or in Britain, fear of the paramilitaries, fear of the security forces, fear of the neighbours, fear of putting your head above the parapet – for very real reasons.

Our society was characterised by a level of fear which did not exist here in the Republic or in Britain, fear of the paramilitaries, fear of the security forces, fear of the neighbours, fear of putting your head above the parapet – for very real reasons. Hopefully, those days are gone. It is my sincere hope that we have now reached a time when all those who can assist the PSNI or my office in resolving some of the unsolved murders of the past will do so, be they Republicans, Loyalists, Catholics, Protestants, members of the military, the security service or retired police officers. We must all play our part.

In so doing, we can, in a limited way, help the thousands who still suffer following the murders of their loved ones. We cannot talk of closure. We can talk of helping the beginning of the healing of so much pain, so that this pain, in all its dimensions, does not pass from generation to generation.

2. The past is a source from which we can learn how to make the future better. For example, last January, I published a report on a complaint made by a courageous father called Raymond McCord whose son was murdered by loyalist paramilitaries. The report established conclusively that matters had been so handled and managed by certain people within the RUC/PSNI that informants, involved in the most serious of crimes – murder, attempted murder, armed robbery, arson, drug dealing etc. – were not properly investigated or made amenable for those crimes. It was a lengthy and sensitive investigation. As a consequence of the investigation and of matters drawn to the attention of the police, we were able to document and agree with the PSNI 40 different changes in working practices between 2003 and 2007. In addition to this, the services of 24 per cent of informants were dispensed with – 12 per cent because they were not producing information to police, and 12 per cent because the PSNI had found that they had been too deeply involved in criminal activity for their continued employment to meet the standards set by law, and the obligations of the PSNI under their own ethical code.

This meant that PSNI was left with 76 per cent of its existing informants and, of course, others have been recruited since. The importance of the McCord investigation was that, whilst I recognised that police across the world use informants, I also emphasised that society needs the protection to be derived from the legal structures which regulate how informants and their information are managed.

3. It is, of course, the case that we will face our future in the context of what is happening in the wider world and that includes international terrorism. We have seen recently the incidents in London and Glasgow and we will have, as a community, to play our part in welcoming people who come to live here from overseas and ensuring that they do not face hostility or discrimination, whilst at the same time contributing, as necessary and within the law, to the fight against terrorism.

4. One of our big objectives is to ensure that we have a legal system, and particularly a criminal justice system, which is accepted by all our people and which operates effectively and efficiently. If people are to accept the rule of law, rather than the rule of the paramilitary, then they must be assured that the law applies equally to all, that, where crime is committed, it will be properly investigated.

One of our big objectives is to ensure that we have a legal system, and particularly a criminal justice system, which is accepted by all our people and which operates effectively and efficiently.

5. I hope finally that during the next five years we will recover the bodies of the disappeared and that their families will be able to lay them to rest and to mourn for them by their graves.

In conclusion, then, my hopes are high that we will move from sectarianism, suspicion and hostility, to become a community which actively cares for all its members, which welcomes visitors and, whilst sharing what it has learned from its past with those who seek to resolve trouble in their own land looks forward to the future.

Ian Paisley Jnr. MLA

Junior Minister in the Offices of the First and Deputy
First Ministers, NI Executive

*Born in Belfast and educated at Greenwood Primary School, Shaftesbury House
College, Methodist College, Queen's University (BA Hons. MSc (Irish Politics)).
Began his career as a political researcher and political aide to his father, the Rev.
Ian Paisley MP, MEP, leader of the Democratic Unionist Party. DUP member
of the Northern Ireland Forum for the constituency of North Antrim 1996-8
and re-elected in 1998. Appointed with two other DUP representatives to the
Northern Ireland Policing Board in 2001. A member of the DUP negotiating
team in the talks leading up to the formation of the power sharing Executive in
May 2007. Appointed Junior Minister in the Offices of the First Minister and
Deputy First Minister with special responsibility for children and the elderly.*

A Great Opportunity to Shape the Future

I want to take a few moments to reflect on what has happened over
the last number of months, and particularly since power was devolved to the representatives of the people of Northern Ireland on
May 8th.

During the Assembly election campaign, Democratic Unionists
pledged to work towards an agreement that would deliver lasting
devolution for the people of Northern Ireland. Such an agreement
could only come about if it were underpinned by support for the rule
of law and recognition that the only way forward was through commitment to exclusively peaceful and democratic means.

The road to agreement was long and, at times, difficult. Anyone
who understands unionist politics will know that the pressure on us
was not to do things quickly, but to do them right. But the patient
approach has transformed the political situation in Northern Ireland
and laid the foundations for a prosperous and peaceful future, one
which allows the people of Northern Ireland to put their best foot
forward. Many challenges lie ahead and, as elected representatives of
the people, we must demonstrate that government is making. a real
and meaningful difference to the lives of people.

In July, Northern Ireland's First and Deputy First Ministers hosted
the British-Irish Council Summit at Parliament Buildings, Stormont
and the North-South Ministerial Council in Armagh. The meetings
were a visual demonstration of the commitment of local ministers to
work together to achieve the best possible outcome for Northern Ireland plc. However, that commitment did not require the evidence of

The road to agreement was long and, at times, difficult. Anyone who understands unionist politics will know that the pressure on us was not to do things quickly, but to do them right.

BIC or NSMC summits. I believe the DUP is a party of its word. We have honoured our word and are delivering for the people and governing on that basis. By participating in both meetings, all involved recognised that Northern Ireland can benefit from both our continued East-West relationship and from practical co-operation with our nearest neighbour, the Republic of Ireland.

Quite understandably down the years, Unionists have eyed cross-border co-operation with suspicion. But Unionists have confidence now – confidence in their leadership and in the policy direction they are being taken. Unionists know Northern Ireland has much to gain through good relations with the Irish Republic – if it is grounded on a pragmatic and appropriate basis. The work carried out by elected representatives on behalf of constituents on both sides of the border is very similar. On this matter of confidence, I was struck by an aside made by Bertie Ahern at the North South Ministerial Council in Armagh when he said: "Confidence is not a government policy – it just happens". Indeed, for Northern Ireland, confidence is growing and we must capitalise upon that once-in-a-generation opportunity.

The return of devolved government has presented us with both an opportunity and a responsibility to ensure that the needs of local people are met. This is the challenge - to be able to govern in a way that makes real and meaningful difference. We must not be afraid of reform. Now is the time to seize the moment to:

- provide the high quality public services which the people of Northern Ireland expect and deserve.
- grow a competitive, outward looking economy,
- rebuild our infrastructure,
- tackle poverty, intolerance and racism, and
- deliver improvements in key services such as Health and Education.

But Unionists have confidence now – confidence in their leadership and in the policy direction they are being taken. Unionists know Northern Ireland has much to gain through good relations with the Irish Republic – if it is grounded on a pragmatic and appropriate basis.

These are the priorities the Executive has committed to tackling urgently, but this is by no means an exhaustive list of the Executive's priorities for the future.

The Executive is currently working on developing its key priorities for government and they will be published for public consultation in a draft Programme for Government later in the year. At the same time, we plan to launch the draft Budget for 2008-11 and a draft Infrastructure Investment Strategy for Northern Ireland. Having a blank page is both a challenge and a great opportunity to shape the future and not be dictated to by the past. Someone else correctly observed: "We must cherish the past, adorn the present but create the future." Today we are doing exactly that – creating a better future for the people.

We will strive to achieve an economy which is characterised by higher levels of innovation and business expenditure, research and development and a private sector that will grow and be restructured to be more in balance with the size of the public sector. We must seek to achieve increased levels of high value-added foreign direct investment and increased tourism levels. We want to gain a reputation for a flexible and skilled workforce supported by an effective education system which greatly increases employability; and to ensure that the social and economic well-being of the region is enhanced by a quality infrastructure and related public services.

Accelerated productivity growth is fundamental to increased competitiveness and to long-term sustainable economic performance. Economic development policy will be increasingly focused on productivity and on moving the economy away from competition, based on costs, to one where the emphasis is on innovation, creativity and improved workforce skills. We will also seek to address the problem of economic inactivity by removing the barriers to work through childcare initiatives, transport strategies and improving individual skill levels. To be successful, the economy needs to become more dynamic and entrepreneurial, be driven by external competition and exports and become less reliant on local markets and public spending.

We will also seek to address the problem of economic inactivity by removing the barriers to work through childcare initiatives, transport strategies and improving individual skill levels.

The Smithsonian Festival

We are determined to promote Northern Ireland as an attractive place to live, work and invest. Ministers from the Northern Ireland Executive recently visited Washington to promote Northern Ireland's contribution to the Smithsonian Folklife Festival. This was a great opportunity to demonstrate that Northern Ireland is a creative, confident, outward-looking region capable of partnering and doing business with US organisations and of creating a future legacy of linkages and relationships that will be mutually beneficial to Northern Ireland and the USA.

The festival involved talented local people telling the story of what it is like to live and work in Northern Ireland through music, dance, song, crafts, storytelling and, through exhibitions, of everyday life, of our work, culture, food and cooking. We hope that participation at this festival will counteract outdated perceptions through the presentation of positive images and show that a transformation has taken place and is continuing to take place in Northern Ireland. To that end, the government will soon be publishing a considered resume of the work carried out and opportunities identified during that important week in Washington DC.

Of course, our NI Bureau, based in Washington, plays an important part in working to develop a positive profile of Northern Ireland among US policy-makers by ensuring that the policies of the Northern Ireland Executive and its associated institutions are known and understood. The Bureau also ensures that Northern Ireland Ministers and Departments have up-to-date information on policy developments in the US and pursues opportunities for co-operation and partnerships. The Executive will wish to consider how we can use the opportunities offered to us through the Bureau more fully to derive full advantage from the long standing "special relationship" between the USA and both Northern Ireland and the Republic of Ireland. To that end, a new CEO will soon be appointed and the Government intends to develop a platform for the Executive in New York and further west. We must also capitalise upon the opportunities open to us in the various British embassy and consulate offices across the US and avail of any opportunity, courtesy of the Republic of Ireland embassy staff headed up by people we have come to know such as Neil Burgess and Michael Collins.

Relationship with Europe

Over recent years, Northern Ireland has benefited significantly from EU funding, particularly through our former Objective One status and the EU Peace programme. As the EU's policies begin to focus more on the newer accession countries, we must ensure Northern Ireland's case of special need, as it emerges from decades of conflict, is not forgotten. Hence the invitation to the EU President and our pressure on the Union for more funding. This means our relationship with the EU must change and develop if we are to gain full benefit from our EU membership.

A Shared Future

This society has seen huge progress. However, unfortunately, some are still engaged in attacks on churches, Orange halls and other forms of sectarianism and racism.

This society has seen huge progress. However, unfortunately, some are still engaged in attacks on churches, Orange halls and other forms of sectarianism and racism. Since the start of July, over 50 Orange halls have been damaged as a result of such attacks. Needless to say, such behaviour, from wherever it comes, raises community tensions. We must continue to challenge and confront this behaviour and the mind-set that leads to it. Those with knowledge of such attacks must help the police in apprehending the culprits.

As a Junior Minister in the Offices of the First Minister and Deputy First Minister, I also have an important co-ordination role for children and young people and for the elderly. The Executive is absolutely committed to ensuring that all children and young people, especially our most marginalised and disadvantaged, are given the opportunities they need to achieve. This is the fundamental focus of the 10-year strategy for children and young people and we will continue to seek opportunities to make this vision a reality. We also hope to publish an updated action plan for the Older People's Strategy in the near future, which will ensure, amongst other commitments, that services are delivered which improve health and quality of life for older people and that they have a decent and secure life in their home and community.

Conclusion

This is an exciting – and challenging – time for Northern Ireland. Achievement of a lasting settlement and political stability through the Assembly and the Northern Ireland Executive will allow Northern Ireland to begin to develop and to move forward into a new future. Much work needs to be done if we are to seize the benefits of devolution and make them work to the advantage of all the people of Northern Ireland.

Given the presence tonight of the outgoing Police Ombudsman, and I do wish her well for the future, it is important that I do reflect that soon we must confront head-on the issue of the future devolution of policing and justice powers. I believe my party was correct for insisting on in-built guarantees that this could not happen until there exists sufficient confidence amongst the people to take on these controversial powers. We have made progress but let's not get carried away believing that these powers must now come to us immediately. There is some distance to go.

In his now famous "Wind of Change" speech, Harold MacMillan said, "the legacy of history belongs to those who are dead and to those who are yet unborn....We must face the differences but let us try to see beyond them down the long vista of the future".

Achievement of a lasting settlement and political stability through the Assembly and the Northern Ireland Executive will allow Northern Ireland to begin to develop and to move forwards into a new future.

Martin McGuinness MP, MLA

Deputy First Minister, NI Executive

Born in Derry. Left school at fifteen to work as butcher's assistant. Became involved in the civil rights protests and, following the outbreak of unrest in the North, became involved in the Republican movement. Second-in-command of the IRA in Derry at the time of Bloody Sunday. Was a key figure in negotiations with the British Government in the '80s and played a leading role leading up to the declaration of the IRA ceasefire in 1994. A leader of the Sinn Féin team in the talks that led to the Good Friday Agreement in 1998. Minister for Education in the power sharing Executive up to the suspension of the Executive in 2001. Re-elected as MP for Mid-Ulster in the Westminster elections of 2005 and played key role in inter-party talks as Sinn Féin Chief Negotiator. On May 8th 2007, became Deputy First Minister in the new DUP-Sinn Féin-led power sharing Executive.

We Have Begun to Script a New History

We have made remarkable progress since I spoke here last year and we should for a moment consider the events of the past year. March 26th was a remarkable day. May 8th was another. They were landmarks on the road that we must travel on a journey towards creating a society at peace with itself which can look forward with hope and a determination to building a better future for us all. It is a mark of how far we have already come that these days and events are milestones marking the road to a better future rather than the millstones of division they may have been in the past.

There were further good days in July of this year with meetings of the British Irish Council and the North South Ministerial Council meeting. They, too, were further leaps forward on the road towards our shared goal of establishing stable sustainable political institutions.

As the joint leaders of the new administration, the First Minister and I have pledged our determination to work together for the good of all our people. We want to live in peace and we want to work to build structures and institutions which will guarantee peace for the future and allow us all to pursue our legitimate political aspirations. I believe that the First Minister and I are part of an administration that is full of dedication and commitment to deliver in the here and now for all of the people. And I think that this work demonstrates a society not just in transition but a society in transformation.

As we look to the future, then, what are the priorities that we face

> I believe that the First Minister and I are part of an administration that is full of dedication and commitment to deliver in the here and now for all of the people. And I think that this work demonstrates a society not just in transition but a society in transnsformation.

for the next five years? Paramount of course is building on what I see as the great foundations which have already been laid. To do that we most work together and by doing so I believe that we can make progress at a rate that few if any could have imagined just a short time ago.

The political progress made has already produced tangible results such as the major investments in our infrastructure that were announced this week following the North-South Ministerial Council. We are a small island. We have to work together to succeed. The announcements made after this week's Ministerial Council meeting in Armagh is evidence of this. In a short time, working together across the island we have ensured much needed investment in roads from Monaghan, through Tyrone and Derry and into County Donegal. Work on the Ulster Canal, which will be a massive boost to our tourism industry, will now commence. This is a project for which people have been campaigning for years. This is real progress, bringing real benefits to communities marginalised by geographical and political isolation. But this is, I believe, only the start. The events of the past few months offer us a template of what can be achieved in the coming years.

We have recently returned from the USA where a united team of Ministers drawn from all parties on the Executive gave tangible expression to our new political reality. I cannot begin to tell you the impact that that united front made, not just on the many high powered political representatives we met but also on business leaders. I am confident that the impression made there will bear fruit, particularly as we prepare for the most important investment conference ever to take place in the North.

These sorts of initiatives benefit us all. Recently, we had the announcement of further highly skilled jobs in Derry – positions that will be filled by people from throughout the North West. These concrete developments are just part of the story. They are not merely an end in themselves. The building of our economy is essentially about providing us with means to care for all our people.

As we move forward, we must do so mindful of the needs of all of our people and especially those who need our help the most- the young, the elderly, the vulnerable, the marginalised, our new communities. Our success as an administration will be measured by how we cater for the needs of these groups and others. Healing the wounds of division between the two main traditions is of course vital and, in this regard, we have to be particularly mindful of those who have suffered over many years of conflict. This I pledge to do.

We are also, however, living in a time when this island and this society is becoming increasingly multicultural and multiethnic. Peo-

Healing the wounds of division between the two main traditions is of course vital and, in this regard, we have to be particularly mindful of those who have suffered over many years of conflict. This I pledge to do.

ple from other lands continue to join us and enrich us by their presence. The First Minister and I, in our very first engagement, invited representatives of our ethnic minorities to Stormont to thank them for the contribution they and their communities were making. This message is one which we will continue to send out. Intolerance and fear of difference has been a blight on our island for too long. We are determined that, as we move forward, we can do so respecting difference, celebrating diversity and, by so doing, building a vibrant and prosperous community.

Opening the Smithsonian festival in Washington, which showcased the vast array of diverse cultures, music and talent within our society, I said that for decades, indeed centuries, our history was one of conflict and war. That part of our history is at an end. Through dialogue, accommodation and agreement we have begun to script a new history marked by confidence, optimism and creativity.

Our priority in the years ahead is to continue with the good start that has been made. There will of course be those on all sides who will be critical of what we are about. But I would say to them to sit back and honestly reflect upon the journey we have collectively made in recent times. Now is the time to look to our future.

I am an Irish Republican. I want to see a united Ireland. I am also jointly leading, with Ian Paisley, a unique set of political institutions and arrangements which reflect the unique set of political circumstances we have all come through.

I am an Irish Republican. I want to see a united Ireland. I am also jointly leading, with Ian Paisley, a unique set of political institutions and arrangements which reflect the unique set of political circumstances we have all come through. Dr Paisley clearly has a very different view. His unionism like my republicanism is not compromised by the actions we have jointly taken. The arrangement we are now in threatens no one's political aspirations. Indeed, it provides for the first time a common space to discuss and debate our futures on the basis of equality and respect.

One thing I can be certain of is that we will move forward in a dramatically transformed situation with conflict ended and a common desire to build a better future for all of the people that we represent, be they Catholics, Protestants or Dissenters.

Audience for "The Future of Northern Ireland"

Fr Alec Reid and Martin Mansergh TD

Enda Kenny TD
Leader of Fine Gael

Noel Whelan
Barrister, Columnist and Political Commentator

Frank Flannery
Director of Elections, Fine Gael

Chapter 2

Lessons from Election 2007

The Problems that Existed Before the Election Remain
ENDA KENNY TD
Leader of Fine Gael

Fine Gael and Labour Need a New Style of Opposition
FRANK FLANNERY
Director of Elections, Fine Gael

It's Still the Economy, Stupid, which Decides
NOEL WHELAN
Barrister, Columnist and Political Commentator

Enda Kenny TD

Leader of Fine Gael

Born in Castlebar and educated at St. Gerald's School, Castlebar, St. Patrick's Teachers' Training College, Drumcondra and UCG. Formerly a national school teacher, first elected to Dáil Éireann in 1975 following the death of his father, Henry, who represented Mayo constituencies for 21 years. Also elected in 1975 to Mayo Co. Council. Spokesperson on Youth Affairs and Sport 1977-80 and on the Gaeltacht 1982 and 1987-8. FG Chief Whip 1992-4. Spokesperson on Regional Development 1994 and on Arts, Heritage, Gaeltacht and the Islands 1997-2002. Minister of State at the Depts. of Education and Labour 1986-7 and Minister for Trade and Tourism 1994-7. Following the resignation of Michael Noonan in the wake of the general election of 2002, elected leader of Fine Gael and led the party in the election of May 2007 winning back 20 seats.

The Problems that Existed Before the Election Remain

Ireland faces serious challenges over the next five years. On the international stage, many changes will happen. We will have new administrations in Washington and Moscow. These and other world leaders will have to grapple with the challenges of climate change and securing future energy supplies. We will see China, India and other countries becoming real economic powers and locations for investment. These developments will have a significant influence on our future economic prosperity.

On the domestic front, the problems that existed before the recent general election remain – the crisis in the health service, the rise in serious crime and the waste of public money. Despite the denial of their existence by the outgoing government, these are very serious problems which must be tackled but I see no political will in the recently-formed Government to even recognise them, much less provide effective solutions.

... these are very serious problems which must be tackled but I see no political will in the recently-formed Government to even recognise them, much less provide effective solutions.

I fought the general election on a positive platform for change – not change just for the sake of change, but change for the better – better government, better services, better spending, better results leading to a better quality of life for all our people. I believe that our message struck a chord with very many people resulting in an unprecedented seat gain for Fine Gael.

However, the message from our main opponents, Fianna Fáil, was very different. Their message was based on fear and scaremongering. They offered nothing but "more of the same" and dishonest attacks on the proposals of other parties. While these scare tactics may have been enough to persuade some people to stick with Fianna Fáil on this occasion, I very much doubt if these voters expected the dollymixture combination of incompatible parties and individuals which was cobbled together after the election.

This result has not provided Ireland with a new government. Fianna Fáil, which has failed to tackle the problems facing them for the past 10 years, remains the dominant force in government. For proof of this, one needs to look no further than the Programme for Government with, apart from a few cosmetic additions to fool the Greens into believing that they have some influence, is essentially the Fianna Fáil manifesto with a new cover. It offers nothing more than a continuation of the policies of the past. It will not equip this country to meet the challenges of the future so that we can remain successful and prosperous while providing the quality public services our people deserve.

That is why I will fulfil the mandate given to me by well over 600,000 people to fight for the changes needed to move Ireland forward. Fine Gael will build on our excellent result to provide vigorous but constructive opposition to this inherently unstable Government. Our objective is to replace Fianna Fáil as the largest party in the next Dáil and as the main force in the next government.

Among the key issues on which we will focus in the next Dáil term will be the need for an economic strategy to ensure ongoing prosperity.

> **Our objective is to replace Fianna Fáil as the largest party in the next Dáil and as the main force in the next government.**

Economy

Ensuring the continuation of our economic progress is fundamental to the country's future success and to the provision of public services. The National Competitiveness Council's latest annual report on the state of Ireland's economy makes it clear that, unlike the 1990s, Irish exporters are no longer contributing to our economic growth, undermined by infrastructure congestion and runaway inflation. Some of the cost competitiveness figures published by the Council are quite alarming.

The report points out that Ireland's share of world trade peaked in 2002, and has since been in steady decline. As a result, Ireland's balance of payments with the rest of the world shifted from a surplus as recently as 1999 to an estimated deficit of €5.5 billion in 2005, and is forecast to deteriorate to €7.8 billion this year.

The conclusions reached by the NCC report about the state of Ireland's competitiveness are consistent with other authoritative analyses. There is now a consensus in Ireland's economic community that the failure to take the hard decisions that were needed to control costs in recent years has now seriously damaged Ireland's competitiveness, and will make it difficult for Irish-based exporters to compete in world markets for years to come.

Years of seemingly effortless employment growth built on the strong foundation laid in the 1980s and 1990s have lulled this Government into complacency about the threats that we face. We need bold, new approaches to tackle the growing competitiveness challenges facing us. Among the menu of action needed to be taken are:

1. Far greater attention to the competitive conditions in the "sheltered sectors" of the economy than has been the case heretofore

2. Radical change in the regulation of sectors, such as energy, transport and communications, where monopoly power prevails

3. Much greater care to ensure that regulation does not impose an unnecessary burden on small business owners

4. A government which exercises discipline on itself and does not use stealth taxes and charges as an easy way to make businesses pay for inefficiencies.

5. Promoting a more confident and assertive consumer culture.

Immigration

Among the other areas in which we will be highlighting the need for change is that of immigration, a phenomenon which has changed the face of Ireland in a very short period of time. Early this year, I called for a major national debate on this issue so that we can avoid the mistakes made in other countries.

I also set out Fine Gael's core principles for creating an immigration system which is both good for the Irish and good for the immigrants. Immigrants have rights and responsibilities. They should have the right to be free of discrimination and have their contribution to the country recognised, but they have the responsibility to integrate into our community, comply with our laws and respect our cultural traditions. I do not want to see a situation developing in which our immigrant population live separate lives. We have a responsibility to facilitate and encourage this integration.

Immigration must be managed in a way that keeps Ireland safe. We must ensure that Irish laws are understood and adhered to by immigrants. We also need to send a strong message that people who want to come to this country to commit serious crime are not welcome and will be dealt with severely.

Immigration must be a force for improving, not threatening, living standards. We must protect Irish jobs and the rights of those who

> ... the failure to take the hard decisions that were needed to control costs in recent years has now seriously damaged Ireland's competitiveness.

come to work here. Companies that pay below the minimum wage should pay severe fines, and immigration levels from non-EU countries must be explicitly linked to economic conditions and the needs of the labour market.

I welcome the appointment of a Minister of State for Integration as a step in the right direction. However, I am disappointed that it is not based in the Department of the Taoiseach, as I had proposed, given the cross-cutting nature of the issues arising from immigration and the need for a minister to have a strong political mandate.

We must have the courage to debate the issue openly and honestly. The possibility of a slowdown in economic activity, particularly in the construction sector, makes it all the more urgent that we make the policy changes needed to deliver a coherent, coordinated system that works in the best interests of everybody living in Ireland.

Another area which is critical for our future success is education. We need to transform Irish education in order to future-proof our economy and wealth for the next generation. Nothing less than a quantum leap is necessary for Ireland to become a major player in the global, knowledge economy. We must face the major threats to Ireland's future prosperity:

1. The widespread pockets of disadvantage that persist, despite Ireland's wealth

2. The persistent, poor levels of literacy and numeracy

3. The political complacency of "good enough" and the recklessness that "more of the same" will drive our economy and guarantee our wealth in the future.

The philosophy of "good enough" can never be enough for Ireland's children. Many communities are doing well in education but too many others are not. Ireland is transforming before our eyes, but our education system, the key to our future prosperity, is stuck in the last century. To secure our economy, our jobs, our wealth into the next generation, we must move on and fix this dangerous anomaly.

I want to use technology to transform teaching and learning, with the laptop becoming the schoolbag of the future. We must reform the way we educate and identify and reinforce higher standards in our schools. Finally, I want to ensure that critical investment is delivered along with local-support programmes to eradicate educational disadvantage.

Some of the proposals that will help deliver my vision of primary and secondary education for the next generation are:

1. Drive the use of technology in education. Give a laptop to every child entering secondary school and radically redesign course material around new technology

> **We need to transform Irish education in order to future-proof our economy and wealth for the next generation. Nothing less than a quantum leap is necessary for Ireland to become a major player in the global, knowledge economy.**

2. Introduce standardised literacy and numeracy tests for all children

3. Audit teachers in skills and methodologies every five years

4. Instigate premium payments for teachers in the most challenging schools

5. Given the extra demands being imposed on our secondary schools we should work towards lengthening either the school day or the school year.

But "good enough" is short-sighted and selfish. I want the next generation to do even better.

If we don't have the courage and vision to transform education, the economic and social consequences will be dire. We've worked hard for what we have. But "good enough" is short-sighted and selfish. I want the next generation to do even better. They will, but only if we transform education. We have to embrace new technology. We must reform and finally we need to invest wisely to provide the opportunities for all our children.

Frank Flannery

Director of Elections, Fine Gael

Born in Co. Galway and educated at St. Clement's College Limerick, UCG and UCD where he took an MBA. Joined the Rehab Group in 1973 and became Group Chief Executive in 1981. Held this position until he stood down in 2006. Established Rehab Lotteries in Ireland and Charity Lotteries in the UK. Has served on the RTE Authority, the National Rehabilitation Board and St. Luke's and St. Anne's Hospitals' Boards. He is a former chairman of the Disability Federation of Ireland. He has been involved with the Fine Gael Party since 1977. Was a member of the Strategy Group 1981-2 and of the so-called National Handlers up to 1987. He is a trustee of the party and a member of the Executive Council.

Fine Gael and Labour Need a New Style of Opposition

Election 2007: The Facts

I suppose, in giving this talk on the lessons of the election, I'm reminded of Harry Truman who said: "It's what you learn … after you know it all … that counts."

In addressing the issue of lessons to be learned from election 2007, I first must set out the basic facts and figures. Naturally, I must start with the very positive fact that FG was the only party to win seats in the election, going from 31 seats in 2002 to 51 seats in 2007 – a stellar achievement by Enda Kenny.

In contrast to FG, all other parties, bar the Greens, actually lost seats: FF lost three going from 81 to 78, with Labour, Sinn Féin and the Socialist Party losing one each. The Greens, of course, managed to hold on to their six seats, albeit with different personnel. The most dramatic election losses were incurred by the PDs, who went from eight to two. The Independents were casualties, too, down from 13 to 5. In terms of FG's gains, we won six seats from Fianna Fáil, five from the PDs, five from Independents, two from Labour, and one each from Sinn Féin and the Socialist Party.

More Votes for Everyone Except the PDs

One of the most significant features of this election was the voters themselves. They turned out in big numbers. Just over 2 million people voted compared to 1.8 million in 2002 – an increase of just over 11 per cent.

One of the most significant features of this election was the voters themselves. They turned out in big numbers. Just over 2 million people voted compared to 1.8 million in 2002 – an increase of just over 11 per cent.

– 43 –

Why was there such an increase? Well, there are a number of reasons. Certainly, a higher, potential electorate would account for some rise. But there is also the impact of the improved electoral register and, of course, the vigorous and robust campaign. We had a real contest.

In looking at the total number of votes cast in real terms, it is also instructive to look at the percentage increase in total votes cast for each party. Fianna Fáil maintained its overall share of the vote. Because it did, the number of real votes it received also went up by just over 11 per cent.

On the other hand, FG made significant gains, pulling a total, first-preference vote of 564,000. That's the highest since 1982, and a substantial 35 per cent increase – over a third of an increase – on the number of votes for FG in 2002.

The Labour Party's real increase was 4.5 per cent, while Sinn Féin increased their votes by 18 per cent aided by a significantly larger number of candidates. The Green Party increased their votes by 35 per cent. And, of course, the real losers were the Progressive Democrats. Their votes fell by almost a full quarter, i.e. 23 per cent.

> On the other hand, FG made significant gains, pulling a total, first-preference vote of 564,000. That's the highest since 1982 ...

Mining the Exit Poll

For the purpose of this presentation, I am going to draw from the Lansdowne Exit Poll conducted for RTÉ. Conducted on polling day, this poll had over 3,000 respondents. It was extremely accurate in predicting the final first-preference vote figure, although it somewhat underestimated the FG result.

Given the accuracy of the top-line figures, a further analysis of the more in-depth figures, revealed some interesting conclusions. I should say that, by and large, I am going to focus on the Fianna Fáil and Fine Gael votes simply because the sample sizes for those parties can give us some comfort about the solidity of our conclusions.

Loyalists, Switchers and New Voters

In general terms, using the Lansdowne data, I believe we can break those who voted for Fianna Fáil and Fine Gael into three broad categories – what we'll call loyalists, switchers and first-timers.

1. The "loyalists" are those who voted for the party in 2002 and who voted again for them in 2007.
2. The switchers are those who voted for a different party in 2002, but switched to Fianna Fáil or Fine Gael in 2007.
3. The first-timers are either first-time voters or those who, for whatever reason, didn't vote in 2002.

So how did Fianna Fáil and Fine Gael fare with these categories?

FF: Solidifying the Core

Analysis of the Lansdowne figures suggests that of Fianna Fáil's 41.6 per cent points, 30 points represent consistent Fianna Fáil voters – in other words, people who voted FF in 2002 and again in 2007. Just under 4 points, represent the people who switched to Fianna Fáil and 7.5 points represent those who were voting for the first time or did not vote in 2002. These figures suggest that Fianna Fáil retains a very solid core vote, which, undoubtedly, the FF machine managed to get out in this election.

There has been a lot of comment about a campaign late surge to Fianna Fáil, and the reasons for that surge. It's true that FF picked up the vital 2 to 3 points it needed in the closing week – and the polls taken during the campaign bear that out. Notably, this reversed a trend, which had become the norm, whereby FF lose support during a campaign.

That's the *what*. But working out *why* they picked up that support is a more complex task. Indeed, the Lansdowne Poll which allows us to cross-reference the key policy issues, with the date on which people decided how they would vote, produces no conclusive evidence that it was the economy, or stable government, or the choice of Taoiseach, or the debate, or the Westminster speech, or the meeting with Dr Paisley, or any other single issue that motivated voting decisions in the last week of the campaign.

It was a combination of all of the above, plus an effective (if unreal) FF message that the widespread desire for change could be combined with the powerful desire for security, by successfully suggesting that the FF/Labour option was always really there – with FF representing safety and security and Labour providing change.

FF mounted a vigorous campaign, based mainly on fear, together with a powerful on-the-ground canvass in the last week, when survival was a strong motivator. All of this secured a shift among that vital few per cent who, in the end, plumped for FF, going from wanting change to fearing change. They opted for the status quo.

FF mounted a vigorous campaign, based mainly on fear, together with a powerful on-the-ground canvass in the last week, when survival was a strong motivator.

Fine Gael: Winning Switchers and New Voters

The comparable figures for Fine Gael's 27.3 points of the vote are that 15 represent consistent Fine Gael voters, 7 represent people who switched to Fine Gael in the election and just over 5 represent first time voters or those who did not vote in 2002.

With a growing population, and evidence of the growing volatility in the electorate, Fine Gael's success in attracting these votes is encouraging for the future. Equally encouraging for the future is that FG's vote has a somewhat more even pattern of support throughout the age spectrum compared to Fianna Fáil, whose vote rises from just 35 per cent of 18-24 year olds to 49 per cent of over 65 years olds. Fine Gael's range is from 23 per cent of 25-34 year olds to 31 per cent of those over 65.

Where the Transfers Went

Certainly, the first-preference votes tell their own story, but Fine Gael's own analysis of the destination of transfers gives some interesting insights. We analysed over 630,000 votes distributed. Almost 11 per cent were non-transferable; Fine Gael was the primary beneficiary, receiving 31 per cent of all votes distributed, followed by Fianna Fáil with 26 per cent – a much smaller share than their share of first preferences.

In light of the subsequent Government formation, it's ironic to see that less than 9 per cent of Green transfers went to Fianna Fáil, whereas almost two-thirds went to the Rainbow of Fine Gael, Labour or the Greens.

In light of the subsequent Government formation, it's ironic to see that less than 9 per cent of Green transfers went to Fianna Fáil, whereas almost two-thirds went to the Rainbow of Fine Gael, Labour or the Greens. In fact, the internal transfer rate among the three so-called Rainbow Parties, at 68 per cent, was more than ten points better than the internal Fianna Fáil rate.

One other interesting phenomenon: Sinn Féin voters traditionally don't transfer in great numbers to other parties. This time, 18 per cent were non-transferable (compared to a national average of 10.6 per cent) and whilst Fianna Fáil received the highest share, at 24 per cent, Fine Gael and Labour weren't far behind, receiving 22 per cent and 21 per cent – which indicates a significant change in the voting pattern of Sinn Féin supporters.

In summary, the outgoing Government parties won just over 44 per cent of first preferences, but only 28 per cent of all votes transferred. Sixty per cent of all transferred votes went to Opposition parties or candidates.

Issues: Health and the Economy

In the run-up to the election, it was clear that the Alliance had chosen public services, particularly the health service, as its key battleground. The Government chose the economy. In terms of the issues identified by the exit poll, it is clear that health remains a dominant electoral issue.

It is interesting to note that the importance of health for voters has actually increased from 2002, when it was also rated as the most significant issue. In contrast, crime receded in 2007 compared to 2002.

As always, managing the economy remains one of the top three issues in every election.

An analysis of those who switched votes in 2002 to 2007 and who cite "health" as their first issue suggests that this was a net gainer for Fine Gael (and Labour to a lesser extent) while being a net loser for Fianna Fáil.

Not surprisingly, those who rated the economy as their top priority, voted overwhelmingly – 57 per cent – for Fianna Fáil. So both sides can claim some success in driving the fight onto their battleground.

More on the Economy

A number of commentators have, I believe, mistakenly suggested that Fine Gael, or the Opposition generally, should have focused more on the economy in the course of the election. Notwithstanding the fact that the Alliance produced a detailed and fully-costed economic blueprint ahead of the election, which no other Government option matched, two key points have to be made on this:

1. Firstly, that health was the most significant policy issue affecting how people voted. Fine Gael did disproportionately well among those voters who cited health as the most important issue in the election.

2. Secondly, the economy was still the Government's strongest card. That is why every day they tried to shift the debate to the economy, in the same way that we tried to focus attention on health. As things turned out, the Government lost 9 seats and Fine Gael won 20.

Those who argue, after the event, that "more" should have been done on the economy forget one of the standard assumptions in economic study and analysis, and that is "ceteris paribus" or "all things being equal".

This simplistic assumption allows, for academic purposes, that you change one variable in a mix without impacting on the others. Of course, the reality is that this is simply not the case, that once one has chosen the best strategy, considering all variables and based on all the research, data and evidence that presents itself, you can't do more of one thing without affecting your strategy elsewhere.

A New Dáil

One outcome of the election has been the changed face of Dáil Éireann on both the Government and Opposition benches. On the Government side, we have now moved from a two-party Government

> Not surprisingly, those who rated the economy as their top priority, voted overwhelmingly – 57 per cent – for Fianna Fáil.

which, over its 10 years, has been quite compatible to a three-party Government, supported by four Independents, which, despite the accepted wisdom, may have the seeds of some instability sown within it.

Stability in Government

Stability is often cited as the hallmark of Bertie Ahern's governments. In fairness, the 1997-2002 Government, albeit operating with the support of Independents, was extremely stable – perhaps because the Minister for Finance was, to all intents and purposes, a Progressive Democrat and he had significant support around the cabinet table from like-minded Fianna Fáil ministers.

By moving the Progressive Democrat ministers to health and crime portfolios, Fianna Fáil cleverly isolated their most sensitive attack points and helped to insulate themselves from the worst of public ire on these topics.

The 2002-2007 Government was less stable, but the stability it had was rooted more in its numerical advantage. By moving the Progressive Democrat ministers to health and crime portfolios, Fianna Fáil cleverly isolated their most sensitive attack points and helped to insulate themselves from the worst of public ire on these topics.

The only issue that ever seriously troubled the stability of the 2002-2007 Government was the Taoiseach's personal finances and, to paraphrase what another political leader said once, it hasn't gone away, you know!

Looking ahead, and especially after the honeymoon period is over, it is certainly possible that tensions within this Government will arise. Last night I heard Enda Kenny talk about how the most fragile eco-system of all was the one around the cabinet table!

The Green Party, in particular, has always been a party of protest and opposition. Its membership base and core supporters are used to opposing many long-standing Government policies. Once the first flush of enthusiasm passes, I expect that the Green ministers will turn a little greener, as they find that effecting change is not as straightforward or simple as they might have thought. I would expect they will be looking for some symbolic decisions to keep their power-base content. How Fianna Fáil responds to the Greens totemic requests will be interesting.

We should also remember that the local elections are just two years away and the issues that have delivered the Greens some success in local elections are not ones that tend to rest easy with their Fianna Fáil companions in Government.

Less Fragmentation in Opposition

On the Opposition side, there has been significant change. Look at the Opposition benches and you see that FG are back with a bang.

The Opposition is also less fragmented. We have to remember that in the past five years, Fine Gael, with just over 30 seats, was vying with the Labour Party, Greens, Sinn Féin and the Independents for air space and share of voice.

One-party State?

One issue which may well arise in the coming months and years is whether we are living in a one-party state. Since 1987, Fianna Fáil has been the dominant Government Party with the exception of 2½ years in the mid-1990s. Once again, Fianna Fáil are back in power, and the implications of such continuity must be watched very carefully. Since the election, we have seen the Taoiseach wield unlimited power in a number of areas:

- In his selection of Government partners
- In his approach to Independent deputies
- In extending his olive grove – hardly a branch – to a deputy who had been "excommunicated" from the Fianna Fáil party
- In increasing the number of Ministers of State to satisfy his backbenches
- In his appointment of a Leas Ceann Comhairle of the Dáil, and
- In other areas, no moaning on the economy, please. The economic Emperor still has some clothes.

The clever construction of this Government puts him in the position that any party unhappy with this exercise of power can be done without. But this type of unbridled power has its dangers and it would not surprise me if the electorate again use the local elections to give FF a bloody nose and remind them who is ultimately in charge. They need to learn, perhaps, that democracy is not just when the people speak, it's when the Government listens.

Fine Gael's Campaign: The Lessons Learned

Finally, I would like to focus for a few minutes on my own party's campaign and the factors which gave us our success. With your indulgence, I will keep the mistakes we made to myself.

We started our campaign early. Some of you might remember the storm of controversy in January when we launched a billboard attack on the Government. We made no apology for setting out our stall and reminding the Irish people, especially in the aftermath of another generous budget, where the Government had failed to deliver.

In the months after January we maintained a strong line of attack on the Government, through the Dáil and media channels. We stayed

One issue which may well arise in the coming months and years is whether we are living in a one-party state.

on the offensive, on message and we drove coverage onto our battle-ground. We defined the election around services and healthcare, in particular. That attack phase significantly disrupted Fianna Fáil's run in to the election and I need only point to the FF Ard Fhéis as an example of how that party was not in control of the agenda.

By contrast, Fine Gael had a stunningly successful Ard Fhéis. The leader's speech, introducing his "Contract for a Better Ireland", along with his pledge to be accountable for its delivery, was the single most positive force in increasing the FG vote. Hand in hand with FG's own campaign, the Alliance with the Labour Party meant that the voters now had an alternative Government on offer. Our campaign itself used the enormous energy and drive of Enda Kenny to its maximum. Enda Kenny's campaign defied many of its armchair critics who seriously underestimated his campaigning ability.

Enda Kenny's campaign defied many of its armchair critics who seriously under-estimated his campaigning ability.

So What Are the Lessons Learned from Election 2007?

1. It was a vigorous election with lively debates on radio and television. The public's interest in issues was maintained and the campaign had enough twists and turns to maintain public interest. The public's engagement shows that Irish democracy is alive and well.

2. An incumbent government is very hard to shift in a time of economic prosperity and popular sense of well-being. Selling a change message in such times is more difficult than defending the status quo. It's like playing into the wind for both halves.

3. Fianna Fáil remains a determined, capable political force and still – by some distance – the leading party in Irish politics. It will never relinquish power easily and its current chameleon quality of being able to accommodate allies from any quarter makes the task of giving Ireland a change of government an even more challenging one.

4. Given all the advantages on the Government side, the Alliance did very well, gaining a net 19 seats and inflicting net losses of 9 seats on the Government – a swing of 28 seats.

5. This resulted in the defeat of the outgoing Government but was not sufficient to prevent Fianna Fáil forming a new Coalition Government with the Greens.

6. Fine Gael had, in many ways, a spectacularly good election, successfully defending all its 31 seats and gaining 20 new seats, including six directly from Fianna Fáil. Its campaign was professional, energetic, focused and brilliantly led by Enda Kenny who finally emerged during the election as a major political force. As a result Fine Gael is rejuvenated, upbeat, despite narrowly missing

out on government and determined as never before to continue its growth and development and ultimately to win government.

7. Fine Gael and Labour need to develop a new and more effective style of opposition and proposition. The consolidation of the opposition will make this a feasible task and the fact that Labour didn't take the FF shilling – or to paraphrase Pat Rabbitte, didn't "waltz with FF" – might well be a key factor for the future.

8. The era of maverick independents and small niche parties is probably over. This new phase will likely be dominated by the three traditional parties.

9. Finally, the challenge of giving Ireland a real alternative to Fianna Fáil continues. The experience of the Christian Democrats in Italy in the second half of the twentieth century shows the dangers of one party being permanently in power and the way a system can become corrupted. But surely that could never happen in Ireland!

Of course, the parties, the hacks and the pundits take their politics terribly seriously. But today, in closing this address on the lessons of the election and what they taught us, let me finish with some thoughts from the ultimate source of wisdom, Buddha:

> Let us rise up and be thankful, for if we didn't learn a lot today, at least we learned a little, and if we didn't learn a little, at least we didn't get sick, and if we got sick, at least we didn't die; so, let us all be thankful.

Fine Gael and Labour need to develop a new and more effective style of opposition and proposition.

Noel Whelan

Barrister, Columnist and Political Commentator

Born in Wexford and educated at UCD (Politics and History) and Kings Inns (Law). Formerly political adviser at Fianna Fáil HQ and Special Adviser at the Dept. of An Taoiseach. He practices as a barrister on the Dublin and South-East circuits and writes a weekly political column for The Irish Times. He has published a number of books including Politics, Elections and the Law *(2001) and the Tallyman series of election guides the most recent of which was:* The Tallyman's Campaign Handbook – Election 2007. *He is a frequent contributor to radio and television news and current affairs programmes.*

It's Still the Economy, Stupid, which Decides

Election 2007 leaves us with a political system in which:

- Fianna Fáil looks almost invincible and looks like it could be at the fulcrum of government formation for the foreseeable future.
- Fine Gael has recovered and is revitalised. It is however stuck again in opposition. While it looks like it could make additional gains at the next election, these again may not necessarily be at the expense of Fianna Fáil and therefore Fine Gael again may not be in government.
- Labour is still stagnant and, with no obvious solution to and only a limited understanding of its dilemma, may actually go into reverse.
- The Green Party is in government and it is their performance in government more than anything else which will determine their future success or failure.
- Sinn Féin is on the rise in Northern Ireland and in government there but has flat-lined in the Republic and is isolated on the opposition benches.
- The Progressive Democrats are teetering on the brink of extinction.
- Independents are smaller in number but have more influence because four of them are shoring up the government.

There are in my view four other key lessons which can, at this stage, be learnt from election 2007:

- We need to take affirmative action to tackle the problem of the under-representation of women in Dáil Éireann.

> Labour is still stagnant and, with no obvious solution to and only a limited understanding of its dilemma, may actually go into reverse.

- We need to remember that the issue at the start of the election campaign is never the issue at the end of the election campaign.
- We need to realise that it's still the economy, stupid, which decides our elections.
- We need to appreciate that "likeability" matters in political leaders but likeability alone is not enough.

We need to realise that it's still the economy, stupid, which decides our elections.

14 June 2007 – First Day of the 30th Dáil

The first sitting day of a new Dáil is always described as historic. For the last two decades these opening sessions of our parliament have been captured in audio and visual format for posterity and for live broadcast on television and radio.

The first sitting of the 30th Dáil on 14 June 2007 was genuinely historic. For the purposes of considering the lessons to be learnt from election 2007, I want to zoom in on a number of the images and moments from that day which, to my mind, crystallised how dramatic the results of election 2007 had been and how the consequences of this election and its immediate aftermath will impact on our politics not only for the next five years but also in the longer term.

Many New Deputies but a Dáil which is Still Very, Very Male

As the deputies poured in on the afternoon of the 14th of June to take up their seats for the first session, the extent to which the membership of the Dáil had been changed by the election result became very evident. There were 49 TDs in the chamber on the opening day of the 30th Dáil who were not members of the 29th Dáil. Some of these 49 were deputies returning to the Dáil having lost out in 2002, and indeed there were a few who had lost their seats in even earlier elections. Most of the new deputies however were people who had never held a Dáil seat previously. Overall, it represented a significant transfusion of new blood into the Dáil membership.

Fianna Fáil had 19 new deputies who were sitting in the Dáil chamber for the first time. Fine Gael had 15 completely new deputies and Labour had three. The Green Party's one new face was their deputy leader Mary White who is also their first ever woman deputy and their first deputy representing a rural constituency.

The Fianna Fáil benches included three sets of siblings – Noel Ahern representing Dublin North West and his brother Bertie elected for Dublin Central, Brian Lenihan re-elected for Dublin West and his brother Conor also back for Dublin South West. For the first time ever, there were three siblings from one family in the chamber – Michael Kitt who regained the seat he and his father before him had held in Galway East, his brother Tom re-elected for Dublin South and their sister Anne Brady-Kitt elected for the first time for Kildare North.

The Fine Gael benches included the novelty of a married couple among its membership – Olwyn Enright who had been re-elected from Laois Offaly and her husband, Joe McHugh, a newly-elected deputy for Donegal North West.

For the first time, a wheelchair user was elected to Dáil Éireann, namely Sean Connick, a New Ross-based businessman who was a newly elected Fianna Fáil deputy from Wexford. His election required a minor redesign of the chamber to enable wheelchair access to the Dáil floor.

As the cameras panned across the benches once all deputies had taken their seats the thing which struck one most was how little colour there was among the ranks of the seated deputies. It was again a wall of mainly dark suits, with very little of it broken by the more colourful attire which can signal the presence of female members.

There are fewer female deputies in the 30th Dáil than there were in the 29th Dáil. This should act as a wake-up call. One lesson we should take from the results of Election 2007, therefore, is that something needs to be done about the paltry levels of female representation in our parliament.

For decades Ireland has languished near the bottom of the league table in terms of female representation in our national parliament. While in Scandinavian countries for decades now, one-third or more of their parliament is female and in most other western European countries one-fifth of their membership is female, we have never had more than one-eighth of our parliamentarians who were female. It cannot be assumed that our political system's derisory record on female representation at national level will be resolved simply by the passage of time.

Much work has been done by political scientists and those specialising in equality and gender studies to identify the reason behind our consistently low levels of female participation in politics. Some have attributed it to the fact that Ireland has traditionally been an agrarian, patriarchal society with low levels of female participation in the workforce. For those who subscribed to this interpretation, the 1992 election when an unprecedented 20 women were elected to the Dáil was seen as the great breakthrough. It was assumed that, as Ireland's society and economy modernised, so too would the configuration of its parliamentary representation.

Now, however, a decade and a half later, in the post-Celtic Tiger era, when our society has reached Scandinavian-like levels of female

... we have never had more than one-eighth of our parliamentarians who were female. It cannot be assumed that our political system's derisory record on female representation at national level will be resolved simply by the passage of time.

workforce participation, little has changed in the gender composition of the Dáil.

Of course, progress can be pointed to in other aspects of politics; it is significant that the Presidency has been held by women for the last 17 years and that, until September 2006, the position of Tánaiste had been held by a woman for a decade. We have indeed been blessed in the main by the calibre of the women who have been elected but there have been too few of them.

The main reason for this appears to be that the parties, especially the larger parties, are selecting very few female candidates. One of the most interesting features of the planning and preparation for this election has been the increasing centralisation of the candidate selection process. Headquarters and/or a national executive committee now have the most significant role in influencing, and in many instances deciding, who the Dáil candidates can be. However, even this trend has not led to any dramatic shift in the selection of female candidates which, for example, it has led to in other countries with similar parliamentary systems and similarly low levels of female membership of parliament. Only 13 per cent of the Fianna Fáil candidates were female compared to almost a quarter of the Progressive Democrats candidates and the Green Party candidates. The other parties come in at between 16 and 18 per cent.

We have surely come to a point where, if we genuinely want to see a transformation in parliamentary representation to more accurately reflect the gender breakdown of the population, we need to take affirmative action. Each of the political parties should be required to field a specific quota of female candidates in all future elections. One could seek initially to do this by asking the parties to write such quotas into their rulebooks but, if necessary, it should be made a legal requirement or a condition of state funding. A target should be set that the candidate line-up fielded by each party in the next election should include at least one-third females and one-third males. This would be a significant achievement and should be possible. Nothing short of this type of positive discrimination will resolve the problem of the enduring low levels of female representation in Dáil Éireann.

There is a growing body of literature in the field which contends that the relatively low levels of female participation in our politics is one of the consequences of the way our society and our economy are organised. It is more difficult for women to juggle the tasks of work and family in Ireland than in many other western European countries – managing a "third" job of engaging in community and/or political activity is almost impossible for most of them.

Changes, therefore, are required in how our politics is organised to make it easier for women to participate. The necessary changes to

There is a growing body of literature in the field which contends that the relatively low levels of female participation in our politics is one of the consequences of the way our society and our economy are organised.

how our politics is organised at party, parliamentary and constituency levels will only happen if there are more women involved in the making of the decisions about how politics is organised. It is a classic chicken and egg conundrum.

Of course, there are many who will argue against such positive discrimination – some of the most vociferous opponents of female candidate quotas are women who are already members of the Dáil and who see themselves having done it without the assistance of affirmative action and argue that it is up to the electorate to decide who they want. I am not arguing that the choice of TD be taken from the electorate but I am arguing that the electorate be given more women among those from whom it is asked to chose. Other initiatives have been tried and failed. The time for the imposition of quota systems for female candidates is a concept whose time has come.

A Changed Party Breakdown

In this election Fianna Fáil held vote share at 41 per cent and, despite indications in earlier polls, was down only three seats. Not only did Fianna Fáil comfortably hold seats that had wrongly been seen as vulnerable but it gained additional seats.

In commuter-belt constituencies, where Fine Gael and Labour claimed the mood for change was reflected strongest on the doorsteps, not only did Fianna Fáil hold its own but the party picked up extra seats in Meath East, Kildare North and Dublin North. Another twist was that Fianna Fáil's success was not achieved by containing the Fine Gael rise but occurred in circumstances where Fine Gael also had a good day. It was the smaller parties – all of them – who were squeezed.

Fine Gael had a good election. Their vote was up five per cent from 22.5 per cent to 27.3 per cent and the party's gain of 20 seat was particularly dramatic. However, it is important to remember that Fine Gael did not win the election. Fine Gael did no more than undo the damage done to their Dáil representation five years ago and, while a Fine Gael gain of 20 seats was impressive and defied many who had predicted their demise after 2002, it did leave the party on the opposition benches, probably for another five years.

... to win the next election Fine Gael will need to be offering a better set of policies than the current government – a set of policies which are more credible and comprehensive than those they offered in this election.

However, to win the next election Fine Gael will need to be offering a better set of policies than the current government – a set of policies which are more credible and comprehensive than those they offered in this election. They must also offer a set of policies and a vision for Ireland which is more distinctive from Fianna Fáil than that which they advanced in the lead-in to this election. When Tony Blair took over the leadership of the British Labour party, when Bill Clinton won the Democratic Party's presidential nomination and when David Cameron took over the leadership of the British Conservative Party, they each effected a revitalisation of their party's organisation and campaign method but more importantly they also put in place a transformation of their party's content – a series of significant policy changes – which repositioned their parties and distinguished them more from their opponents. A similar task remains to be done by the Kenny leadership team.

The Labour Party's vote in the election was down just over half a percentage point from 10.7 per cent to 10.1 per cent and they lost one seat going from 21 to 20. Depending on how blunt one wants to be about it, the Labour Party is either "becalmed" or "stagnant". Giving the annual Jim Kemmy lecture in July 2007, Pat Rabbitte himself opted for the word "flatlined". Although it has three relatively young new deputies after this election, the Labour parliamentary party is still largely a collection of men and women over fifty who jealously guard their one-man or one-women constituency fiefdoms. At least in this recent speech, Rabbitte has recognised the extent to which Labour's vision of itself is detached from the aspirations of the mass of the Irish electorate, particularly that portion which, as working class, might have been expected to vote Labour, but which is now increasingly lower and even upper middle class.

... the Labour parliamentary party is still largely a collection of men and women over fifty who jealously guard their one-man or one-women constituency fiefdoms.

The Green Party's vote was up 1 percentage point but they held just the same number of seats with Mary White's win in Carlow-Kilkenny compensating for the loss of Dan Boyle's seat in Cork South Central. The small rise in their vote was due in no small part to the fact that they ran more candidates this time out. Although the party vote appeared to have reached 9 or 10 percentage points in the first months of this year, the party didn't achieve such support during the election itself. Its issues were sidelined during what was at times a bizarre election campaign, with the first half dominated by the Taoiseach's personal finances and the second half by the head-to-head contest between the alternative taoisigh. Although the smaller parties and Independents came under pressure in the election, the Green Party did best at holding its ground. In the circumstances, it was no mean achievement to hold six seats. The Green Party's real success in 2007 came in the weeks after the election when they got the opportunity to begin government negotiations with Fianna Fáil. Once they got that opportunity the Green Party used it well.

The Progressive Democrats by comparison lost a third of its vote and three-quarters of its Dáil representation. They were the biggest losers of the election and with the party's leader, deputy leader and president each having announced since that they are giving up politics altogether, the Progressive Democrats are teetering on the brink of national political extinction – or negotiating the dividing line between being a niche party and a non-party.

For Sinn Féin the election was also disastrous. The extent of the disaster for them is not evident from the actual results of the election itself. Their Dáil seat numbers declined from five to four and their vote rose marginally from 6.5 per cent to 7.4 per cent. This small rise, like that for the Green Party, was due to the fact that they ran more candidates this time out. The disaster for Sinn Féin was that their performance was so bad relative to their expectation. This was an election in which Sinn Féin expected to make significant gains and the failure to do so has significantly damaged their brand, north and south of the border.

The disaster for Sinn Féin was that their performance was so bad relative to their expectation. This was an election in which Sinn Féin expected to make significant gains and the failure to do so has significantly damaged their brand, north and south of the border.

The election was a disaster for the Independents, the numbers of whom were cut from 13 to five. This fall in the number of independents, the fact that four of the independents have done deals to support the Fianna Fáil-led government and that the Greens are in government means that the "technical group" which was such an interesting entity in the 29th Dáil – and was often so ably led by Joe Higgins at leaders' question time – will not be a feature of the 30th Dáil.

Ahern is Elected Taoiseach for a Third Term

One of the most dramatic moments of the afternoon of June 14th was when the acting Green Party leader, Trevor Sargent, rose to second the nomination of Bertie Ahern as Taoiseach. He did so from a seat amidst the government benches, beside his party colleague Mary White who was beside Mary Hanafin. The Green Party has matured in 2007 and taken the final significant step on a long journey from a protest movement to political party to a party of government. Sargent and his parliamentary party colleagues managed and led their membership in a sophisticated way during the negotiations for government and the subsequent special conference which overwhelmingly ratified the decision to enter government. While many bemoaned the fact that the Green tinge of the Programme for Government was not stronger, the party made the right decision. The Green Party has secured two cabinets posts. Their departments are in the key areas of policy concern for the Green Party and they are going to run those departments for five years. That is two more departments than Fine Gael or Labour have run for ten years.

With the support of his own Fianna Fáil deputies, the Green Party's deputies, the two Progressive Democrats and no fewer than four independents going through the Tá lobby for him, Bertie Ahern was comfortably re-elected Taoiseach. Ahern has many political achievements to his credit after ten years in office. History will look back on this as one of his most striking. Securing a third term as Taoiseach and building a majority which enables his party to be in government again for another five years is a truly remarkable achievement in the context of modern politics and the intense media environment in which it operates. Events have undermined government with solid majorities before – the collapse of the Reynolds-Spring Government in 1994 being the most dramatic example – but it will take a truly extraordinary series of events to take this government down. My advice is to mark in your diary that the next general election will be in 2012, probably again on the third Thursday in May.

Ahern's victory both in the election and in the subsequent negotiations on government formation are a tribute to his political skill and determination and a product of his obsession with politics. His election as Taoiseach for a third term confirms that likeability matters in Irish politics. To succeed, a party needs to be led by a leader who is liked by a large cross section of the electorate. Fianna Fáil had this lesson confirmed to them in this election. Fine Gael also learned it this time around. The Progressive Democrats also learned it to their cost.

The other lesson of the election is that the issue which dominates at the start of an election campaign is never the issue at the end of the election. Bertie Ahern's personal finances dominated the coverage of the first ten days of the election campaign but it did not determine the election. In the final week, this election turned to a consideration of the issue it was always going to turn to: whether re-electing an Ahern-led government or electing a new Kenny-led government was the best way to ensure the continuation of a strong economy. Having dallied with change, the electorate opted instead for continuity.

Securing a third term as Taoiseach and building a majority which enables his party to be in government again for another five years is a truly remarkable achievement in the context of modern politics ...

Sinn Féin's Parliamentary Importance

Later that evening, there was another moment which symbolised the consequences of the election result for Sinn Féin – the only one of the smaller parties not in government.

When Ahern returned from Áras an Uachtaráin to lead the traditional parade of new Ministers into the Dáil chamber, the House, and indeed the live TV and radio audiences, waited for the Taoiseach's formal announcement of his new Cabinet. The expected order of business was interrupted when Sinn Féin's Caoimhghín Ó Caoláin rose to object to the arrangements for the debate on the appointment of Ministers, and demanded that he and his party be given speaking rights.

Ó Caoláin sought to force the matter to a vote so the new Ceann Comhairle, John O'Donoghue, went through the required procedure of calling those in favour to shout "Tá" and those against to shout "Níl". O'Donoghue then asked those deputies saying Tá to stand to see if their number met the 10 deputies required to trigger a division of the House.

Just the four Sinn Féin deputies stood. Small in number and isolated, they couldn't even force a vote on whether they could speak. It was a stark physical representation of how disappointing the election and its results were for Sinn Féin.

A New Tánaiste

When he came to name his cabinet the first thing that Ahern did was announce that Brian Cowen would again not only be Minister for Finance but also Tánaiste, becoming the first Fianna Fáil member to hold the post since the late 1980s. Cowen had been a steady hand on the steering wheel during Fianna Fáil's wobbly campaign, particularly during the first ten days when a clearly distracted Bertie Ahern was swamped in the controversy surrounding the purchase of his house. Cowen was also responsible for developing and delivering the systematic attack on the content (or, as he saw it, lack of content) in the "Rainbow's" policy position. During the campaign Cowen delivered a series of consistently effective media performances and good calls.

I get the sense that there has been a significant shift in Cowen's standing among many middle class, middle ground and female voters over the last few months. Cowen has long been a darling of the Fianna Fáil grass roots. His clapometer at party Ard Fhéiseanna has been ringing off the scale for a decade and a half. However, his direct, combative and partisan style may have been off-putting for some in the wider electorate. In recent times however his ability, intelligence, steady management of the economic brief and the political skill he displayed during this election campaign have gained him a greater standing.

Three years (if it is three years) is a long time in politics and so a Cowen succession cannot be taken for granted.

Whether all this plays out in a scenario where Cowen succeeds Bertie Ahern as Taosieach remains to be seen. There are many in Fianna Fáil who would see it differently and at least three other Fianna Fáil ministers have short-term leadership ambitions. Three years (if it is three years) is a long time in politics and so a Cowen succession cannot be taken for granted.

Conclusion

Despite what some Fianna Fáil spin doctors and some self-serving commentators sought to suggest after the election, this was an election which Fianna Fáil could have lost and came close to losing. They won it because large swathes of the middle classes – not only in the commuter belt but throughout the country – decided that a Bertie Ahern-led government is something they wanted more of, that historical stories about Ahern's personal finances did not matter but that securing their future economic possession did. Fianna Fáil, with a strong candidate line-up and with an organisation which had fire in its belly, flamed by a sense that they and their leader had been wronged by the media, was best positioned to derive maximum benefit from this swing-back when it came.

They won it because large swathes of the middle classes – not only in the commuter belt but throughout the country – decided that a Bertie Ahern-led government is something they wanted more of ...

Brian Cowen TD, Tánaiste
and Minister for Finance

Joan Burton TD, Labour Party Deputy
Leader and Spokesperson on Finance

Jim O'Hara,
General Manager, Intel Ireland

Brian O'Connell, Managing Director,
Westpark Shannon Ltd

Chapter 3

Sustaining the Celtic Tiger

Taking Account of the Competitiveness Imperative
BRIAN COWEN TD
Tánaiste and Minister for Finance

The "Knowledge Society" Offers Huge Potential
JOAN BURTON TD
LABOUR PARTY DEPUTY LEADER AND SPOKESPERSON ON FINANCE

Productivity is Absolutely Critical to Future Success
JIM O'HARA
General Manager, Intel Ireland; President, American Chamber of Commerce in Ireland

Integrated Planning and Visionary Creation
BRIAN O'CONNELL
Managing Director, Westpark Shannon Ltd.; Co-Founder/ Chairman, Atlantic Way

Brian Cowen TD

Tánaiste and Minister for Finance

Born in Tullamore and educated at Mount St. Joseph's College, Roscrea, UCD (BCL) and Incorporated Law Society. Formerly a solicitor, first elected to Dáil Éireann for Laois-Offaly on the death of his father, Ber. He was Minister for Labour 1992-3, Minister for Transport, Energy & Communications 1993-4, Minister for Health & Children 1997-2000 and Minister for Foreign Affairs 2000-2004. He succeeded Charlie McCreevy as Minister for Finance in 2004 and was reappointed to the position following the 2007 election when he was also appointed Tánaiste. He was a member of Offaly Co. Council 1984-92.

Taking Account of the Competitiveness Imperative

We have seen tremendous economic and social progress in Ireland in the past ten years or so and we have put in place solid foundations for a modern, forward-looking economy. Over the next five years we will face many challenges the greatest of which will be to consolidate and sustain the remarkable progress we have made and provide a better quality of life for all.

The challenge of the next five years from an economic viewpoint is, I believe, two-fold in nature. First, we must strive to ensure that we consolidate and retain the progress of the past ten years in terms of the creation of well-being, most obviously in terms of employment and incomes. Second, we must build on that progress by using the resources at our disposal now to make our country an even better place in which to live, to work, and to invest. In essence, the challenge is about competitiveness.

I am more than aware of the concerns that have been expressed about an apparent weakening of competitiveness in Ireland in recent times. **The sight of factory gates closing as some manufacturing facilities sought out lower-cost environments abroad has made for powerful television images.**

These closures can have a huge, detrimental social and economic impact, particularly where they take place in smaller communities and their replacement with higher value-adding, more sustainable employment opportunities is a priority for government and its agencies. However, we do need to keep these events in context. The employment market remains strong and unemployment remains well below that of our fellow EU members despite the remarkable pace of inward migration witnessed in the past number of years. While it might not make for powerful television, the simple fact is that Ireland continues to be an attractive location for international investment. Last year, IDA Ireland reported an employment increase of almost 3 per cent in the companies it works with. In addition, new R&D and innovation projects have involved spending of almost €500 million being supported by the agency. In total, 71 new projects were negotiated with new and existing clients of the IDA entailing an investment of €2.6 billion over the coming years which will create new jobs across the country in industries where Ireland has a competitive advantage. Ireland remains very successful at attracting and retaining some of the best mobile investment in the world. The challenge for us all now is to retain and build on that advantage.

When we think about competitiveness, escalating costs are the first thoughts that leap to mind. But countries cannot compete on the back of low costs alone. I for one do not want to live in a low-cost, low-wage economy. I do want Ireland to be a country that competes not on the back of endless rounds of cost reductions but rather on the stronger grounds of profitability and value creation.

Cool-headedness and restraint are what are required in wage-setting expectations and behaviours at all levels of both the private and public sectors.

It is important that we do not price ourselves out of the international marketplace. For that reason, it is absolutely vital that we do not respond to the current increase in headline inflation, an increase which is largely caused by external factors such as energy prices and interest rates, by pushing wage rates higher. The damage to our competitiveness of higher energy and interest costs would be compounded if we pushed wage growth higher too. Cool-headedness and restraint are what are required in wage-setting expectations and behaviours at all levels of both the private and public sectors.

The regulated sectors are the areas where the state has the greatest impact on cost levels. While we cannot ignore the realities of what is happening in international commodity markets, I do want to be confident that the various regulatory regimes are operating efficiently, are balancing the needs of both producers and consumers and are supportive of the Government's broad policy objectives. That is why the Government has set as a priority a formal review of the regulatory environment which is now underway.

Costs are important and we must do everything we can to contain them. However, in the medium and long terms, our success will not be driven by a narrow cost competitiveness but by a wider definition which takes account of our skills and our infrastructure. Successful countries compete ultimately on the grounds of the quality of their labour skills and the quality of their capital. That reality has been and remains the focus of the Government's programmes for many years now, most obviously in the form of the National Development Plans. The current plan, launched earlier this year, involves a quantum leap in terms of scale of funding and size of ambition. It addresses the longer-term competitiveness issues with both purpose and force.

On skills, it commits over €25 billion to human capital which will see unprecedented resources being invested in education, training and upskilling. These resources will be used to ensure access to the highest possible standards of education for all and to meet the labour skills requirement of the future.

On economic infrastructure, the Plan commits €55 billion to ensure that we have the transport, energy, environment and communications infrastructure necessary to sustain and support our quality of life and our future economic development.

On social infrastructure, the Plan works to achieve a fair and equitable distribution of the fruits of economic success among all sections of our community and commits over €33 billion to this objective.

At the National Development Plan's core is the issue of competitiveness. The political and economic realities are clear. We will only be able to sustain and improve our quality of life if we are competitive. It is our greatest challenge and our greatest priority.

The political and economic realities are clear. We will only be able to sustain and improve our quality of life if we are competitive. It is our greatest challenge and our greatest priority.

The Plan will directly enhance the quality of our skills and the quality of our capital and its on-time, on-budget delivery are critically important to our future well being as an economy and as a society. However, it is only one half of the Government's competitiveness platform. The National Development Plan commits the resources to improving labour skills and our capital endowment while the taxation system allows workers and investors to retain much of the income generated by their efforts and their investment.

We have adapted to a world where capital is highly mobile, characterised by the free movement of investment across jurisdictions. Ireland has a pro-enterprise taxation structure for business to promote domestic and international investment in creating jobs. That is why we have a 12.5 per cent corporation tax rate. That is why we will retain control over corporation tax and that is why we will resist any move whether direct or covert to introduce a harmonised system of taxes on enterprise across the European Union. We make our own fiscal choices. These have the support and endorsement of the electorate. In the same way that we do not seek to impose our fiscal choices on others, so too should others desist from seeking to impose their own fiscal choices on us.

Today, skills too are increasingly mobile with some of the most talented individuals seeking out employment and business opportunities without too much concern for geography. There was a time when people had no choice but to leave this country. This generation of Irish people is the first where everyone has the opportunity to build a good life for themselves and their children in their own country. As a politician and as an Irishman, I am very proud of that new reality. Having built a strong economy which meets the needs of our own people, we now have the opportunity to encourage talented people to choose to live in this country, people whose labour and capital can help to secure our prosperity for years to come. If we are going to attract and retain the best mobile labour skills in the world, whether of an indigenous or international variety, we have to encourage them through low taxes on work and enterprise.

Ireland's fiscal regime is the result of deliberate choices made to incentivise and encourage behaviours with positive outcomes for our society. Let nobody be in any doubt that our economic success is built on the hard work of the Irish people and the policies of low taxes on labour and enterprise. That economic success has generated the resources which we have pumped into improving our health, education and welfare services and which are now being used to fund the bulk of the €184 billion in developmental expenditures committed to in the National Development Plan.

If our taxation system is to be most effective as an incentivising instrument, it must do more than impose a moderate burden. The rates and levels at which we levy tax must be credible not just today but in the future. Low taxation is most effective as an incentive for good behaviours if it can be delivered within a sustainable fiscal framework. The best guarantee that low taxation can be delivered over the long term is the maintenance of a prudent budgetary policy which aims to deliver broadly balanced budgets year in, year out. Budgetary prudence is not some sort of economic preoccupation. It is central to our competitiveness strategy and its continued pursuit is vital to our economic success.

From my perspective, the Government's responsibilities on competitiveness lie in the areas of infrastructure improvement, skills enhancement, low taxation and sustainable fiscal policy. Given our achievements to date and our plans for the future, I believe that any fair-minded person will accept that this Government has more than acquitted itself on these fronts.

There is a common belief that responsibility for improving competitiveness lies solely and exclusively within the bailiwick of government. Yes, the government has a lead role to play in ensuring that Ireland's competitiveness is enhanced but that challenge can best be addressed in a broader context which involves all of the social partners working together. Clearly, partnership involves more than one player and I believe that the competitiveness challenge can best be met if we work together. There is a responsibility on private business to invest and to innovate in order to ensure that the goods and services it provides are competitive in terms of price and quality. Such

If we are going to attract and retain the best mobile labour skills in the world, whether of an indigenous or international variety, we have to encourage them through low taxes on work and enterprise.

competitive behaviour must also include investment in the skills of the work force to ensure that the value added in private industry is at its maximum potential.

The trade union movement, too, has obligations on the competitiveness front. These obligations include a willingness to engage positively with employers in introducing practices which are designed to improve productivity and efficiency and to engage in wage negotiations in a way which defends the long-term interests of their members while taking account of the competitiveness imperative. Most immediately, it is vital that we do not respond to externally-driven inflationary pressures by pushing wages, and later prices, higher across the economy. That would do nothing to improve our competitiveness and could actually threaten employment levels.

Finally, there is a particular responsibility on the public sector to work to improve Ireland's competitiveness. This requires a real, active commitment to the modernisation agenda.

Finally, there is a particular responsibility on the public sector to work to improve Ireland's competitiveness. This requires a real, active commitment to the modernisation agenda. It demands that our public service responds positively and openly to the evolving needs of industry and wider society to ensure that our bureaucracy acts in a way which supports and drives national policy objectives. Any proposed pay increases can only be sustained from a competitiveness viewpoint if they are awarded in return for real enhancements in productivity. Any other settlement would not be acceptable.

The government has ambitious plans and projects which we will implement and deliver over the next five years. I hope that the other partners, private business, trade unions and the public sector, deliver on their potential and their responsibilities. Working together, we can realise the ambition that the quality of life of this country's citizens, all its citizens, will rank among the best in the world. That is the real opportunity before us, and how we respond to the competitive challenge will determine how successful we are in realising our country's ambition.

Joan Burton TD

Labour Party Deputy Leader and Spokesperson on Finance

Born in Dublin, educated, Sisters of Charity, Stanhope Street and UCD (B. Comm.). Fellow of Institute of Chartered Accountants. Formerly accountant and lecturer, first elected to Dáil Éireann in 1992. Minister of State at Dept. of Social Welfare 1992-4 and at Depts. of Foreign Affairs and Justice 1995-7. Elected to Dublin City Council in 1991 and to Fingal Co. Council in 1999. Nominated spokesperson on Finance by Pat Rabbitte in 2002. Elected Deputy Leader of the party in October 2007.

The "Knowledge Society" Offers Huge Potential

I was disappointed by the economic debate in the election campaign. Unfortunately, stamp duty was the only topic that got serious and, I may say, undeserved attention. At the launch of the FG-Labour economic document it was the only subject that elicited media questions. Other serious economic issues such as inflation and energy got scant attention.

Today, I want to take up a couple of issues that will have a bearing on the economy's long term prospects. I have a particular concern about the role of education policy in achieving sustainable growth and sharing the proceeds of growth in the coming decade.

I'm not at all sure that we are getting either an adequate economic or social dividend from our current spending on education, even with no less than six ministers assigned to the Department of Education. The report on Future Skill Needs has some very timely reminders of what is needed and how far our institutions are failing to meet these needs. In *The Irish Times* recently, one industrialist expressed serious misgivings about the quality of some graduates he meets. It would be a foolish Minister who fell back on the usual tired mantras that we have the best educated workforce on the planet. I don't believe that.

It really is disturbing to observe the lack of interest among talented students in subjects like mathematics, science and engineering. These subjects simply do not have the status they ought to have. Perhaps it is not surprising. There are no engineers or scientists in the cabinet that I know of and certainly too many lawyers. I can immediately think of only a few TDs of any party who are in those professions. So, maybe young people see a disparity between rhetoric and reality in the economic and social status we give to scientists and engineers. An inventor will rarely get the celebrity status of an actor

> I'm not at all sure that we are getting either an adequate economic or social dividend from our current spending on education, even with no less than six ministers assigned to the Department of Education.

or a successful writer. The medical or legal consultant can command high fees but the engineer and scientist is employed usually on a salary and certainly do not feature on the list of highest earners. The end result is that the demand for college places is skewed towards these high status professions and we have universities and colleges reducing the points requirements for science and engineering to fill available places. That cannot be healthy.

I accept it is not possible to force students to pursue studies in areas which they want to avoid like the plague. But we need to do more to enhance the status of those professions and skills. Interestingly, Gordon Brown has created a full cabinet slot for a minister devoted to innovation, third level education and skills. It is part of the Lisbon agenda to devote resources and political attention to this area. I am conscious that Minister Cowen has turned his mind to the policy and resource gaps that cause a shortage of key skills but we have a long way to go.

The Expert Committee on Skill Needs has published some interesting and ambitious targets. One of these is to have a 72 per cent participation rate for post secondary education and another is a 90 per cent completion rate for the Leaving Certificate. These are important targets but hugely difficult to achieve. We already have a near 60 per cent participation rate at third level and this is very high already. The UK is struggling to get beyond 55 per cent. The standard international yardstick from UNESCO is that universal participation is roughly equivalent to a 50 per cent participation in third level for the relevant age group.

To go beyond that to an over 70 per cent level will need a thorough examination of policy to encourage young people to stay on in education and go on to college. This is easier said than done. The school drop out rate among young males in urban areas is very high indeed and I don't think the Department is paying adequate attention to tracking this and is reluctant to answer Parliamentary questions on it. This group can be classified as a "hard to reach" group and show many signs of resisting all proposals to encourage them to persist in formal education.

These young men display a distinct resistance to "top-down" educational policies they consider to have little interest or relevance to their own lives. A famous UK study highlighted the kudos that could be won by the simple act of quitting school and the corresponding contempt shown to those who persevered. The "loser" image has become commonplace and puts an immediate tag on many working class young males. Furthermore, it places the blame for their hopeless position entirely on themselves. This identity exercises a powerful attraction to this group of boys and is an element of peer group

The school drop out rate among young males in urban areas is very high indeed and I don't think the Department is paying adequate attention to tracking this and is reluctant to answer Parliamentary questions on it.

pressure on them to keep away from any involvement with formal education.

There is a certain sense of exasperation apparent among policy makers towards this attitude. This is a group who appear to disdain all the best efforts directed at improving their educational and hence their economic and social positions and this rejection, in turn, reinforces the group's "doomed to failure" image. The public pariah status that often follows only makes the situation worse.

Personally, I don't think either official policy or the major educational institutions make enough efforts to remedy this. The underlying culture and environment within institutions can seem hostile and unfriendly to students from non-traditional backgrounds and standard access programmes only scratch the surface in changing this. I do acknowledge the huge efforts of many individual programmes such as the one in Clondalkin organised by Brian Fleming, a former TD but there is a more deeply rooted issue here that needs to be addressed. The plain fact is that there is no level playing field for all students even though there are no tuition fees.

The plain fact is that there is no level playing field for all students even though there are no tuition fees.

Changes in employment patterns such as the export of many traditional manufacturing jobs to lower cost locations has created a situation where a numerically significant group of young men are in a position of limited use value to the modern global economy. It is one thing to suggest lifelong learning and other educational opportunities as the way out of this cul de sac. It is quite another thing to facilitate easy access to the cultural capital that can make sense of these opportunities, especially where peer pressure may lead to an altogether different pathway that celebrates "drop out" and rejection.

There may well be a "sting in the tail" effect in operation here that could make the situation worse rather than better. Dismissive tags such as low aspirations and under-achievement are attributed in quite a casual fashion with the result that a public stigma attaches to those who reject the higher education path or who "drop out". This implies a culpability on their part for turning their backs on Government-inspired policies that are ostensibly for their benefit. I would argue that there is a fundamental injustice in such an approach and that it makes scapegoats and victims of this group, thus creating a separate unintended social problem out of policies that are designed to solve another. Furthermore, it designates a low status to all other forms of education and all other forms of personal ambition that do not involve formal credentials. To get anywhere near the 72 per cent target for post-secondary participation means reaching out to this hard-to-reach group and while finance is a barrier in some cases it is not by any means the only barrier.

In my view there is a deep flaw in the underlying education philosophy that is presently promoted by the Lisbon agenda. It is far too heavily fixated on exclusively economic goals and this is acting as a brake on the system's capacity to actually deliver on the targets. This approach is the new theory of human capital promoted in the Lisbon agenda and by bodies like the OECD and stresses the overriding importance of a highly skilled and flexible workforce to national economic success. According to this viewpoint, education is classified as an individual benefit first and foremost replacing the more traditional belief of education as a social good. I believe there is a conflict of purposes here that does need to be resolved or clarified.

On the one hand, the purely economic goals stress the importance of supplying the skills associated with a modern economy and these include a wide range of cultural and artistic skills as well as traditional technical skills. On the other hand, the system needs to incorporate a much wider range of social groups if it is to meet its numerical targets and also sustain a stable and content society.

One view could be called the "knowledge economy" and it offers huge potential as well as financial and economic benefits both to the country and to those who take part in it. I prefer to argue for the "knowledge society" that draws in all social groups and in the longer term could secure more lasting benefits. I think some Nordic societies have achieved high ratings in the international competitive league tables by going for this approach and this involves attention to and investment in pre-school education and patient attention to those who come into the early drop out risk categories. It also means a more concerted effort to bring adult learners in from the cold at our third level institutions. I think the efforts made for this group are quite half-hearted. I keep meeting constituents who go to college with high hopes but are unable to stay the course due to unforeseen barriers that should not be there.

... in the coming years education policy could be as important a factor for long-term economic progress as business tax incentives or indeed physical infrastructure improvements.

In general, I want to stress that in the coming years education policy could be as important a factor for long-term economic progress as business tax incentives or indeed physical infrastructure improvements. I mean education at every level because we cannot have full success at higher levels until issues at earlier levels are addressed. I see that august bodies like the National Competitiveness Council put an emphasis on investment in pre-school and the early years of primary education as essential pre-conditions for later achievement. I was disappointed that the programme we set out for investment in pre-school got minimal attention at the election but I do urge that it gets attention in future budgetary plans. It is just as significant as the metro or the M3 for Ireland's future economic prospects. These physical investments get the lion's share of attention in public policy but this will change and may indeed change sooner rather than later. I certainly hope so.

I want to mention energy security as an issue as well. The Stearn report on the economic implications of Climate Change got a lot of attention last November but I don't think its message has yet caused the kind of policy changes one might expect from its conclusions.

Targets and studies are one thing. We have those by the dozen. In fact, we are drowning in the amount of expert opinion available but the pace of policy change is much slower. The EU has set a target for 20 per cent of all energy in the member states to come from renewable sources by 2020. That is all energy and not just electricity. Electricity is just one part of the total energy picture. I think there is a fatal ambiguity in the official attitude to renewables. There is serious doubt about the capacity to meet that target and about the possible costs mainly due to the belief that the energy system will need to have a back up capacity for times when the wind doesn't blow. That is a fair point if we look at it solely from a single country perspective.

If it is looked at from a more general European perspective we get a different picture. Last year, the German government published a study of the effects of linking the electricity networks of all the countries in Europe. The purpose of the exercise would be to release access on a much wider scale to renewable sources with adequate guarantees of supply stability. The wind may not blow enough all the time in one country but the same could not be said for the whole continent. I am impressed by the determination of many railway companies in Europe to create trans-Europe links for high speed trains in France, Germany and Spain. It is the proof that the serious technical problems can be overcome. The same could be true for trans-Europe power links. Every country in the network would then be able to rely on stable and predictable supplies from elsewhere. The German study suggests that by spreading the demand across a much wider network, 80 per cent of Europe's electricity could be reliably produced from renewable power.

It is here where real innovation can take place through our higher education institutes and specialist institutes such as one recently opened in Co Louth by Martin Naughton. This is knowledge-driven investment in the very best sense. For example, to find effective ways of switching transport away from fossil fuels is just one vital component of progress. The Welsh Centre for Alternative Technology has just published a ZeroCarbonBritain document with a quite awesome list of suggestions for innovation that are scientifically necessary, socially possible and technically achievable. All that is left is the biggest task: how to make it politically thinkable.

Climate change is more than a challenge. It is a fantastic window of opportunity for innovation. Governor Arnold Schwarznegger of California seems to have got the message and is adapting his policies

The German study suggests that by spreading the demand across a much wider network, 80 per cent of Europe's electricity could be reliably produced from renewable power.

to take economic advantage from it. I suppose it takes the Terminator to truly meet the challenge of global termination.

The election is over and it would be futile to rehash the economic arguments, few enough as they were. There are many issues that may arise in the coming five years that will offer opportunities to question the economic competence of this strange new Government and I certainly look forward to the debates to come.

Jim O'Hara

General Manager, Intel Ireland; Vice-President,
Intel Corporation; President, American Chamber of
Commerce in Ireland

Worked for Digital Equipment Corporation for 17 years including five years in the USA before joining Intel in 1991 as part of the Fab 10 start-up team. He became plant manager for Fab 10 in 1996 and subsequently managed both Fab 10 and Fab 14, now known as Ireland Fab Operations. He took over the role of general manager in April 2002 and is responsible for Intel's operations in Ireland which employ directly and indirectly 5,500 people with $7 billion investment. He is a member of the governing board of IBEC. In May 2006, he was conferred with an honorary degree of Doctor of Science by NUI Maynooth.

Productivity is Absolutely Critical to Future Success

At the outset I want to be absolutely clear that this is no major, deep economic or sociological thesis but rather a personal reflection on the economic landscape, as I understand it, and an outline of the challenges that now face us and what we need to do to address them. I have no great "grá" for those who highlight problems without suggesting remedies for consideration. I will also endeavour to do that in this brief paper.

We are truly fortunate living in the Ireland of today. Many here will remember that less than two decades ago the economic landscape looked very bleak. The miracle that is the Celtic Tiger has transformed all that. The most recent quarterly bulletin of the Central Bank suggests unemployment will remain at the current 4 per cent level – in other words full employment. At the same time, it forecasts GNP and GDP growth in 2007 in the order of 5 per cent (GNP 4.75 per cent and GDP 5 per cent) with a slight reduction in growth in 2008 to 4 per cent. These figures are good but they mask the significant turbulence facing the economy as some industries become less viable and successful companies adapt to the new environment. Significant change is required to move Ireland into its next economic phase. We are an open economy and very much subject to global trends and shifts. To make the point, the positive growth figures I just quoted are excellent but are just half of the growth forecast for India and for China in the same period.

Significant change is required to move Ireland into its next economic phase.

Many leaders and their decisions can be given credit for the economic miracle but most of us today would agree that no one policy change led to this spectacular result. The genesis was "a general tendency of many policies to increase economic freedom" which "caused Ireland's economy to grow rapidly". The genesis of today's success was laid over many years by visionary politicians and leaders being willing to take risks in the present to reap rewards in the future. We owe a deep debt of gratitude to those people amongst whom I'd include T.K. Whittaker and his desire to reduce tariffs, Declan Costello and his push for a just society, Seán Lemass and the 1965 Anglo-Irish Trade Agreement, Donagh O'Malley and free secondary education, the decision to join the EU and in more recent times Desmond O'Malley's insight that lower personal and enterprise taxes can, paradoxically, stimulate an increased exchequer tax take. I would also include Alan Dukes for his Tallaght strategy which, in their obituary for Charlie Haughey, no less an authority than *The Economist* wrote that it had "… allowed the fierce spending and tax cuts that began to transform Ireland from a banana republic into a Celtic Tiger", and, last but not least, the often unnamed civil servants who negotiated, prioritised and allocated the huge volume of cohesion funding (over €8 billion) we received from the EU.

My adult life has taken place throughout this economic transition and in many ways my own personal career path mirrors that of the nation. I see myself as someone who made progress almost in step with Ireland's economic progress. In the 1950s, while Costello envisaged a fairer society and Whittaker argued for the elimination of tariffs, I was in school. In the late 1960s, I took my first job with Brunswick Corporation, one of the earlier US investments in Ireland. In 1972 as the Republic voted to join the EEC, I joined Digital in Galway. By the late 1980s when Ireland's economy was stabilising, I was in the US with Digital Corporation. There I joined Intel as part of the start-up management team for the Irish Fab 10 project. The rest, as they say, is history!

I think it is important not to view our recent success through rose-tinted glasses. Irish economic history has not all been smooth sailing. As a nation we have many times been forced to re-invent and re-brand ourselves. Many well known industrial names have been and gone over the years including Ford Motor company, Dunlop, Ferrenke, Wang and Digital. Yet this has neither diminished our desire to be the leading location for inward investment in Europe nor stymied our economic performance. Today, we face another challenge which we need to proactively confront if we want Ireland to remain a strong and vibrant economy.

I think it is important not to view our recent success through rose-tinted glasses. Irish economic history has not all been smooth sailing. As a nation we have many times been forced to re-invent and re-brand ourselves. Many well known industrial names have been and gone over the years including Ford Motor company, Dunlop, Ferrenke, Wang and Digital.

We should not hide behind clichés like "the economy is now resilient". Ireland faces another transformation of its economic landscape and it will be difficult. It will again require strong leadership, risk-based decision-making, far-reaching policy initiatives and the commitment and collaboration of a variety of stakeholders to see us through this change successfully.

A large part of our recent success was due to American investment. Today, over 600 US companies employ over 100,000 people directly in Ireland and are responsible for a further 225,000 indirect jobs. To stress the importance of US companies to Ireland let me quote a few statistics. In 2006, the exports of US firms were valued in excess of €200 million per day or over €70 billion. Last year, US companies paid €6.5 milion every single day to the Irish exchequer in corporate tax or over €2.4 billion and contributed a further €36 million per day or €13 billion in expenditure to the Irish economy in terms of payrolls, goods and services employed in their operations.

Despite the intense media focus on foreign companies moving their operations out of Ireland, let me give you the actual figures from a recent survey of over 40 American Chamber members – yes, indeed, 8.7 per cent of them indicated that they were considering relocating all of their Irish operations overseas and of course this is the headline. However, of the rest, 15.4 per cent were considering further major investments in Ireland and a staggering 84.6 per cent were considering ongoing investment in their existing plants in Ireland. So, it is not all bad news from the foreign manufacturing companies in Ireland.

However, that positive perspective is only one side of the coin. Ireland does not tend to separate indigenous from foreign-owned company statistics. Doing so is informative as it allows me to highlight a couple of important facts:

Our export base is almost totally dependent on foreign-owned companies who accounted for 92 per cent of Irish exports last year up from 87 per cent in 2004.

1. Our export base is almost totally dependent on foreign-owned companies who accounted for 92 per cent of Irish exports last year, up from 87 per cent in 2004. However, our manufacturing exports showed no increase last year. Indeed, Paul Tansey wrote earlier this year in *The Irish Times* that "Ireland's Celtic Tiger economy, where growth was led by exports, expired in 2001". He goes on to state that we've ignored this fact because growth based on indigenous activity such as construction continues.

2. Of the 86,000 jobs created in the economy last year less than 10 per cent were in companies in the tradable services and goods sectors of the economy. Of those 86,000 jobs, just under 6,000 (7 per cent) were in export-related sectors. Export-led growth has stalled. Our export sector is both heavily concentrated and stalling and we are not yet replacing it.

3. I am indebted to Alan Gray, Managing Partner of Indecon economic consultants, for a recent report on productivity to AMCHAM members. It noted startling differences in productivity and value-add per employee between Irish and US-owned companies in two key sectors of our economy, Pharma/Chem and ICT/Electronics. US firms in the electronics/computer industry in Ireland demonstrate very high levels of value added and net output.

A second structural feature is the exceptionally high productivity per person employed in these US-owned companies as measured by net output per person employed.

Both industries benefit from the transfer of high value intellectual capital to their Irish operations. They are in effect knowledge-based industries but the knowledge capital is developed and owned outside Ireland. And it is mobile.

We are in yet another transition phase. The early Celtic Tiger expansionary period was fuelled by the significant gains of the export-driven phase. This has been replaced by significant investment in spending on physical infrastructure and expanding our housing stock. Currently we are moving into a tentative "consumption-driven" phase with its inherent uncertainties. We need to accelerate into the "innovation phase" and drive towards a knowledge-based economy that grows our economy.

Let me repeat what I have been saying for a while: we have serious issues to tackle. Our cost competitiveness has gone from a strength to a weakness. The cost of services in particular must be reduced. Energy prices are out of alignment with our European neighbours. The strength of the euro versus the dollar is a growing problem. Our inflation rate is twice the EU average. All these issues make it increasingly difficult to carry on business here. The excellent productivity gains, which were hard won over a sustained period, are not enough to offset rising costs. This makes it very difficult for the 84.6 per cent of companies considering ongoing investment in existing plants to sell this investment to their parent corporations.

Let's go back and look closely at that P word, "productivity", because it is absolutely critical to future success in every area of our economy. Consider this fact: between 2001 and 2005 the increase in the average industrial wage was 19 per cent in the same period that public service salaries have risen by 37 per cent (made up of €2.5 billion or 24.3 per cent in general rounds and €1.3 billion or 13 per cent in benchmarking). That 37 per cent cost increase becomes 59 per cent when you add the salaries of the additional 38,800 (18 per cent) extra staff (€2.2 billion or 21.6 per cent) added in the period. So I don't think I'm being overly controversial by suggesting the "P" word needs to become everyone's mantra. I don't see why the methodol-

Consider this fact. Between 2001 and 2005 the increase in the average industrial wage was 19 per cent in the same period that public service salaries have risen by 37 per cent ...

ogy of benchmarking against the best and setting out concrete goals and timelines by which to close any gap and take a productivity lead – the approach which has served private industry and particularly American companies extremely well – shouldn't also work across all sectors of the economy. We must improve our productivity if we are to maintain the high living standards to which we have become accustomed. As a matter of urgency we need robust productivity enhancements throughout the economy.

Ireland is at a cross-roads in its economic development. Dealing with productivity may maintain the status quo but future economic growth is dependent on innovation and the commercialisation of ideas. Particular attention needs to be focused on enhanced support for R&D, education and building on our natural strengths.

We need to recreate our value proposition in order to differentiate ourselves and to continue to attract appropriate investment. One of the key objectives in the Government Strategy for Science, Technology and Innovation Report (SSTI) calls this out as follows:

> Ireland by 2013 will be internationally renowned for the excellence of its research and will be to the forefront in generating and using new knowledge for economic and social progress, within an innovation–driven culture.

Earlier this year, American Chamber launched a detailed policy document on the same theme, entitled Retuning the Growth Engine. At its launch I said,

> In today's global trading environment, intense competition from emerging economies means we need to look to new areas of innovation and added value to sustain our economic success story. Put bluntly, Ireland needs to continue to offer something distinctive in order to attract and retain multinational companies' innovation investment.

The proposition outlined in detail in the document is to build this renewed growth based on a "virtuous circle" comprised of five key elements: education, research, convergence, commercialisation and fiscal policy.

Education

Investment in education is the strategic enabler of any knowledge-based economy. Ireland needs to take whatever actions necessary to be in the top 10 per cent of OECD countries at all four education levels. We must provide an ethos of innovation, integration and inclusion combined with life-long learning.

We must improve our productivity if we are to maintain the high living standards to which we have become accustomed. As a matter of urgency we need robust productivity enhancements throughout the economy.

Research

Our centre of wealth and value creation needs to move to research and innovation if we are to engender serious economic growth and be successful in the global economy. This requires a robust fourth level under-pinned by significant strategic investment in collaborative research. The new robust fourth level must foster entrepreneurial skills and be enabled by a modern IP infrastructure coupled with incentives for risk-taking and innovation.

Commercialisation

We must transfer wealth creation to indigenous companies and make new collaborations with existing companies, creating robust global ventures in their own right. This needs to be supported by a creative fiscal, legal and commercial framework. Value must be created in collaborations between large and small enterprises. All our fourth level education and research institutes, regardless of size, must engage in this commercialisation.

Convergence

There is a need to look in a new fashion at ways of exploiting the very positive results of the large FDI investment in our economy in order to explore and fully leverage emerging areas of technology and market convergence. The large base of ICT and Medical device companies in Ireland suggests intelligent medical devices or digital health innovations as potentially fruitful examples.

Fiscal Policy

... I am optimistic about our future but we need to acknowledge and aggressively address the difficulties we face.

Our tax and incentive regime needs to reward risk-taking, capability development, IP and technology transformation and commercialisation while rewarding individuals for investing in their own educational development. These changes will be big and they will only come about in our small open economy through collaboration at all levels: MNC and SME, public private partnerships, academia and industry (e.g. CSETS).

Finally, as I said at the outset, I am optimistic about our future but we need to acknowledge and aggressively address the difficulties we face. Now is the time to take concrete action that will have far reaching positive consequences into the future.

- First, let's get our productivity up to world class in all sectors of the economy.

- Second we must grow significantly our investment in Research & Development but, even more importantly, we must structure our R&D sector to ensure it is world class.

- Thirdly, let's figure out what it takes to have a best in class education system at all levels and put the changes and spending in place to get us there as soon as possible.

- Fourthly, in addition to closing our infrastructure deficit Ireland should become the showcase for the world as a digital nation. We must use technology to drive innovation and productivity improvements across every area of education, enterprise and governance.

... in addition to closing our infrastructure deficit Ireland should become the showcase for the world as a digital nation.

Having made these decisions, we will fast come to the realisation that Ireland's problem is not so much a policy deficit but a delivery deficit. As we embark on a new National Development Plan we must take urgent action from today to ensure timely and efficient delivery on all infrastructure deficits.

If we follow these simple imperatives we can successfully make the necessary transition to a strong knowledge-based and innovative economy.

Brian O'Connell

Managing Director, Westpark Shannon Ltd.;
Co-Founder/Chairman, Atlantic Way

Born in Crecora, Co. Limerick and educated at Mungret College, Co. Limerick. Started general contracting in 1975 operating throughout the Mid West Area including Cork and Dublin in the 1980s and 1990s. Set up a development business in 1990 and has spent the last 10 years putting the land bank and the concept of Westpark together, which will create a campus of 1,000,000 sq. ft with investment of €200,000,000 employing 3,500 people.

Integrated Planning and Visionary Creation

Background

Over seven years ago it was evident that our region was not capitalising and creating the best sustainable environs to attract its share of Foreign Direct Investment. Seeing the influx and opportunities in the greater Dublin Area, the IFSC and City West, we were being quickly left behind.

Having identified a most unique and attractive site within the Shannon Free Zone, literally five minutes' drive from Shannon International Airport, I assembled a number of consultants and design team members to develop the concept of Westpark.

Location

We knew we had something special and the design brief and challenge was to create a high density campus, that could have panoramic, 360° views, of the Airport, the Shannon Estuary and the surrounding hinterland from wherever you were positioned within the campus. Working closely with Shannon Development, we recognised that it would be a major challenge and take time to profile and market Westpark. We negotiated a 10-year planning agreement with Clare County Council.

This allowed us time to profile and market both nationally and internationally, a location that had become somewhat tired, and needed to regenerate its former history and glory (bearing in mind that 45 years ago, the Shannon Free Zone employed 15,000 people, generated 80 per cent of GDP and was built out within seven years) Today it employs almost 8,000 people.

The Westpark Campus has seven magnificent towering buildings, and the overall square footage of the Campus is close to 1,000,000 sq. ft., providing an ideal location for Corporate HQ, offices, R&D facilities and laboratories. It is recessed into the hill allowing wonderful parkland amenities and walkways, which will be complimented with a full leisure amenity and wellness centre.

Infrastructure

Substantial upfront capital has had to be invested in providing the IT infrastructure that our market and new foreign direct investment rightly demand. Full Tier 1 connectivity, independent and resilient from our new state of the art telehouses, relay directly back to Dublin and onwards globally. We also have the first regional data centre being fitted out and it will be operational in 2008 – an investment in power and energy in the provision of a 110 KV station is being provided within the Campus again giving ample power for the future.

The first phase of the Campus, the first building was complete by October 2006. We are now currently building out two additional units and our patronage uptake is superb. Premium clients such as Digital River (new FDI to Ireland), GE Capital, Schwarz Pharma, Genesis, and recently, new regional Headquarters for Enterprise Ireland (decentralising from Dublin).

Westpark is proud to have such world class tenants in our campus which undoubtedly will act as a huge magnet of attraction for other companies and future foreign direct investment which will create 3,500 jobs.

> Substantial upfront capital has had to be invested in providing the IT infrastructure that our market and new foreign direct investment rightly demand.

Investment

Private sector funding of over €200 million will be required to build out this Campus. Our upfront investment for the first building of €35 million has been expended. Yes, our project has given many sleepless nights but it also gives a great sense of achievement and pride to see the original concept becoming a reality, and positioning itself as the catalyst for the rejuvenation of the region.

Atlantic Way

Atlantic Way is a voluntary movement of people who have a strong desire to make things happen. It is represented by key private and public sector bodies who seek to maximise the development potential of the Western Region by supporting and promoting best practice in every aspect.

By checking on our marketing collateral you will see that we have purposely used a rippling effect North of Galway and South of Limerick. Atlantic Way seeks no boundaries, wishes no boundaries, instead it aspires to remove boundaries. In line with Government National Spatial Strategy, Limerick and Galway will be the two City Gateways. Our motto is: "support those doing the good work, encourage lateral thinking and vision, and above all join up the thinking process".

Infrastructure Pillar

The roll out and completion of integrated infrastructure will allow the growth and opportunity of a regional counter-pole of up to 800,000, people which can have expansion potential into the future.

- Accelerate completion of the N18 by 2010
- Completion of full autonomy of Shannon Airport
- Galway Outer Orbital Road
- Shannon Airport – Foynes/Askeaton River Crossing (N19/N69 – N21/N23)

The roll out and completion of integrated infrastructure will allow the growth and opportunity of a regional counter-pole of up to 800,000, people which can have expansion potential into the future.

Atlantic Way, includes two cities, numerous towns, an international airport, a relatively under-used Shannon Estuary with deep sea berthage and leisure facilities. Let me also show you a future infrastructural opportunity of a bridge connection from Shannon Airport across the River Shannon to Limerick/Foynes.

Social Inclusion Pillar

- Commence rejuvenation of RAPID areas.
- Support recent Government initiative of Limerick City Rejuvenation Boards.
- Foster private sector support, leadership and vision.
- Promote private sector initiatives/taxation initiatives to encourage participation.

We held a preliminary meeting on our draft proposals of Atlantic Way with the Taoiseach at the end of January 2005. At that stage, we had three pillars. The Taoiseach strongly advised us to go away and reflect on social inclusion.

I am glad to report that, not alone have we got the fourth pillar, but we have also got a huge groundswell of genuine dedicated support, to work in partnership with all of the bodies, and in particular with Government, to find a substantial and sustainable solution to this problem.

Recent initiatives, including the creation and actions on the John Fitzgerald Report and the new appointment of Mr. Brendan Kenny, along with setting up the various boards in Limerick City, is a huge, courageous and visionary move by Government that is sincerely welcomed and is one that will be whole-heartedly supported to give it every possible opportunity to succeed.

Knowledge Enterprise

- A best in the world science and innovation annual conference
- Nurture indigenous home grown billion euro corporations
- Roll out regional Tier 1 connectivity and advance broadband MANS throughout.
- Encourage educational up-skilling opportunities.

Remarkably, this has been the most challenging and difficult of the pillars. The topic of this seminar is very appropriate and timely because in Atlantic Way we have a serious concern that time is running out. Just for a moment strip out and remove all of the housing activity, all of the commercial retail – there are very few sustainable jobs being provided outside of service and housing industry.

We have achieved great success, capitalised on great opportunities, but we must now urgently advance our knowledge enterprise pillar. We work closely with the Atlantic Technology Corridor, the universities/third level centres and I would like to acknowledge their commitment and support.

We have achieved great success, capitalised on great opportunities, but we must now urgently advance our knowledge enterprise pillar.

Tourism

- Government support for regional marketing budget (€53 million over five years)
- Iconic tourism projects for Galway
- Iconic tourism projects for Limerick/Shannon.
- Regional creation of walkways and pathways throughout western tourist routes.

The region has worked positively and cooperatively with Government in progress and conclusion on the open skies and bi-lateral agreement. The implementation of the marketing fund over the next five years to ensure not just sustainability but further growth of tourism is critical.

Government Priorities for the Next Five Years

The new Government has committed itself to a substantial Programme for Government across the whole spectrum of our lives with 800 pledges across 29 different sections – it is ambitious, comprehensive and innovative. Distilling through the programme there is but one brief section on balanced regional development. There are some small key steps in the right direction – mention of a linked metropolitan corridor from Waterford/Cork/Limerick/Shannon to Galway to develop a national counter-pole to Dublin supported with further roads, rail links, joining gate way towns; a gateway innovation fund of €300,000,000 to support innovative projects, urban investment schemes and a City Docks Development scheme. In summary, abstracting the spend, the planning of this regional development looks almost insignificant and irrelevant to the huge demand on Government who have to retro design and fit infrastructure into a sprawling and polluted city, that has become totally traffic gorged and grid locked.

A Vision of the Region

> Any project deserves integrated planning and visionary creation. We must have collaborative and a joined-up process to ensure that we can roll out a vision that will create a serious *wow* factor of what this region can and should be in the year 2020.

Any project deserves integrated planning and visionary creation. We must have a collaborative and a joined-up process to ensure that we can roll out a vision that will create a serious *wow* factor of what this region can and should be in the year 2020.

The creation of a serious counter-pole in scale and size – Galway, Shannon, Limerick – is very achievable and close to realisation. The completion of the N18 Limerick–Galway Road by 2010 will increase the access to Shannon International Airport to almost 800,000 people. The city conurbations can and should be master planned to be extended upwards to 200,000 over the next 10 to 20 years.

Planned infrastructure needs to be clearly identified and integrated with current and future products, not just connecting towns but the existing and future creation of clusters of living, recreational, working and educational centres allied with tourist hotspots.

Government Fund to Facilitate Implementation

Government must support the opportunity to seed the future harvest of collaborated co-ordinated concepts, that will bring not just success to the region but to the whole island of Ireland. We acknowledge and appreciate the leadership of the Government and its commitment to fourth level education funding. The creation of Science Foundation Ireland and the €680 million committed so far to R&D and capability development have been of strategic importance to upskilling both current and future FDI employees. We believe that many highly skilled employees within FDI companies have entrepreneurial skills. Government and potential entrepreneurs might generate more Irish-based enterprises. We also believe there is a need to devise creative ways of fostering the growth of more Irish-based billion euro corporations.

Agility and Flexibility

So, how then do we deliver the agility, the flexibility and the adaptability so that together, Government, Local Authorities, the public sector and the private sector can work closely together, plan together and deliver regionally together?

In some ways, it is merely an extension of that successful national partnership which has given us successive national agreements. Let us now innovate again and develop strong, flexible regional groups such as the Atlantic Way, broadly representative but regional champions first. Think regional, act national should be the informal motto. With a small staff, a strong regional team and a direct line to government a great deal is possible. Mind you, some of the compartmentalised departmental structures which we still have today are unsuited to the sophisticated whole-life or whole-picture contexts we live and work in today.

Government must encourage the public sector to adapt and become empowered to work in partnership in the regions with authority to kick ass and get the job done. The government wisely decided to decentralise personnel. Now we want them to follow their own logic and decentralise decision-making and funding, because that is definitely for the betterment of the regions and therefore for the country.

Think regional, act national should be the informal motto. With a small staff, a strong regional team and a direct line to government a great deal is possible.

Aidan Punch
Director of Census, Central Statistics Office

Prof Brendan Walsh
Chairman, National Statistics Board

Chapter 4

Census 2006 – The Implications for Government

Census 2006 – Some Noteworthy Findings
AIDAN PUNCH
Director of Census, Central Statistics Office

The Census, Decision-makers and Policy
PROF BRENDAN WALSH
**Senior Research Fellow, UCD; Chairman, National
Statistics Board; Emeritus Professor of Economics, UCD**

Aidan Punch

Director of Census, Central Statistics Office

Born in Cork and educated at Colaiste Chriost Rí and UCC where he obtained a degree in Mathematics and Statistics. Joined the CSO as a statistician in 1972. Completed a Masters in Public Administration in UCD in 1986. Currently Director of Census. Secretary to National Statistics Board on its foundation in 1986. Chair of European Population Committee 2002-3. President of Statistical Inquiry Society of Ireland

Census 2006 – Some Noteworthy Findings

Clearly, there is a wealth of data already available from Census 2006 with more to follow.[1] What then are the implications of the Census 2006 results for Government? To answer this question we need to re-examine the main reasons for holding a census. Fundamentally, the census is a stock take of the population at a particular point in time – in this case 23 April 2006.[2] One of the primary uses to which the census results are put is to re-draw Dáil constituency boundaries. I will leave it to my fellow contributor, Professor Brendan Walsh, to look at what implications the 2006 census results are likely to have for this important work.

Apart from the constitutional imperative, a major advantage of the census is its ability to provide results at small area level and also to provide information on minority groupings.

Apart from the constitutional imperative, a major advantage of the census is its ability to provide results at small area level and also to provide information on minority groupings. Allied to this is the ability of the census to provide a sampling frame for specific topics such as disability. The responses to the disability questions in the 2006 census enabled a sample of approximately 15,000 persons to be drawn from all those persons who ticked "yes" to any of the disability categories. These persons were interviewed in September/October 2006 as part of the National Disability Survey carried out by CSO. This was the first occasion on which such an approach was adopted.

The choice of topics from which to select is quite broad, covering 30 individual questions and 11 questions on household characteristics. In theory, the results flowing from all the census questions need to be examined closely by policy makers at national and regional level as they are likely to have important consequences for how society is being organised and therefore for the Government's agenda in the coming years. The topics covered in the present paper appeal to the author as being worthy of particular attention. They are:

• The results of a new question on voluntary activities

• A renewed look at the data on commuting

- Unemployment at small area level, and
- How migration is impacting on the family in Ireland.

Voluntary Activities

Following the usual public consultation process which precedes a census operation a new question in relation to voluntary activities was introduced for the 2006 census. There has been a lot of conjecture in the media to the effect that with the pressure of modern living Irish persons have become more individualistic and are giving less of their limited free time to undertake voluntary activities which benefit the community and society at large. While the 2006 census results did not enable us to pronounce on how the situation has been evolving over time, as it was the first time for the question to be asked, it does, however, establish an important benchmark on which to base future comparisons.

The results showed that voluntary activity is alive and well and living in Ireland. One in six persons aged 15 years and over reported that they were involved in one of the five voluntary activity categories distinguished in the four weeks before the census, with identical proportions for males and females overall. Females participated to a greater extent in social or charitable organisations and voluntary work with a religious group or church while the male participation rates were higher in sporting organisations and political or cultural organisations. The widest variations between male and female activity rates were recorded in sporting activities with overall participation rates of 7.4 per cent and 3.3 per cent, respectively.

Middle-aged males and females (i.e. those aged 45-54 years) were the most active voluntary workers with the relevant proportions being 22.9 per cent for males and 22.5 per cent for females. Older teenagers aged 15-19 years also performed with distinction with one in seven females and one in eight males in this age group doing some voluntary activity. Those in their early twenties contributed least in proportionate terms to voluntary activities.

A final distinction worthy of note is the extent to which persons in different social classes give of their time to voluntary work. One in four persons in the social class, professional workers, undertook some voluntary work in the four weeks before census day. The proportions decline as we move down the social class structure to 23.1 per cent for the managerial and technical class to 17.3 per cent in the case of the non-manual category. Persons coded to the skilled and semi-skilled social classes had similar participation rates, 13 per cent and 12.9 per cent, respectively while the lowest percentage (9.5 per cent) was recorded by those coded to the unskilled category. While

> Middle-aged males and females (i.e. those aged 45-54 years) were the most active voluntary workers with the relevant proportions being 22.9 per cent for males and 22.5 per cent for females.

the census does not throw any light on the reasons behind participation or non-participation in voluntary activities, the differential between the various social classes suggests that availability of time may not be an explanatory factor.

Commuting Patterns

There tends to be a preoccupation with commuting in the popular media. Tales in relation to commuting dominate the airwaves with the popular perception being of hard-pressed parents dropping their children off at crèches or at child-minders early in the morning and then battling their way through rush hour traffic only to renew the battle on the return journey later on that evening. While there is no denying that this practice occurs and is the daily diet of some persons, the question is whether the popular perception is the norm.

Census 2006 sought information on the means used to travel to work, school or college, the time slot in which the person left home, the distance travelled (to the nearest kilometre) and the journey time in minutes. In addition, the full work-place address was requested in the case of workers which, when analysed geographically and associated with the person's place of residence, allows a detailed origin/destination matrix to be compiled for the 1.9 million workers identified in the census. Householders were also asked the number of cars owned or available for use by one or more members of the household. What do the results based on the responses to all these questions tell us of our current plight?

Certainly, there are more cars on the road – 1.96 million in 2006 compared with 1.6 million four years earlier. However, this increase needs to be seen in the context of the underlying growth in population of 320,000 and more specifically the increase of 274,000 in the number of persons at work over the same period. Not surprisingly, the car is the favoured means of transport to work accounting for 57 per cent of workers compared with 55 per cent in 2002. Taken in conjunction with van and lorry drivers, almost 65 per cent of workers drove to work in April 2006.

Regarding distances being travelled to work, the evidence from Census 2006, reproduced in the following table, indicates little change since 2002 in the average distance travelled from home to work. In fact, the average distance travelled by workers living in rural areas actually declined slightly. In interpreting the results, it should be borne in mind that the non-response rate to the question was 20.4 per cent in 2006 compared with 12.2 per cent in 2002. Clearly, the changeover to kilometres was mainly responsible for this higher level of non-reporting. While it is not possible to be prescrip-

Taken in conjunction with van and lorry drivers, almost 65 per cent of workers drove to work in April 2006.

tive, what can we say about the non-respondents and their impact on the results? In my opinion, there is a higher likelihood that those who did not respond to the question travelled shorter rather than longer distances as anyone travelling a long distance to work is likely to have a good idea of the distance travelled, regardless of whether it is in miles or kilometres. So, therefore, the average distances reported may be overestimates of the true values and, given the higher non-re-porting in 2006, it is likely that the extent of overestimation is higher in the later period.

Table 1: Average distance in kilometres travelled to work, 1991-2006

Year	State	Urban	Rural
1991	7.7	7.0	8.5
1996	10.7	9.1	13.1
2002	15.7	12.5	21.3
2006	15.8	12.8	20.9

Turning to the length of time taken, which is probably a more mean-ingful indicator of the stress suffered by individuals during their dai-ly lives, the following table tells the story.

Table 2: Time taken to travel to work, 2002 and 2006

Time spent travelling	2002	2006	Change	Change share
Under ¼ hour	395222	470483	75261	27.5%
¼ hour - under ½ hour	428087	505841	77754	28.4%
½ hour - under ¾ hour	260173	317152	56979	20.8%
¾ hour - under 1 hour	110861	124320	13459	4.9%
1 hour - under 1½ hour	101052	131144	30092	11.0%
1½ hours and over	41455	56275	14820	5.4%
Not stated	176464	181866	5402	2.0%
Total	1513314	1787081	273767	100.0%
Average time taken (minutes)	26.8	27.5	0.7	–

Of the increase of 274,000 in the number of persons at work between 2002 and 2006 over half spent less than a half an hour travelling to work. So clearly, workers are choosing to live closer to their work places or work closer to where they live. This is not to ignore the ad-ditional 45,000 workers who spend over an hour getting to work each day. When reporting the situation most of the attention seems to focus on the worst cases while making light of those whose situation is rather more tolerable.

Unemployment Blackspots

As previously mentioned, one of the advantages of the census is its ability to provide data at small area level. Focusing on unemployment, the relevant data is got from the responses to the long-standing question on the present principal status of persons aged 15 years and over. The question inquires whether the person is working, looking for their first job, unemployed, a student, looking after the home/family, retired, unable to work or some other status. It is important to stress that the measure of unemployment derived from this source differs substantially from the official measure based on the results of the Quarterly National Household Survey (QNHS). The unemployment rate compiled from the 2006 census was 8.5 per cent compared with 4.3 per cent based on the QNHS International Labour Office (ILO) measure for the second quarter of 2006. The reasons for the difference are explained in the census report on the principal socio-economic results. In any event, the census provides a comparable measure of unemployment across all small areas in the country. The small areas in question are the 3,440 Electoral Divisions (EDs).

An ED was described as an unemployment black spot if its unemployment rate exceeded 20 per cent on a census basis. In order to avoid misleading results based on particularly small labour markets, it was decided to include only those EDs with a labour force of 200 persons or more in this analysis. Using these guidelines some 62 small areas in 14 different counties met the relevant criteria. The average unemployment rate for the 62 EDs combined was 24 per cent – nearly three times the national average – with Dublin, Cork, Limerick and Waterford cities accounting for 35 of the EDs in question.

Limerick City provided four of the top 10 unemployment black spots in the country – John's A (42.6 per cent), Glentworth C (35.1 per cent), Galvone B (34.5 per cent) and Prospect B (31.7 per cent). Dublin City provided three – Cherry Orchard A (33.6 per cent), Priorswood B (28.7 per cent) and Ballymun B (28.5 per cent). The remaining three top 10 slots were filled by Sailearna (33.2 per cent) and Scainimh (30.4 per cent) in the Gaeltacht area of Galway County and Mín an Chladaigh (29.9 per cent) in the Donegal Gaeltacht.

Given that the same yardstick was also used to determine unemployment black spots in 2002, it is of interest to compare the results of both censuses. This is done in Table 3.

> The average unemployment rate for the 62 EDs combined was 24 per cent – nearly three times the national average – with Dublin, Cork, Limerick and Waterford cities accounting for 35 of the EDs in question.

Table 3: Unemployment blackspots, 2002 and 2006

County	Number of unemployment blackspots		Average unemployment (persons)		Average unemployment rate (%)	
	2002	2006	2002	2006	2002	2006
Clare	2	1	170	254	21.0	21.2
Cork City	11	5	163	236	24.7	24.6
Donegal	18	8	105	127	25.2	22.0
Dublin City	15	13	341	405	24.0	24.5
Fingal	1	1	119	146	23.1	25.9
Galway County	6	6	134	88	27.6	25.0
Limerick City	11	11	147	141	24.8	26.8
Limerick County	1	1	93	151	22.9	24.2
Longford	1	3	277	198	22.1	23.9
Louth	4	1	445	226	22.1	21.3
Mayo	5	2	95	182	29.9	24.5
South Dublin	1	3	463	499	22.4	21.7
Waterford City	6	6	125	116	24.5	23.6
Other counties*	6	1	166	243	21.0	21.5
Total	88	62	188	221	24.0	24.0

At an overall level, the number of black spots declined, although in many cases the unemployment rate for the EDs in question is still high compared with the national average figure. The average unemployment rate for the combined total of black spots was identical at 24 per cent in 2002 and 2006 although the absolute number of persons unemployed increased by 17.6 per cent during the relevant period.

Of the 62 unemployment black spots identified in 2006, 44 were black spots in 2002 as well. The list is given in the Appendix. Although the overall unemployment rate for the EDs in question declined from 25.1 per cent in 2002 to 24.2 per cent in 2006 the persistence of unemployment on such a relatively high scale calls for specific targeted measures for the relevant areas.

Of the 62 unemployment black spots identified in 2006, 44 were black spots in 2002 as well.

The Impact of Migration on the Family

The final section of the paper looks behind the recent figures on migration to gauge possible impacts on family formation. First, the benchmark data; the number of usual residents who were born outside the country has nearly trebled over the last 15 years, from an estimated 213,700 in 1991 to 612,600 in 2006 with over half of the increase occurring in the last four years. Those born abroad now represent 14.7 per cent of the usually resident population compared with 6.1 per cent 15 years earlier.

One of the hot topics being debated at present is to what extent those who have come here to live are likely to remain in the event of an economic downturn. The available evidence shows that most of those immigrating are young single persons, e.g. 68 per cent of the 122,000 who immigrated into Ireland in the twelve months before the 2006 census were single and 62 per cent of these were in their twenties. By definition these persons are mobile and therefore would be likely to return to their country of birth or move elsewhere if economic circumstances in this country were not to their liking. As a counterweight to this, however, it is of interest to look at what impact inward migration has had on family formation in Ireland as immigrants in stable family-type situations here are more likely to have established deeper roots and therefore may consider staying.

Analysing the number of young children under 5 born in Ireland by reference to the country of birth of their parents may help to shed some light on this. The following table provides such an analysis distinguishing the following country groups: Ireland, UK and other countries.

... most of those immigrating are young single persons, e.g. 68 per cent of the 122,000 who immigrated into Ireland in the twelve months before the 2006 census were single and 62 per cent of these were in their twenties.

Table 4: Usually resident Irish-born children aged 0-4 years by country of birth of parent(s), 1991-2006

Country of birth of parent(s)	1991	1996	2002	2006
Both parents born in Ireland	198,554	161,450	153,797	159,554
Lone parent born in Ireland	17,619	21,927	27,143	39,473
One parent born in Ireland - the other in UK	25,826	26,631	30,498	32,363
One parent born in Ireland - the other abroad outside UK	3,914	4,740	7,786	11,318
Both parents born in UK	2,372	2,827	4,051	4,408
Lone parent born in UK	1,918	2,398	2,916	3,035
One parent born in UK - the other abroad outside UK	507	631	1,201	1,646
Both parents born abroad outside UK	869	1,009	6,674	18,254
Lone parent born abroad outside UK	229	383	1,596	5,010
Total children aged 0-4 years	251,808	221,996	235,662	275,061

The proportion of births where both parents were Irish born has declined from 79 per cent in 1991 to 58 per cent in 2006 while at the other extreme the share of births in which none of the parents were Irish increased from 2.3 per cent to 11.8 per cent over the same period. Lone parenthood has increased for all categories shown with the numbers for those in which the parent was born abroad outside UK being significant. Also of significance is the 18,254 Irish-born children aged 0-4 at the time of the 2006 census where both parents were born abroad outside the UK.

The emerging evidence is therefore pointing to an increase in the extent to which persons born outside Ireland are putting down family roots here. However, the rate of increase has not kept pace with the overall increase in migration.

Conclusions

Four topics were chosen from among the many covered by the most recent census.

- In the case of voluntary activities there is evidence of strong civic engagement notwithstanding the pressures of modern society. Of particular note is the engagement by teenagers.
- While traffic congestion and commuting difficulties are certainly pre-occupations the case may tend to be overstated. The increase in average commuting times between 2002 and 2006 was not that remarkable with indications that a slightly higher share of workers are taking less than 30 minutes to get to work.
- Despite the economic successes being experienced there are still deprived areas where unemployment is persisting at relatively high levels.
- The impact of increasing inward migration is feeding through to data on family formation with, according to the last census, the proportion of young children where both parents or the lone parent are Irish-born now standing at 72 per cent.

The emerging evidence is therefore pointing to an increase in the extent to which persons born outside Ireland are putting down family roots here.

Endnotes

1. A further nine subject matter volumes are planned for release between July and November while the remaining SAPS are due for release in October 2007.

2. The method used to enumerate the population is the so-called de facto approach i.e. every one who is in the State on census night is covered and persons are counted where they are on that night. By asking questions in relation to usual residence and in respect of those temporarily absent at the time of the census it is also possible to get a measure of the usually resident population.

Appendix

Electoral Divisions (44) which were unemployment black spots in 2002 and 2006

Electoral Division	County	Unemployment rate 2006	Electoral Division	County	Unemployment rate 2006
John's A	Limerick City	42.6%	Mount Sion	Waterford City	24.1%
Glentworth C	Limerick City	35.1%	Ballymun C	Dublin City	23.8%
Galvone B	Limerick City	34.5%	Ballymun A	Dublin City	23.6%
Cherry Orchard A	Dublin City	33.6%	Farranferris B	Cork City	23.4%
Prospect B	Limerick City	31.7%	Mayfield	Cork City	23.3%
Scainimh	Galway County	30.4%	Cherry Orchard C	Dublin City	23.1%
Mín an Chladaigh	Donegal	29.9%	Carraig Airt	Donegal	23.1%
Priorswood B	Dublin City	28.7%	John's B	Limerick City	22.5%
Ballymun B	Dublin City	28.5%	Tallaght-Killinardan	South Dublin	22.5%
Cnoc na Lobhar	Mayo	27.3%	Morrisson's Road	Waterford City	22.0%
Ballybeg North	Waterford City	27.1%	Ballybough A	Dublin City	21.4%
Ballymun D	Dublin City	26.7%	Leitir Mhic an Bhaird	Donegal	21.3%
Priorswood C	Dublin City	26.4%	Prospect A	Limerick City	21.3%
Dún Lúiche	Donegal	26.2%	Ennis No. 2 Urban	Clare	21.2%
Blanchardstown-Tyrrelstown	Dublin-Fingal	25.9%	Gort an Choirce	Donegal	21.1%
Knocknaheeny	Cork City	25.3%	Newport's Square	Waterford City	20.5%
The Glen A	Cork City	25.3%	Lisduggan	Waterford City	20.3%
Rathbane	Limerick City	24.8%	Mountjoy A	Dublin City	20.3%
Gurranebraher B	Cork City	24.7%	An Cnoc Buí	Galway County	20.2%
Ballynanty	Limerick City	24.6%	Killeely A	Limerick City	20.2%
Longford No. 1 Urban	Longford	24.4%	Raphoe	Donegal	20.1%
Garmna	Galway County	24.4%	Na Croisbhealaí	Donegal	20.0%

Prof Brendan Walsh

Senior Research Fellow UCD; Chairman, National
Statistics Board; Emeritus Professor of Economics UCD

*Graduated from UCD in 1961, obtained a doctorate in economics from Boston
College in 1966 and taught at the University of Massachusetts and Tufts
University before returning to Ireland to take up a post as economist at the
Economic and Social Research Institute (ESRI) 1969-80. He was appointed
Professor of National Economics at UCD in 1980. He has served overseas as an
economic adviser with the Harvard Institute for International Development and
as a consultant with the World Bank, the OECD and the Commission of the EU.
He has published several books including* The Macroeconomy of Ireland *and
has written extensively on the Irish economy in academic journals.*

The Census, Decision-makers and Policy

Introduction

The use of census statistics to guide rulers and policymakers reaches
as far back as the origins of writing. Some of the earliest fragments of
written languages from the Middle East are enumerations of various
sorts. There has always been a close link between counting people
and levying taxes on them. Caesar Augustus' desire to enumerate
his subjects for tax purposes was, of course, the reason for the city
of Bethlehem's place in history. William Petty's *Political Anatomy of
Ireland*, published in 1672, was designed to help in the division of the
spoils of the Cromwellian settlement. The new American Republic
enshrined in its Constitution the requirement to take a decennial census so that "representatives and taxes shall be apportioned … among
the several states in accordance with their population".

The growth of population and industry in the nineteenth century
spurred interest in the potential contribution of statistics in fostering
progress, very much along the lines of the recent OECD conference.
This spirit was exemplified by the efflorescence of Statistical Societies, especially in the north of England, of which, however, the Dublin
Society proved the most enduring. It was founded in 1847 and, under
the name of the Statistical and Social Inquiry Society of Ireland, it still
flourishes. In fact, both Aidan Punch and I are past Presidents of the
SSISI. In her history of the Society, aptly named *In a Spirit of Earnest
Endeavour*, Mary Daly summarises the philosophy that guided the
Society:

> There has always been a close link between counting people and levying taxes on them. Caesar Augustus' desire to enumerate his subjects for tax purposes was, of course, the reason for the city of Bethlehem's place in history.

The founders of the Society believed that statistics and economic analysis would provide scientific answers to the major problems of the time. If this seems naively optimistic . . . the supposed scientific nature of statistics, and their apparent ideological neutrality, seemed to offer a better way forward.

This nineteenth century view saw policymakers as rational, unselfish individuals using the best available evidence to promote the greatest good of the greatest number. Modern political economists are by and large a sadder, and perhaps wiser, lot. They believe that politicians and even bureaucrats have their own goals that are not necessarily aligned with the common good. Politicians are driven by electoral imperatives and bureaucrats have career objectives and strive to increase the power and influence of their own institutions. And, to make matters worse, the public's interest in, and ability to interpret, statistics is limited.

All of which is by way of warning you not to expect too great an improvement in the economic decision-making process to follow from the comprehensive and timely flow of reliable data now emerging from the Central Statistics Office as the results of the 2006 Census of Population are published.

The 2006 Census was the twenty-third in a series that stretches back to 1841. Following the postponement of the 2001 Census due to the foot and mouth disease epidemic, the cycle is now back on a five-year basis and the preparation for the 2011 Census will be getting underway next year. Our policymakers are ensured a regular flow of valuable information about a rich array of topics, available in a timely and user-friendly manner.

The Census has been an important source of enlightenment and an influence on policy in the past. An interesting historical example of its role is provided by the introduction of a question on religion in the 1861 Census. This shed light on the contentious issue of the share of members of the tax-supported Church of Ireland in the population. The results of this Census played a role in the disestablishment of the church in 1869.

As an aside, the Nazis used religious information from censuses for far less benign purposes in the 1940s, which is part of the reason for the refusal to include a question on religion in the US census.

As an aside, the Nazis used religious information from censuses for far less benign purposes in the 1940s, which is part of the reason for the refusal to include a question on religion in the US census. However, Ireland's bona fides in this area is shown by the disappointment of the Jewish community that their faith was not listed as an option to tick in the recent Census. The matter was something of a storm in a teacup, as respondents had ample space to write in their religious affiliation.

The Census and the Constituencies

Turning to specific issues where census results should influence the political process and decision making, the most obvious is the drawing of the constituencies in which elections are contested.

Articles 16.2.2 and 16.2.3 of the Irish Constitution give the Census of Population a role in the drawing of constituencies for Dáil Éireann. These articles state that the ratio of TDs to population shall be not less than one for each 30,000 of the population and not more than one for each 20,000 of the population and that the actual ratio shall, so far as is practicable, be the same in all constituencies. In the 1961 *O'Donovan v Attorney General* case, the 1959 Electoral Amendment Act was deemed not to have taken sufficient account of the changes in population during the 1950s, which had resulted in constituencies in areas of declining population being over-represented relative to those in areas of growing population. The biggest discrepancy was between Dublin South West, which had 23,128 people per deputy, and Galway South with only 16,575 people per deputy. The ratio was 40 per cent higher in Dublin South West than in Galway South.

Things have moved since then, or have they? The 1997 Electoral Act provided for the establishment of a Constituency Commission "upon the publication by the Central Statistics Office, following a Census of Population, of the Census Report setting out the population of the State classified by area". The purpose of this Commission is to redraw the constituencies to take account of demographic shifts and ensure that the provisions of the Constitution are implemented. While this precludes the sort of crude gerrymandering that occurs, for example, in drawing the districts for elections to the US House of Representatives, it has not eliminated the traditional reluctance to redraw the constituencies on the basis of the most recent available information on demographic shifts.

The task of achieving rough equality in representation across constituencies has undoubtedly been rendered more difficult by the rapid but uneven population growth recorded in recent years. However, the failure to take the preliminary Census 2006 results into account ahead of the 2007 election showed scant regard for the spirit of the Constitution. The preliminary Census results were published on 19th July 2006. It presented estimates of the population of the constituencies, and the population per TD, as of April 2006, using the constituencies established in Electoral (Amendment) Act, 2005. This Act had redrawn the constituencies on the basis of the results of the 2002 Census of Population. The final report on the population by area from the 2006 Census was released on 26 April 2007. However, the General Election was held on 24 May 2007 in constituencies that took no account of either the preliminary estimates or the final results of

> The task of achieving rough equality in representation across constituencies has undoubtedly been rendered more difficult by the rapid but uneven population growth recorded in recent years.

the 2006 Census. Instead the constituencies used were based on the 2002 distribution of population, without any adjustment for the unprecedented demographic changes that occurred in the succeeding five years.

The legality of conducting the election on the basis was challenged in the High Court in April 2007. The main defence offered by the defendants for not revising the constituencies in the light of the preliminary census results – available some nine months before the election – was the possibility that the final results would materially differ from the preliminary ones and that the constitution and Electoral Acts were unclear as to whether the census returns referred to the preliminary figures or to the final figures.

But the reality is that, as has been the case with previous Census results, in no constituency was the difference between the preliminary and final numbers material. The largest absolute downwards adjustment was in Dublin South West, minus 612 persons; the largest upwards adjustment in Meath East, plus 545 persons. All the final results fell within ±0.6 per cent of the preliminary results. Indeed, the discrepancies between the preliminary and final population estimates were very minor. Moreover, they pale into insignificance when compared with those between the 2006 and 2002 populations of the constituencies.

There was an unprecedented 8.2 per cent increase in the national population over these four years and the rate of population change varied from -4.3 per cent in Dublin North East to +26.9 per cent in Dublin West. As a result, the ratio of population to TD was 36 per cent higher in Dublin West (30,967) than in Dún Laoghaire (22,833). Furthermore, the national population increased by a further two per cent between the time of 2006 Census and the date of the election, so that the election was fought with even more glaring discrepancies in the population/TD ratio between constituencies. Most probably Meath East joined Dublin North and Dublin West above the Constitutional limit of 30,000 persons per TD.

This issue will not go away. If the newly-elected Dáil runs for five years, the next General Election will be contested in mid-2012. The situation will then be much the same as it was this year – the preliminary but not the final results of Census 2011 will be available. Holding the 2012 election in constituencies redrawn on the basis of the final returns of the 2006 Census risks working with a variation in the population/TD ratio just as glaring as that which existed during the recent election.

To avoid this unsatisfactory situation, heed should be paid to last month's High Court judgment by Mr. Justice Frank Clark, who urged "there should be 'urgent consideration' of whether the Electoral Act

If the newly-elected Dáil runs for five years, the next General Election will be contested in mid-2012. The situation will then be much the same as it was this year – the preliminary but not the final results of Census 2011 will be available.

1997 should be amended to allow measures to begin from the time of publication of preliminary rather than final census figures." (*The Irish Times*, 8 June 2007). It would seem that the Oireachtas could establish a new Constituency Commission and instruct it to use the preliminary results of the 2011 Census to draw the constituencies for the 2012 election. This would minimize variation in the population/deputy ratio and strengthen the democratic credentials of our electoral system.

The Census and Population Projections

The problem just raised arises from the fact that published census results have inevitably something of an historical flavour. I want to turn now to a forward-looking application of census results, namely, the preparation of population projections. Since the early work of R.C. Geary on the "future population of Saorstát Éireann" in 1935, the Irish Central Statistics Office has had an interest in population projections. It now follows the practice of preparing projections of the future population and labour force every five years based on the latest Census results.

These projections are based on the age structure of the initial population – as revealed in the most recent Census – and assumptions about (i) mortality, (ii) fertility, and (iii) net migration. Inevitably, the future contains surprises not foreseen in the assumptions and the outcomes tend to differ significantly from the projections. The projections based on the 1971 Census underestimated the growth of population in the 1970s due mainly to an unanticipated inflow of population in the second half of the decade. Conversely, the projections based on the results of the 1981 Census failed to anticipate the economic disasters of that decade and the return to crisis-level emigration, which led to a falling population towards the second half of the 1980s. An independent projection, prepared by DKM economic consultants in 1987, fell into the trap of assuming the gloom and doom of the 1980s would continue forever, and hence projected a sharp decline in population – from 3.5 million in 1986 to a 3.3 million in 2011. In reality, the population grew to 4.2 million in 2006! The highest projected 2011 population foreseen in the most recent published projections from the CSO (December 2004) was 4.5 million. In view of the fact that in recent years the population has been increasing at an annual rate in excess of 2 per cent – or almost 100,000 persons a year – this upper limit looks likely to be surpassed, unless of course the slowdown in the economy turns nastier than anticipated and the recent strong net immigration suddenly dries up or even becomes a significant net outflow, which is not beyond the bounds of credibility.

The highest projected 2011 population foreseen in the most recent published projections from the CSO (December 2004) was 4.5 million. In view of the fact that in recent years the population has been increasing at an annual rate in excess of 2 per cent – or almost 100,000 persons a year – this upper limit looks likely to be surpassed, unless of course the slowdown in the economy turns nastier than anticipated and the recent strong net immigration suddenly dries up or even becomes a significant net outflow, which is not beyond the bounds of credibility.

Net migration is of greater relative importance in Ireland than in other countries and – crucial from the perspective of population projections – it is also more volatile. In the second half of the 1980s, net emigration averaged 0.8 per cent of the population – fully offsetting the excess of births over deaths. In the inter-censal period 2002-2006, net immigration averaged an amazing 1.1 per cent of the population and contributed 58 per cent of the growth in the population. Volatile migration makes population projections an unusually hazardous undertaking. Who, in the early 1990s, would have believed business plans based on assumed population growth rate of over 2 per cent? Who today would believe that we should plan for a stationary population over the next decade?

The costs of getting it wrong are enormous – the extrapolation of pessimistic demographic trends from the late 1980s undoubtedly played a role in our under-provision of infrastructure in the 1990s. The consequences of assuming that our "strong demographic fundamentals" would underpin the housing boom for as far as the eye could see are now coming home to roost.

Work is now well advanced in the Central Statistics Office to prepare projections of the population and labour force for the interval 2011-2041. The targeted publication date is end-2007. It could be argued that this is the most vital application of the census for policy purposes. The statisticians use the most up-to-date information from the recent Census to prepare a range of estimates of what the future population will be. In principle these numbers should guide policy makers in relation to a variety of topics, especially in relation to infrastructure. The projections provide guidance not merely to the future size of the population, but also its age distribution, for example. Projections of the growth in the elderly population can be taken as very reliable, since it "only" involves applying assumed mortality rates to the existing population – but none the less the costs of extending the Medical Card to all aged over 70 were wildly miscalculated in 2002. More difficult are the projections of the numbers of school age, because they require assumptions about fertility and migration, as well as information about the future population of child-bearing age.

And those who believe that the government should be able to micro-manage matters into the future clamour for ever more detailed projections, with particular emphasis on the regional dimension. But the more detailed the projections, the greater the number of assumptions on which they are based, and the greater the margin of error attaching to them.

It is regrettably easy to identify recent examples where policy makers made poor use of available demographic information. One that springs to mind is the failure to take into account the predictable –

and predicted – peak in the number of students leaving the second level educational system in planning the capacity of the third level system.

The decline in the numbers doing their Leaving Certificate could have been anticipated from the number of births registered, the Census results and the population projections. But the pressures from various lobbies led to a very significant expansion in the number of places at third level which came on stream just as the demand for places began to weaken. The result has been difficulty in filling the available places, especially in some of the more peripheral (in terms of location and subject matter) courses, competition for overseas students and weaker school leavers to take up the slack.

Conclusion

The Census of Population is a rich source of information that is of potentially great value to decision-makers. But vested interests and inertia often reduce the application of up-to-date information in the essentially political process of policy making. The cost to the tax payer is high.

The decline in the numbers doing their Leaving Certificate could have been anticipated from the number of births registered, the Census results and the population projections.

Dr Edward Walsh, Founding President,
University of Limerick

Padraig McManus, Chief Executive, ESB

David Taylor, Chief Executive,
Sustainable Energy Ireland

Eamon Ryan TD, Minister for
Communications, Energy &
Natural Resources

Chapter 5

Providing Our Energy

Padraig McManus

Chief Executive, ESB

Born in Kildare and educated at Naas CBS, UCD (B. Eng. Electrical). MD, ESB International 1973-81 and Charles T. Main (Middle East 1981-3. Various management positions in ESB 1983-2002. Appointed Chief Executive 2002. Fellow, Institute of Engineers, Board Member Irish Management Institute.

ESB Has a Role to Play in Ensuring Energy Security

In recent years, the energy challenges facing us have been raised in popular awareness to a degree not experienced since the "oil crisis" in the 1970s. Energy matters have topped the agendas of the last three G8 Summits at Gleneagles, St Petersburg and Heilgendamm. Put simply, the challenge is to secure adequate, reliable and affordable supplies of energy whilst meeting the constraints on emissions and address environmental concerns, in particular climate change.

These are formidable global challenges and global approaches are needed. Ireland is but one voice in an international community but nevertheless, working mainly through the European Union, Government can continue to ensure our concerns are articulated and recognised.

Energy policy is built on three major pillars – environmental sustainability, energy security and competition. In other words, energy policy must address each of these areas. Lately, however, environmental sustainability and energy security – being ends in themselves – are increasingly recognised as pre-eminent. Let me deal with each of these in turn.

There is now widespread global consensus that mankind is creating an unacceptable risk for our environment. Concerns regarding climate change issues including global warming have increased following the latest assessments by the UN Inter-Governmental Panel on Climate Change and other authoritative commentators such as Sir Nicholas Stern. The International Energy Agency finds our current pattern of energy usage unsustainable – not to mention our future growth. It is simple: if we are to maintain our way of life and continue to grow our economies, we must reduce the amount of energy we use *and* the amount of carbon released from the energy we do use. We need to "de-energise" and "de-carbonise" our economy.

The Spring European Council set a unilateral Community-wide reduction target of 20 per cent by 2020 as a minimum "placeholder"

> It is simple: if we are to maintain our way of life and continue to grow our economies, we must reduce the amount of energy we use *and* the amount of carbon released from the energy we do use. We need to "de-energise" and "de-carbonise" our economy.

pending international negotiations on the successor to the Kyoto Protocol in 2012.

There is no doubt that Ireland will now have to "buck the current trend" of our national emissions. Put simply, the EU Climate/Energy package "ask" of Ireland which post-dates the measures contemplated in either the recent White Paper and, to a large extent, the revised National Climate Change Strategy, will be of a magnitude never previously considered. The question now is: "Can we meet our allocated targets without endangering the national economy?"

First and foremost, we need to ensure that a pragmatic approach is taken in talks with our EU partners to setting Ireland's target. Thereafter, we all must undertake a review of energy policy, costing all options and prioritising for implementation each one on a least-cost basis, in the interest of national competitiveness. ESB has a role to play in implementation and we are eager to do so.

Of all the options, it almost seems trite to say it, but there is no better way to do this than to consume less energy in the first place! The Government is running an excellent campaign – the Power-of-One – and public awareness is key to success. However, the magnitude of the target – i.e. 20 per cent reduction in energy consumption – will mean a point of departure from existing practice; in fact, it requires in effect starting a "new industry". ESB has been a thought and action leader on energy efficiency and demand-side management for decades. ESB has the experience, capability, track record and scale and, with appropriate authorisation, we can facilitate "kick starting" this industry in a manner that will deliver our reduction targets.

So much more can be achieved in this area. We need to make the financial impact of energy consumption visceral. Wouldn't it be great if you could see in your own home the actual cost of your consumption, rather than waiting two months for an ESB bill? Building on an existing pilot, our ambition is to do precisely that and roll out nationwide SMART meters for our customers.

Utilities in Europe are facing a new reality: the power generation sector will have to be essentially net "carbon-free" by 2050. This is an extraordinary engineering challenge and is the subject of global research and development. ESB's strong engineering ethos and capability gives us confidence that this challenge will be met. ESB will use its scale and capabilities to be a leader in carbon management in Ireland, e.g. through our involvement in renewables.

I will now turn to energy security. As you are aware, Ireland is not endowed with abundant fossil energy resources and we are over 90 per cent dependent on imported fossil energy. We run the risk of physical interruption and price duress, although I acknowledge our suppliers are reliable. However, we have potential in our indigenous

Of all the options, it almost seems trite to say it, but there is no better way to do this than to consume less energy in the first place!

renewable resources – biomass, bio-energy and wave – and we have already begun large-scale utilisation of wind. Further interconnection with Britain will facilitate growth in the use of these resources. In this regard, it is imperative that we get this done as soon as possible. Developing these sources will promote diversity. Over time ESB will be basically switching our imported oil dependence for indigenous renewable sources. Think about it – switching oil for renewables and the attendant complications and risks. Overcoming these issues is what we do at ESB.

The Government has set a target of 33 per cent of electricity generation from renewables by 2020, including 500 MW of wave power. Each of these technologies is at a different stage of the development cycle and a great deal more investment is needed. ESB has a role in ensuring that each plays its part. ESB has a significant share – we are number 1 or 2 (depending on how you count it) – of the current renewable market and we will continue to have a strong role. In addition, we plan to convert our existing peat stations to make them capable of burning biomass. All of these promote diversity and improve our security of supply.

All of this will take time: it is my belief that we will need to "dig-in" for the long haul and address these issues over a 25 to 30 year time horizon, always being mindful of security-of-supply and protection of national competitiveness.

Availability of infrastructure is a key component of energy security. To support the economic growth, ESB has spent over €5 billion on the network over the last decade – a phenomenal investment. There was much doubt initially as to whether ESB could actually deliver investment of this order, but we succeeded and kept pace. ESB has a major role to play in expanding and developing the electricity networks to keep pace with the growth in renewables and other distributed generation.

I will now turn to the final pillar of energy policy, competition. Competition is the way by which we can best ensure that investment needs are met. ESB has been supportive of the introduction of competition in the electricity market in Ireland since it first opened in 2000. In fact, ESB has been exemplary amongst our peers in Europe on the way in which we have approached and facilitated competition.

We have supported and particularly welcomed the opening of the single electricity market of Ireland and Northern Ireland next November. We look forward to further market development including closer integration with those of Britain when further interconnection comes about.

We have supported and particularly welcomed the opening of the single electricity market of Ireland and Northern Ireland next November. We look forward to further market development including closer integration with those of Britain when further interconnection comes about.

Interconnection is a key enabler and we urgently need to accelerate implementation. I believe we need to be more ambitious and double the planned capacity with Britain. We also need to take seriously the possibility of interconnection with France, even as early as 2020, integrating with the European networks as an ultimate goal.

We have acknowledged from the outset that ESB's position in the market had to reduce. We voluntarily agreed to reduce our market share from 100 per cent to 60 per cent by the end of 2005, and we did. We have entered into a commitment that we will divest a further three stations (Tarbert, Great Island and Poolbeg) by 2012 and we will do it. These and other actions are intended to engender market confidence and to create the conditions for bringing in more players into the electricity sector. ESB intents to be an active participant in vibrant competitive electricity market on this island.

I suppose no discussion on energy policy would be complete without mention of nuclear power, which is legally proscribed, and clean-coal technology. Our company has had an interesting history with nuclear and both the company and country have come a long way since we last debated nuclear at Carnsore Point. Interestingly, a wind farm owned by ESB now stands on that site. There has been a lot of development in nuclear technology, safety and waste management. There are many folks advocating that we have a nuclear debate.

While dialogue is always welcome, and without pre-judging the outcome of debate, I would sound a minor caution that we must not get distracted from tackling the significant challenges "on our plate" at present. However, I believe that with more research, nuclear and clean-coal will be among the options in our long-term policy mix.

In conclusion, I think Ireland has taken many of the right steps required to guarantee our country's supplies into the future. We are now focused on implementation which is fraught with technical and engineering challenges. This is precisely where ESB can best make a contribution. In particular, ESB can uniquely contribute and support Ireland playing its part in the climate change by deploying its considerable engineering capability on achieving net zero-carbon power generation by 2050. It's a tall order, but I am convinced that we can do it if we apply ourselves, starting now: 2050 seems a long time away but we are in an industry with long investment cycles.

ESB can uniquely contribute and support Ireland playing its part in the climate change by deploying its considerable engineering capability on achieving net zero-carbon power generation by 2050.

ESB has a significant part to play in ensuring energy security, in particular by developing our portfolio of renewables and by continuing to develop the electricity networks and to grow the indigenous renewable generation. Finally, building on our past successes and current initiatives, ESB has a role to play in reducing demand. We will continue to help our customers to save for themselves.

In summarising, my advice is that we all should:

- Pay particular attention to the EU talks on burden-sharing in relation to emissions reductions.
- Re-examine recent energy policy decisions in light of the new targets and identify and fully cost the options for priority implementation.
- Pay particular attention to improving overall energy efficiency – it offers the cheapest solutions in the short-term.
- Continue the public awareness programmes on energy use.
- Further expand R&D capability on key aspects of energy sources, transformation, storage and use.

Extract from the Programme for Government

Energy

A reliable and affordable supply of energy is central to many elements of economic and social life. The Government is committed to securing both long-term energy security and a low carbon future for Ireland. We will achieve the following commitments across three energy pillars:

Security of Supply

We will:

- Ensure that electricity supply consistently meets demand.
- Ensure the security and reliability of gas supplies.
- Enhance the diversity of fuels used for power generation especially renewables.
- Ensure the development of a landbank of state owned power generation sites to facilitate the entry of new independent generation.
- Deliver the East/West and second North/South electricity interconnectors.
- Deliver electricity and gas to homes and businesses over networks that are efficient, reliable and secure.
- Create a stable, environment for hydrocarbon exploration while increasing the return to the State.
- Mitigate the impact of any energy supply disruptions by ensuring that contingency measures are in place.

Environmental Sustainability

We will:

- Dramatically accelerate the growth of renewable energy sources in the electricity, heat and transport sectors of the economy.
- One-third of all electricity consumed will come from renewable energy by 2020.
- Remove any regulatory barriers to combined heat and power and district heating systems.
- Introduce co-firing at each of the three peat stations with up to 30 per cent biomass by 2015, which will reduce greenhouse gas emissions from those three stations by 900,000 tonnes per annum and will also extend the life of those stations.
- Implement in full the National Bioenergy Action Plan for Ireland, which will reduce greenhouse gas emission by at least 2 million tonnes per annum.
- Promote the enhanced deployment of green energy technologies and the sustainable use of energy in transport.
- Introduce a biofuels obligation scheme by 2009.
- Work with our EU partners to require biofuels used in transport to comply with an environment certification system which incorporates sustainability criteria in terms of biofuels production
- Promote the sustainable use of energy in transport.
- Maximise energy efficiency and energy savings across the economy with a target of 20 per cent energy savings by 2020 and 33 per cent for public sector.
- Introduce new national building standards in 2007 to ensure that new housing has 40 per cent lower heat energy demand than existing building standards and revise them again in 2010 to achieve a 60 per cent target in further years.
- Incentivise people to move towards greater energy efficiencies in their homes especially through improved attic and wall insulation.
- Ensure that the ESB installs a new smart electronic meter in every home in the country which will allow people to reduce their bills by cutting back on unnecessary use of electricity.
- Facilitate the introduction of net metering to allow consumers to sell electricity back into the grid from any renewable power supplies they have.
- Stimulate the development of alternative energy sources.
- Support Energy Research Development and Innovation Programmes.

- Maintain the REFIT scheme and keep it under review to encourage investment in wind farms, biomass and anaerobic digester power plants in order to provide a stable environment for energy enterprises.
- Provide for a distributed grid connection system to encourage the development of small scale and community-owned renewable power supplies.
- Devise a price support scheme to support and encourage investment in the development of wave and tidal power.
- Keep under examination the possibility of appropriate support measures for offshore wind.
- Work with the European Commission and other national grid operators to develop an offshore wind farm grid connection system to power the rest of Europe.
- Establish a dedicated Ocean Energy Development Unit. The Unit mandate will be to develop the sector and work to a target of at least 500 MW of wave and tidal energy by 2020 with an interim target of 75 MW in 2012. Aim to create an export-oriented Ocean Energy sector focused on the technologies associated with this exciting sector through R&D supports and grant funding of start-up production in the sector.
- Support the establishment of community methane digesters to reduce pollution and simultaneously produce methane gas which can be used in CHP plants – this could also go some way to relieving the need for slurry storage required under the Nitrates directive.
- Ensure that the new all-island energy market is designed to ensure the maximum use of renewable energy in the system.
- Amend the remit of Science Foundation Ireland to include a third research pillar in the area of sustainable energy and energy efficiency technologies.
- Review the remit and operation of Sustainable Energy Ireland

Energy - Competitiveness
We will:

- Deliver competition and consumer choice in the energy market in support of economic growth and national competitiveness.
- Oversee the successful introduction of the Single Electricity Market in 2007.
- Keep the electricity and gas network infrastructures, as strategic national assets, in State ownership and ensure that these assets are never privatised.

- Oversee the transfer of transmission assets to EirGrid, establishing it as the National Transmission Grid Company by end 2008.
- Operate natural monopoly electricity network businesses under a risk-related related rate of return, leading to reduced network tariffs which will be passed on in full to electricity customers.
- Reduce the market power held by any one player in price-setting generation plants.
- Ensure a sustainable future for the Semi-State Energy Enterprises.
- Provide substantial financial support to improve the energy efficiency of existing public housing and assist those on low incomes to avoid fuel poverty.
- Expand and develop programmes for energy conservation to ensure the most efficient use of energy.

David Taylor

Chief Executive, Sustainable Energy Ireland

Qualified as a chemical engineer and holds an MSc in Management from Trinity College Dublin. Prior to his appointment as CEO of Sustainable Energy Ireland, which was set up in May 2002, he was the Director of the Irish Energy Centre. He is active in European energy matters and is a member of the IEA Committee on Energy Research and Technology.

"Doing More with Less" – The Case for Energy Efficiency

Ireland's recent achievements in improving the sustainability of electricity supply are commendable but we have to go further in end-use efficiency and in doing so prepare to transform the way we meet our energy needs.

Against the background of the Programme for Government, the National Climate Change Strategy, the Energy White Paper "Delivering a Sustainable Energy Future for Ireland" and the IEA review of Irish Energy Policy published on July 4th, one could be forgiven for saying that the over-riding priority is action. The urgency is to release the power of energy efficiency, to reduce the pressure on energy supplies and ensure that the sustainable energy agenda we are committed to at a policy level becomes an affordable reality. Ireland's recent achievements in improving the sustainability of electricity supply are commendable but we have to go further in end-use efficiency and in doing so prepare to transform the way we meet our energy needs. I will concentrate on the electricity sector and the built environment leaving industry, transport and the service sector for another day.

Energy Policy Goals

Ireland has absorbed a three-fold increase in the price of oil, a significant drop in refining capacity due to hurricane Katrina, and the effects of armed conflict in several oil-producing regions of the world. The economy has continued to grow in parallel. We have, on the face of it, done well. But for many in the developing world the experience is of an unfolding tragedy as the cost of energy and climate change impacts.

Across the world there is a growing sense of unease about the mounting observable and predicted impacts of climate change. People, business and institutions are struggling to come to grips with the true meaning of our over-reliance on oil and gas. The widespread sense that we are addicted to something that is not going to be good for us in the long run has been exploited by the RTÉ series *Future*

Shock and of course is the subject of the Al Gore movie. How are we, as an island nation, to secure our energy future?

Energy White Paper and Programme for Government

The White Paper – "Delivering a Sustainable Energy Future for Ireland" – has set targets for energy efficiency and renewable energy (RE) in energy supply for 2020. In the areas of heat and transport there are milestones for RE to be achieved ahead of 2020. This then is the first substantive priority – to show progress on the targets set.

While the electorate will have broadly assented to the thrust of government policy it has yet to endorse the details or indeed the implied impacts. It goes without saying that the social benefits of that policy will have to be made explicit and that in addition to having achieved widespread and popular endorsement for its achievements the new Government will have done well if in five years' time it has achieved these outcomes strategically.

The priority of this Government has to be the positioning of the sustainable energy policy agenda as a true public good and desirable continuing policy objective.

Energy Prices and Competitiveness

All economic commentators point towards the ongoing risks attendant on the erosion of competitiveness and the consequences for growth, employment and securing the soft growth landing which is desirable. There are repeated calls for action on competition policy to manage inflationary pressures.

Much has been made of the impact of energy prices on industrial competitiveness. However, when SEI looked at the relative cost of energy in the cost structure of manufacturing industry in Ireland we found that 95 per cent of value-added in industry is produced by entities for which energy is less than 5 per cent of their direct costs. Irish industry is not energy-intensive by international standards. The Irish industrial sector is now structurally more robust in the face of rising energy prices. In some cases that adjustment has been bought at a high price as we lost recycling processors - in paper, for example. Costs do matter when you are trying to attract new industry or retain existing marginal industries.

On the other hand, when we look at the cost of energy to domestic consumers we find that for about one-sixth of the population fuel costs account for more than 10 per cent of both their gross and disposable incomes. I have argued elsewhere that those who could af-

> ... when we look at the cost of energy to domestic consumers we find that for about one-sixth of the population fuel costs account for more than 10 per cent of both their gross and disposable incomes.

ford to save most have the least incentive, and it is the case that those who would benefit most can least afford the investment necessary to make the savings. These and similar issues will need to be considered as the Government approaches its Programme for Government commitments on a levy and consideration of a carbon tax.

Security of Supply

The title of this evening's session is "Providing our Energy". Implicit in this title is the notion of security of supply – an aspect of energy policy where expectations of government are high.

Security of supply nowadays implies access to energy resources over reliable infrastructure within a market framework that is regulated in the best interests of the stakeholders and ultimately in the interest of the final consumer. The United Kingdom continues to champion and, by and large, lead Europe in the area of energy market reforms. Its success in this, and our own commitments to the EU-led liberalisation process, may ultimately be the best guarantor of overall energy security in Ireland.

Aside from markets, we rely on short-term arrangements for emergency stockholding which are co-ordinated by the International Energy Agency (IEA). These were successfully used when hurricane Katrina hit production in the Gulf of Mexico and reserve stocks were released to help stabilise oil markets.

As a small population with limited economic power, our current prosperity owes much to the openness of the economy and our conformity with international tax, governance and financial norms. Ireland's dependence on exports and inward investment will be a continuing feature of our industrial policy and economic success. Any tendency to pursue energy nationalism by attempting to go it alone would sit uneasily with this open market stance. In an increasingly security conscious world, strength lies in pooled interdependence and this is one of the key features of EU internal and external energy policy. Competitiveness considerations should weigh heavily when investing for security of supply – the security of our export markets in terms of our ability to compete has to be our first consideration. In this competitiveness respect, the delays to and slow pace at which Corrib gas is being developed is regrettable.

Climate Change

The whole topic of climate change looms large when considering energy policy and it is in this area that the Programme for Government is at its most ambitious. The risk is that in stretching to pursue one

Ireland's dependence on exports and inward investment will be a continuing feature of our industrial policy and economic success. Any tendency to pursue energy nationalism by attempting to go it alone would sit uneasily with this open market stance.

aspect we compromise on others such as security of supply or competitiveness. The Government strategy seeks to mitigate these risks.

I am struck by the difference between the way scientists and economists view climate change. As the scientific consensus about cause and effect grows, the moral imperative to correct the situation grows among scientists. On the other hand, economists tend to emphasis the long-term nature of the issue, the time that remains for new technological responses and, as economists do, put numbers on the downside and upsides. This is very uncomfortable territory, especially when the worst affected are the least powerful.

No doubt the Stern Report was commissioned to bridge this gap and make the economic case for early action. Like the IPCC Reports, it has attracted a broad welcome but has left itself open to criticism on grounds of the assumptions made and the scenarios selected. Predicting or rather modelling possible futures was never going to be easy.

Now more than ever we need action that addresses the central issue with collateral benefits which command the support of many or all of our people. Implicit in this stance is the need for early and proportionate action. "First things first" and "beginning with the end in mind" need to be the ruling ethos.

Robust Policy

In putting forward a minimum target of 20 per cent improvement in energy efficiency by 2020 the Government has aligned itself with EU-level targets that seem to have an appropriate level of ambition. Achievement of these targets will contribute significantly to all three pillars of energy policy. From a consumer perspective, this one policy emphasis, effectively pursued, has the power to contribute to the availability, affordability and environmental acceptability of energy services. It respects economic competitiveness, security of supply and reduces environmental impact. What is now needed is the road map – the sequence of resourced actions that will enable government, with the lightest hand possible, to guide the development of the market in the direction that is good for producers and consumers alike. Seen like this we need to aspire to doing more with less in both the energy and the policy sense.

What is now needed is the road map – the sequence of resourced actions that will enable government, with the lightest hand possible, to guide the development of the market in the direction that is good for producers and consumers alike.

Electricity Sector

The level of ambition is at its highest when applied to electricity supply. An energy efficiency gain of 20 per cent combined with 30 per cent of renewables in electricity supply would allow electricity demand to grow at a little over 1 per cent per annum between now and 2020 while emissions reduce by about 33 per cent of what they might have been or 19 per cent lower than they are today today. At this simple level of analysis there is scope to achieve significant reduction of greenhouse gas emissions as the new policy is applied to the electricity sector. At this junction it is useful to look at some statistics that reflect how these issues have come together in the past.

The recent changes in the efficiency of power generation in Ireland and the reduction in CO_2 intensity of electricity supply are part of the continuing success story of electrical power provision in Ireland. The availability of lower carbon fuel (gas), the development and deployment of new technology (new generation technology such as combined cycle gas turbines, as well as wind turbines) and the growth in electricity demand have been the causal factors.

If we look at the special case of the wind industry in Ireland we can see how rapid the development has been in recent years. Such rapid development is as a result of many preparatory actions. We can see this where the period from 1999-2005 was marked out by stop and start, institution and technical misalignment, and low confidence until in the last two years, as if by magic, the foundations emerge of a real industry contributing more than half of 9 per cent of electricity supply as wind and other renewable generation capacity comes online.

Studies have shown that economic benefits are greater when the opportunity to improve electrical distribution and end-use efficiency are favoured over investment in new supply. The challenge is to structure a process so that the decision makers in the wider electricity market can reap the benefits of energy efficiency in electricity generation, distribution and use. The CER has a particular responsibility with regard to competition and energy efficiency in generation including combined heat and power (CHP). The role of CHP, and more generally distributed generation, need careful treatment within the market structure and rules. The losses in any electricity system are very high indeed and their reduction over time has to be a central element contributing to national climate and security of supply goals.

Every choice of a superior energy product over another less-energy efficient one sends a signal to product designers and suppliers. In this very real sense we will inherit a future based on the choices we make today.

The final consumer can be a powerful influence for product development and innovation. The Government's "Power of One" campaign seeks to position the consumer as the central actor in driving change. Every choice of a superior energy product over another less energy efficient one sends a signal to product designers and suppliers. In this very real sense we will inherit a future based on the choices we make today. The visibility of the "Power of One" campaign, the clarity with which white goods such as washing machines and fridges are labelled in advertising and display will all assist the evolution of consumer purchase choice and behaviour in use. More than any-thing we need role models of prudence rather than extravagance and in this sense the behaviours of business leaders and opinion formers will be crucial.

Building Sector

However, one of the areas where the Government has decided to make a huge leap is in the matter of the building regulations. The in-tent is to revise them so that houses built under the new regulations are 40 per cent more energy efficient than the existing ones. This is a huge step but its impact on our emissions position by, say, 2010 or 2012 will be reduced by the weight of the legacy of existing stock. We may by 2012 build 300,000 or so houses that are 40 per cent bet-ter than today's which when added to a stock of say 1.6 million will improve the average performance of the housing stock by about 4 per cent or 1 per cent per annum below where it might otherwise have been. This is a necessary step to reach the desired goal but clearly we will need to do more. Other interventions will be necessary and as far as possible they should aim to ensure that the services that energy provides continue to be available, affordable and environmentally acceptable over the transition.

SEI championed the "House of Tomorrow" programme and in turn local authorities and more recently Government have moved to set the 40 per cent improvement in energy performance over existing regulations as the requirement from 2008 onwards. This will extract more value for consumers from a market where many intermediar-ies have profited in the past ten years or so. This evidenced-based approach to making policy is very much in line with the mission of SEI. We very much welcome Minister Ryan's invitation to raise the bar on the "House of Tomorrow" programme to 60 per cent above current regulations in preparation for the scheduled upward revi-sion in 2010.

As more emphasis is placed on the development of the centres of our towns and cities we create the possibilities of significantly im-proving energy and overall sustainability. The management of ser-vices to apartment complexes is one area where the Government sees the need for better regulation in the interests of all. I believe that there will be opportunity to consider the role of energy service companies (ESCOs) in this wider context.

SEI's Dundalk 2020 project seeks to achieve government targets earlier by engaging business while fostering co-operation among en-ergy players, local authorities and the community they represent. Since I spoke here two years ago I am pleased to say that the project

As more emphasis is placed on the development of the centres of our towns and cities we create the possibilities of significantly improving energy and overall sustainability.

has been selected for support by the European Commission. Work is underway and I am hopeful that we will see among other things a biomass district heating system established in the Dundalk Sustainable Energy Development Zone. The project is founded on the premise that there is widespread agreement on the wider goals of sustainability but that there are issues of pace, emphasis, responsibility and the sheer practicalities of how much will it cost and who pays that are much better confronted at a local level. We believe that a consensus action-orientated environment and appropriate support framework will achieve more on the ground and provide lessons for all as to what is replicable and under what conditions.

The Greener Homes Scheme has given the whole agenda wings and the 15,000 applicants to date are increasingly favouring solar. This is a surprising result and provided we see a reduction in system and installation costs this could be one of the winning technologies for greening Irish homes. The future prospects for heat pumps and pellet-fuelled appliances are equally dependant on supply chain and other developments, all of which are likely to create employment opportunities in the local and wider economy. There are of course risks in relation to fuel price exposure and there is a cost to being an early entrant. However, it is these considerations that justify the grant in the first place.

> **There is no doubt but that the transformation of the energy performance of the building stock should be a priority for Government through and beyond the life of this Government to say 2020.**

There is no doubt but that the transformation of the energy performance of the building stock should be a priority for Government through and beyond the life of this Government to say 2020. Devising a sustainable and appropriate mix of regulatory, informational and fiscal instruments will be the central challenge. Naming and sequencing the issues to be tackled will be helpful. Sweden has made much of its desire to eliminate oil from the heat and electricity sectors. We could make a start with heat and prompt business to organise around this goal while government addresses the needs of the disadvantaged and those most adversely affected by the policy.

Structuring the Response

The Government is preparing to go to consultation on its action plan for energy efficiency. The plan is partly being prepared in fulfilment of our obligations under the EU Energy Service Directive, but the intention is to go beyond that and show how the White Paper targets are to be achieved. The plan has the potential to be powerfully anti-inflationary in the medium term, it will contribute directly to our climate change targets and it can contribute to a reduction in resource pressure. It could achieve the latter more powerfully if it were to be seen as a model for others to emulate. Is there any more worthy project that is within our capability to deliver right now?

By all means let us have a debate on nuclear energy and other supply-side considerations, but let it not be at the expense of action towards a goal that will contribute to the well-being of our people, our economy and our ability to lead the world in compassionate self-interest.

Dr Edward Walsh

Founding President, University of Limerick

Educated UCC (BEng), Iowa State University (Dphil, MSc.). Engineer with Pye Ltd. UK 1960, Associate, US Atomic Energy Commission Laboratory, Iowa 1963-5, Asst. Professor, Iowa State Univ. 1964-5, Founding Director Energy Research Group Prog., Virginia, Assoc. Professor, Virginia State Univ. 1968-9. Member of numerous international bodies including New York Academy of Science, and the American Nuclear Society. He is also a member of the Royal Irish Academy and of the Company of Goldsmiths of Dublin. His numerous publications include: Energy Conversion *and many papers for scientific journals.*

Irish Energy Policy: Reason vs Emotion

> Opposition to nuclear energy is based on irrational fear fed by Hollywood-style fiction, the Green lobbies and the media. These fears are unjustified, and nuclear energy from its start in 1952 has proved to be the safest of all energy sources. We must stop fretting over the minute statistical risks of cancer from chemicals or radiation. Nearly one-third of us will die of cancer anyway, mainly because we breathe air laden with that all pervasive carcinogen, oxygen ... By all means, let us use the small input from renewables sensibly, but only one immediately available source does not cause global warming and that is nuclear energy.[1]

These statements are made by James Lovelock, Britain's premier environmental scientist and a founder of Greenpeace. They are echoed by Sir David King, Chief Scientific Adviser to the UK Government[2] and by a range of professional and scientific bodies of high standing that have studied the facts. An unlikely alliance has emerged between the nuclear industry and an increasing number of environmentalists.

Looking at the fundamental facts has not been an activity in which we in Ireland have much indulged ...

Bruno Comby, the French environmentalist and President of Environmentalists for Nuclear Energy, states:

> When you look at the fundamental facts, nuclear energy is the only energy which is available in large quantities and is able to deliver the energy which our society needs in a clean manner. In fact it is the only way to do that.[3]

Looking at the fundamental facts has not been an activity in which we in Ireland have much indulged, and the outgoing Minister with the energy portfolio, Noel Dempsey TD, had reason to comment near the end of his term:

> The reality of our opposition to nuclear energy is that it is an Irish problem - an emotional problem rather than a rational one.[4]

Our new Minister for Communications, Energy and Natural Resources, Eamon Ryan TD, has got off to a constructive start and has clearly opted for the rational approach. He is quoted as saying that the crises caused by climate change and the impending decline in world oil supplies means that "we have to look at everything" in terms of energy supplies. He has said recently: "I've no objection to a debate. I was encouraging one for the last number of years because we do need to be well-informed."[5]

Taking on Ireland's energy portfolio is no simple challenge. Ireland has a problem. Its energy infrastructure is near the bottom of the IMD world competitiveness rankings at 46th.[6] While ahead of Romania and Indonesia, Ireland is behind places like Turkey and Poland. Ireland and Italy, two countries without nuclear power, have the highest electricity costs in the EU. Ireland's high energy costs have been mentioned as reasons for the closure or deferral of plants such as Procter and Gamble in Nenagh and the €100 million Coca Cola plant in Wexford. Even at the high end of the spectrum enterprises such as Google and Intel are sensitive to energy costs.

The Finns as usual are ahead of the game. They have had a full energy debate and are now forging ahead with the construction of a new nuclear reactor. The decision was driven primarily by economic,[7] environmental considerations … and the facts. These facts are quite unambiguous. Nuclear reactors do not emit carbon gasses and so do not contribute to global warming. Compared to other means of energy production nuclear power is safe. Death statistics reveal that energy production by hydroelectric and coal are the most dangerous, gas is safer, but nuclear is the safest of all.[8]

Coal is one of the most lethal energy sources. In addition to its serious impact on global warming, large numbers of people die while mining coal, or subsequently from black-lung disease. Last year some 6,000 died mining coal in China – five for each million tons of coal extracted.[9]

While we should have little worry about the stability of Irish dams, the records show that hydroelectric is the most dangerous form of electrical generation. Some 200 major hydroelectric dams have failed, killing some 8,000 people. But few recall these: the 1959 French Malpasset[10] dam accident killed 421. In the Italian Vaiont[11]

The Finns as usual are ahead of the game. They have had a full energy debate and are now forging ahead with the construction of a new nuclear reactor.

dam accident of 1963, 30 million cubic meters of water swept down the Alpine valley. The villages of Longarone, Pirago, Villanova and Rivalta were wiped out, killing 2,600. Two thousand died when the Indian Machhu dam failed in 1979. The litany of forgotten hydroelectric accidents goes on.

Yet few will be unaware of the world's two major nuclear accidents: Three Mile Island and Chernobyl. Neither was caused by a nuclear explosion. In both cases the problem was caused by steam pressure damaging the nuclear reactor vessel. No deaths or injuries occurred during the Three Mile Island accident.

The one at Chernobyl[12] was a radically different matter. The reactor design was gravely defective and the Soviets ignored public safety by omitting the enclosures provided in all western reactors to prevent radiation leakage. Typically, a western reactor is sealed in a four to eight inch thick high-tensile steel pressure vessel. About this is an additional four foot thick leaded-concrete enclosure. These, together with the radioactive coolant systems, are then enclosed in a further one to two inch thick steel containment vessel, which in turn is enclosed in a three foot thick shield building.[13]

The Chernobyl reactor lacked these vital layers of containment structures. As a result, when steam pressure caused the reactor vessel to rupture the radioactive material that rushed outwards escaped immediately into the atmosphere. The graphite moderator went on fire, burned for nine days and the radioactive smoke particles were carried by the wind over large areas of the Soviet Union and Europe. The area within 30 km of the reactor was seriously contaminated. If the Chernobyl reactor had been enclosed in the same way as Three Mile Island this would not have happened.

Contrary to reports of thousands of deaths, the report established that a total of 56 people died from the results of nuclear radiation since the accident in 1986.

Hundreds of thousands of people were evacuated and their lives were drastically disrupted. While the large majority of those evacuated received only minor radiation doses, less than that of a chest x-ray, this was not made known to them for two years. The foreboding that arose from wild media reports of 10,000 to as many as 100,000 deaths, combined with a lack of information about individual health prospects, inflicted serious psychological scars. This sense of doom and uncertainty was finally brought to a conclusion only recently when the World Health Organisation, together with seven other United Nations Agencies and some 100 leading scientists, established the true facts related to the Chernobyl accident.[14]

While the UN report highlights a human tragedy that has caused major disruption to the normal life of the region, it also made it clear that the effects on health and environment were significantly less severe than initially predicted. Contrary to reports of thousands of deaths, the report established that a total of 56 people died from the results of nuclear radiation since the accident in 1986. Forty-seven of these were emergency workers who fought the fire at the nuclear plant during the first day while radiation levels were at a peak. Most of their deaths took place within the following four months. Some 4,000 subsequently developed thyroid cancer. But the survival rate was over 99 per cent and only nine of these have died as a result of radiation. The report, despite previous forecasts, found that there was no observed rise in the incidence of cancer amongst the general population, nor was there evidence of a decrease in fertility or increase in birth defects due to radiation. If nuclear reactors were never built at Chernobyl some hundred thousand people in the area studied could be expected to die of cancer in the normal course of events. The UN team estimate that it is possible that some 4 per cent of these deaths could eventually be attributed to the Chernobyl accident.

The UN report finds that the most significant damage was psychological, and the assistance programmes established in the region in the wake of the accident have fostered an unhelpful culture of dependency creating a major barrier to the region's recovery.

More recently, an evaluation of risks by scientists at Britain's Centre for Ecology and Hydrology[15] concludes that for the emergency workers and those living near Chernobyl (other than the some 200 firefighters and helicopter crew) the increased risk of premature death is around 1 per cent – approximately the same as that of dying of diseases caused by inhaling other people's tobacco smoke or by pollution in major cities. Indeed, Smith and Beresford conclude that:

> Populations still living unofficially in the abandoned lands around Chernobyl may actually have a lower health risk from radiation than they would have if they were exposed to the air pollution health risk in a large city such as nearby Kiev.

A European Environmental Agency report considers environmental risks and estimates that 370,000 European die prematurely due to air pollution caused by transport. The naturally occurring radioactive gas radon is estimated to cause some 200 Irish deaths each year from lung cancer. Yet, although there are some 400 nuclear power reactors in operation, there is no record of any civilian anywhere in the world being killed by radiation from a nuclear power plant in the past 20 years.[16]

There are 103 nuclear power plants in operation in the US and during the 30-year period since most of them were constructed there is not a single civilian nuclear radiation fatality associated with these plants. Yet during the same period 4,559 people were electrocuted in their homes, 21,018 were killed on the railways, 1.5 million on US roads and 2,954 were killed by lightning.

... although there are some 400 nuclear power reactors in operation, there is no record of any civilian anywhere in the world being killed by radiation from a nuclear power plant in the past 20 years.

Ireland's attitude towards nuclear energy fluctuates over the years and is much influenced by international events. In 1968, the ESB announced plans for a 650 megawatt nuclear plant at Carnsore Point, lodged a planning application for four nuclear reactors with Wexford County Council in 1974 and contracted with Urenco for the supply of enriched uranium.[17] Uranium exploration commenced in Ireland and drilling in potential deposits commenced in Donegal and Wicklow. Following the oil shock of 1973, the government's commitment to nuclear energy strengthened and the energy minister Des O'Malley made it clear at the 1978 Fianna Fáil Ard Fheis that the "Flat Earth Society" was not going to determine Ireland's future energy policy. However, the Three Mile Island accident, the Kinsale gas find combined with Des O'Malley's expulsion from Fianna Fáil did – plans for building a nuclear power station were dropped.

Others moved ahead with their plans – today there are a total of 439 nuclear reactors in operation in 31 different countries. The French nuclear programme has been the most successful. Seventy-seven per cent of France's electricity is generated by its 59 nuclear reactors. As oil prices rise, France's energy costs remain stable, providing the country with an important competitive advantage. European energy shortages and spiralling oil prices have put France in a strong position to export nuclear-generated electricity and nuclear reactors. Last year, it exported €3 billion worth of electricity, mostly to Germany. Areva, the world's largest nuclear supplier, is convinced of a nuclear revival – it is hiring an extra 1,000 engineers.

Despite the findings of both an OECD investigation[18] and an Irish government task force[19] showing that there are no major public health risks associated with nuclear activities in Cumbria, Sellafield remains a contentious issue between Dublin and London. As a result of inflamed public opinion and the resultant sticky political situation, it is now difficult for Irish policy-makers to address the twin challenges of escalating oil prices and global warming as other countries are doing.

In addition to the 437 nuclear power plants in operation, 34 new plants are under construction, 70 more are at the planning stage and a further 150 have been proposed. Most countries in the developed world have emerging plans for nuclear. The technology has moved on and there is much interest in the German pebble-bed reactor concept now under construction in both South Africa and China, and under development in the Netherlands. Pebble-bed reactors offer the prospect not only of generating low-cost electricity but also providing the means by which hydrogen can be extracted from ordinary water, using the sulphur-iodine process, providing the much sought after pollution-free fuel for transport and heating.

The pebble-bed reactor[20, 21] represents a major technological breakthrough. The fuel is in the form of fine grains of uranium, each coated with several layers of a ceramic that provides a seal about the uranium that is good for one million years. These coated grains are formed together into spheres the size of tennis balls, which are again sealed in a ceramic. Thousands of these balls are then placed in the nuclear reactor vessel and heat is removed by blowing helium through the gaps between the spheres, thereby in a very simple way eliminating the mass of coolant pipe-work and maintenance problems associated with earlier reactors. Helium is such an inert gas it can be heated to very high temperatures. It leaves the pebble-bed reactors at above 900°C. The hot gas can then be used to drive gas turbines and generate electricity or, as proposed, be used to crack water and extract hydrogen for use as a clean fuel in transportation and heating.

The sulphur-iodine process,[22] which was developed in the 1970s, is a chemical means of extracting hydrogen from water. It requires a particularly high temperature heat source and the pebble-bed reactor provides this. The Chinese, who have been importing such large amounts of oil and gas, are particularly interested. China has licensed the German technology and has a major research and development programme underway. Their initial focus is on electricity generation. Construction of the first of 30 planned 200 MW pebble-bed reactors is due for completion this year and research is underway with a view to building further reactors for hydrogen production.

Given the years of tabloid journalism and the political backdrop, there is not much hope in the short term, without strong political leadership, of Ireland following the lead of other small countries such as Finland, Switzerland, Belgium, Lithuania and Latvia and investing in nuclear energy. In the short term, as the issue is debated, Ireland must reduce its dependence on imported oil and gas. Facilitating Shell in bringing ashore the gas from the Corrib field is the most immediate priority. While wind energy is not competitive with other sources without subsidy, it is wise to encourage investment in renewable energy sources. Sustainable Energy Ireland has recently announced helpful incentives.

Because of its isolated island location, Ireland has weak electrical interconnection to the European grid. As a result our system can only cope with a modest proportion of unreliable energy sources such as wind without additional investment in costly energy storage systems. The planned 500-megawatt electrical inter-connector across the Irish Sea to the UK grid is an important initiative and offers the possibility of increasing wind capacity – again, at considerable cost. Interconnectors are expensive to build and the economic

Given the years of tabloid journalism and the political backdrop, there is not much hope in the short term, without strong political leadership, of Ireland following the lead of other small countries such as Finland, Switzerland, Belgium, Lithuania and Latvia and investing in nuclear energy.

Spiralling energy costs, loss of competitiveness and plant closures, combined with global-warming concerns, are changing Irish attitudes towards nuclear energy.

benefits are marginal. But when the wind is not blowing Ireland's energy shortfall has to be made up by other power plants on stand-by in Ireland or by energy imported from the UK through an inter-connector. The fact that some of it may be generated by the two new reactors proposed for Sellafield[23] will, in the short term until we mature, provide, once again, a UK solution to an Irish problem.

Spiralling energy costs, loss of competitiveness and plant closures, combined with global-warming concerns, are changing Irish attitudes towards nuclear energy. The debate, welcomed by Minister Eamon Ryan, is the essential prelude to rational action.

In time we will look back and see the ban on nuclear energy as hilariously ludicrous as those imposed in Ireland on the works of James Joyce, contraceptives and foreign games.

Endnotes

1. Lovelock, James. *The Independent*. 24 May 2004.

2. Critical mass. *The Economist*. 3 Dec 2005.

3. O'Connor, Fergal. *Business & Finance*. 10 Aug 2006.

4. Gurdgiev, Constantin. *Business & Finance*. 22 Feb 2007.

5. Cullen, Paul. Ryan calls for debate on turning to nuclear power. *The Irish Times*. 19 June 2007.

6. World competitiveness report. IMD. 2005.

7. Economics of nuclear power. Briefing paper 8. www.uic.com. Jan 2006.

8. Ball, Roberts & Simpson, Research Report #20, Centre for Environmental & Risk Management, University of East Anglia, 1994; Hirschberg et al, Paul Scherrer Institut, 1996; in: *IAEA, Sustainable Development and Nuclear Power*, 1997; *Severe Accidents in the Energy Sector*, Paul Scherrer Institut, 2001.

9. Coonan, Clifford. *The Irish Times*. 18 Aug 2005.

10. Goutal, N. Malpasset dam failure. National Hydraulic and Environement Laboratory. Electricite of France. Chatou. France.

11. Vaiont dam disaster. http://seis.natsci.csulb.edu/bperry/Mass per cent20Wasting/VaiontDam.htm

12. Chernobyl Accident. Nuclear issues briefing paper 22. May 2007. http://www.uic.com.au/nip22.htm

13. Safety of nuclear power reactors. Nuclear issues briefing paper 14. http://www.uic.com.au/nip14.htm

14. Chernobyl Forum: 2003-05. Chernobyl's Legacy: Health, Environmental and Social-Economic Impacts. IAEA, WHO, UNDP. 2005

15. Smith, J.T. and Beresford, N.A. *Chernobyl – catastrophe and consequences*. Springer. 2007.

16. *Business & Finance*. 10 Aug 2006.

17. *Country reports: Ireland*. Laka publications. 1995.

18. OECD study says no health risk from spent nuclear fuel. Planet Ark. Reuters News Service.18 May 2000. http://www.planetark.com/daily-newsstory.cfm/newsid/6728/newsDate/18-May-2000/story.htm

19. J. Radiol. Prot. 20 80-81. 2000. doi:10.1088/0952-4746/20/1/607

20. Pebble bed reactor. http://en.wikipedia.org/wiki/Pebble_bed_reactor

21. Next generation of nuclear power? Technology news. ES&T Online News. 25 Jan 2006.

22. Schultz, K.R. Use of the modular helium reactor for hydrogen production. World Nuclear Association annual symposium. London. Sep. 2003.

23. Smyth, J. Sellafield site identified as possible new nuclear plant. *The Irish Times*. 10 April 2006.

Eamon Ryan TD

Minister for Communications, Energy & Natural Resources

Born in Dublin and educated at Holy Cross N.S. Dundrum, Gonzaga College, UCD (B. Comm). Formerly, founder of activity holiday company, first elected to Dáil Éireann in 2002. Elected to Dublin City Council in 1999. Founding chairman of Dublin Cycling Campaign, member of the Dublin Transportation Office Advisory Committee. Re-elected to Dail for Dublin South constituency in May 2007 and a member of the Green Party negotiating team in talks with Fianna Fáil to form a government. Appointed Minister for Communications, Energy and Natural Resources in June 2007.

The Gravity and the Scale of the Challenge Facing Us

In energy policy, you have to think long-term. The cars we buy today will be running in 2020. The power stations we will build in the next two years will be there in 2050. The roads we build will be used in 100 years' time. In making investments in energy infrastructure, therefore, we have to look forward to the coming decades and not just the next five years. This is the kind of timeframe and certainty that is also needed for those making commercial decisions. It makes sense for the market and it makes sense for Government.

The twin challenges of climate change and peak oil will soon dominate the policy decisions we have to make. On both these counts we will face a severe crisis unless we wean ourselves off our dependence on fossil fuels. A long-term view shows us the problems we face but urgent action is required today in order that we can avoid them. We cannot put off these issues for 5 or 20 years. Every single issue needs a long-term view to see that threat but it requires urgent action today to meet it. Every budget and every investment decision should be measured on the basis of whether it is helping or hindering us in breaking our addiction to the wasteful use of coal gas and oil.

Padraig McManus of the ESB is right when he says it will take some time for some of the renewable energy technologies to come to their full commercial fruition However, unless we start now, unless we actually make a collective decision to head in this direction, then we will be too late. We cannot wait for all the right market signals and technological solutions to be in place. We need to take the first step and help create the right conditions by providing incentives and introducing regulations so that individuals and businesses start to

> **The twin challenges of climate change and peak oil will soon dominate the policy decisions we have to make. On both these counts we will face a severe crisis unless we wean ourselves off our dependence on fossil fuels.**

make investment choices which will ultimately and substantially reduce their use of fossil fuels.

We must stand up and face this crisis. The task is not too great, nor
is it too much to ask. It requires action by all strata of society and it requires visionary political leadership. Such leadership has in the past
helped us achieve what no one thought would be possible in a time
frame that nobody expected. When John F. Kennedy said his country
would take people to the moon, no scientist knew exactly how that
could be done. Nonetheless, his sense of direction and urgency made
sure it was achieved. On a blacker note, when that same country was
threatened by war on two fronts they were able to develop in a few
short years a lethal nuclear technology that in less urgent conditions
might have taken decades to develop. The evidence is there that in
a crisis, in an emergency, humankind can collectively work together
to solve problems. We need a sense of collective urgency around the
energy crisis that we now face.

I want to put our dependence on imported oil coal and gas within
a global context. I believe we are now approaching a peak in global
oil production, which will have profound consequences for the world
economy. I have followed with interest the work of the Association
for the Study of Peak Oil (ASPO, www.peakoil.net) which was set
up by a group of academics and former oil geologists, who have no
commercial interest in the area. Five years ago, if you talked to the
International Energy Agency (IEA), which advises western Governments on oil security, they would have strongly refuted the theory
that these so called "peak oilers" were expounding. Today, those official reports are only echoing the concern that supply can no longer
keep up with demand.

The peak in global discoveries of oil occurred in 1964. That's over
40 years ago. All the major fields have now been found. Today, we
are only finding almost one new barrel of oil each year for the five or
six barrels that we are consuming. We face a geological reality that
sooner rather than later the actual production of oil starts to level out
and then decline.

The exact year of a peak in global oil production is not the important thing. Even when we go past the peak we will still have oil available to us. However, we will then be on a steady downward slope in
the availability of the cheap, conventional, easy, light oils – the ones
that power our airplanes, that drive our cars and heat our homes.
That downward slope is expected to be in the region of a two to three
per cent reduction each year. We may be able to get more oil out of
tar sands or out of the polar or deep-sea regions but it will require a
lot of energy just to get these reserves out of the ground.

Within this global context, Ireland is particularly exposed. Sixty

We must stand up and face this crisis. The task is not too great, nor is it too much to ask. It requires action by all strata of society and it requires visionary political leadership.

per cent of our energy comes from imported oil. Every man woman and child in the country is consuming on average ten pints of oil a day. When you include our use of coal and gas we see that almost 90 per cent of our energy is imported in forms of fossils fuels. By comparison, the average figure in the European Union is closer to 50 per cent.

Gas may well be the substitute fuel that will carry us through this period when oil is less readily available. Gas is similar to oil in being a form of energy which has been stored for over 100 million years. We can liquefy it and can now transport it in different ways but it, too, will peak and become much more expensive. What we have to do is use gas as a transition fuel as we move to developing a new non-fossil fuel economy.

I think in the future, when historians look back they will see that the twentieth century was an era dominated by the story of cheap American oil. At their own peak in production in the early 1970s, America was pumping ten million barrels of oil a day. That's the same as Saudi Arabia is producing at full tilt today. They won the Second World War because they had oil. George Bush knows about oil. His Vice-President is also an oil man and when they say we are addicted to oil and we need to wean ourselves off it, we should listen. America's a good example because the 50 states have a long and varied history in oil discovery and use. The pattern of their own rise and fall in production is likely to be replicated internationally. Having peaked in the early 1970s, their production is now down to less than five million barrels of oil a day and decreasing.

The picture in the North Sea is similar. This is of particular importance to ourselves as we get most of our own oil and gas from this area. Having peaked more recently around the year 2000, production levels across the area are now declining by about 7-8 per cent a year. That's why the British Government have re-written two energy papers in the last four years as they realise the extent of the challenge they now face. That is why gas prices spiked here as the market started to realise that the UK was close to not having enough gas to meet their own needs. The situation has since been alleviated by the recent opening of a new connecting gas pipeline to the Norwegian gas fields. However, these too will peak and deplete in the near future which will leave us dependent on a very long gas pipeline coming all the way from Siberia. We have to start preparing now so that we are not utterly dependent on that pipeline for our energy security.

A recent study for the US Department of Energy carried out by Robert Hirche came to the conclusion that a state should radically change its investment plans two decades in advance of a peak in oil production so that is has the right infrastructure to cope with such an event. Coincidently, Sir Nicholas Stern was saying at the same time that we will have to change our investment decisions over the next decade if we are to protect our economy and our society from the effects of global climate change.

The issue of climate change brings a moral as well as an economic imperative. The city of Lima, Peru is situated in a desert to the west of the Andes mountain range. It relies on the glacier waters from those mountains to provide water for the ten million inhabitants of the city. Unfortunately, as the temperatures rise those glaciers are retreating and there is a real question if within decades the people of that city will have enough water to survive. What will we do when that happens? What are the people in China, or Bangladesh or in India going to do when the water coming from the Himalayan glaciers reduces to the extent that the Yangtze or the Ganges or the other rivers in the region cannot provide for the hundreds of millions of people who live alongside them?

There is a real concern if we go above a two degree increase in global average temperatures we may well trigger some feedback mechanisms that you can't stop. The melting of the polar ice caps could reduce the amount of heat being reflected out to space and cause further rapid increases in temperature. The melting of the permanent Siberian tundra could release huge amounts of methane that would cause runaway climate change. The Amazon rainforest might not be able to survive the micro climate changes that are already starting to be noticed which in turn would release hundreds of millions of tonnes of additional greenhouse gases into the atmosphere.

Why is that of concern for us? Because when those positive feedback mechanisms occur and runaway climate change occurs, it does threaten Ireland. We also have a responsibility to act as it is the developed world which is responsible for the emissions over the last hundred years which are still today having an effect in the upper atmosphere. As a country, we have the fifth highest per capita income rates in the world, so we cannot point the finger at anyone else. We cannot just wait for other countries to act. We are all responsible as we live in a truly global economy. The goods we use today mostly come from China. The power plants they are building will provide electricity to support the lifestyle that we enjoy.

In Ireland, two-thirds of our own emissions come from the energy sector and roughly one-third comes from agriculture. In agriculture we have made some cuts as we lower our national herd size but the easier and bigger reductions are going to have to come from the energy sector.

The problem we have is that rather than falling, our use of energy is rising steadily. With the European Union we are committing

> As a country, we have the fifth highest per capita income rates in the world, so we cannot point the finger at anyone else. We cannot just wait for other countries to act. We are all responsible as we live in a truly global economy.

collectively to a reduction in Greenhouse Gases of 30 per cent below 1990 levels by 2020, if there is a wider international agreement. However, the predictions for our own economy are that our use of energy will actually increase a further 30 per cent by that period. The government has set a target of a 3 per cent reduction in emissions per annum. This will bring us towards the reductions we will need to make within a European burden-sharing agreement; however our actual emissions from the energy sector are now growing by some 3 per cent per annum. That's the gravity and the scale of the challenge facing us.

What can we do about it in Government? We can try and go beyond our initial renewable energy targets by providing fixed-price support systems so that the ocean wind wave and tidal powers systems are given the chance to take off. We can provide grants so that people can put in proper roof and attic and wall insulation which is the easiest and cheapest way of cutting our wasteful use of energy. We can put a levy on carbon which provides a clear signal across all markets on the need to switch to cleaner fuels and more efficient devices. We can switch to public transport and improve planning so people have to travel less. We can invest in new energy research. We will set energy standards in homes for new buildings which are 40 per cent higher than the existing ones and then increase them within a short number of years to 60 per cent higher and that will save people money. That'll lead to a better construction industry and that will cut back emissions.

However, if we are to achieve real change then we will first and foremost have to change attitudes and make sure that everyone is aware of the nature and scale of the challenge facing us. This was one of the key reasons why the Green party decided to enter into Government. We need to use our position to explain and persuade.

Hopefully, we will also be able to provide some leadership by making certain sensible and simple changes to the way this country uses energy. I believe the Irish people are ready and willing to follow such leadership so that we can proudly play our part in responding to the greatest political challenge of our time.

> **However, if we are to achieve real change then we will first and foremost have to change attitudes and make sure that everyone is aware of the nature and scale of the challenge facing us. This was one of the key reasons why the Green party decided to enter into Government. We need to use our position to explain and persuade.**

Sean O'Rourke, Chairman of the session "Providing Our Energy"

Brian Cowen TD, Joe Mulholland, Joan Burton TD, Jim O'Hara

Jim O'Leary, Department of Economics
NUI Maynooth

Peter McLoone, General Secretary
of IMPACT

Cormac Lucey, Former Special Adviser to
Minister for Justice, Equality & Law Reform

Colm McCarthy, School of Economics,
University College Dublin

Chapter 6

Reforming the Public Service

*A Critical Evaluation of Aspects of Recent Public Service
Reforms in Ireland*
Jim O'Leary
Department of Economics, NUI Maynooth

Trade Unions Need to Become Advocates of Real Reform
Peter McLoone
General Secretary of IMPACT, former President ICTU

Rationality, Reality and Unreasonableness
Cormac Lucey
**Former Special Advisor to Minister for Justice, Equality
& Law Reform**

The Need for Reform in Economic Policymaking
Colm McCarthy
School of Economics, University College Dublin

Jim O'Leary

Department of Economics, NUI Maynooth

Jim O'Leary was born in Dublin and educated at Belvedere College and UCD. He has a Masters degree in economics. He has worked at the ESRI, the NESC and the Department of the Taoiseach. From 1987 to 2001 he was Chief Economist at Davy Stockbrokers. Since 2001 he has lectured in economics at NUI-Maynooth. He is also a columnist with The Irish Times *and a non-executive director of AIB. He is a former director of Aer Lingus, the National Statistics Board and Gresham Hotels. He was a member of the Public Service Benchmarking Body from its inception until his resignation in April 2002.*

A Critical Evaluation of Aspects of Recent Public Service Reforms in Ireland

Introduction

Contrary to popular belief, the Irish public service is not frozen in aspic, impervious to change and modernisation. Under the influence of successive waves of reform, the public service has changed enormously, and mostly for the better, since the 1960s. The latest wave of reform started with the launch of the so-called Strategic Management Initiative (SMI) in 1994. An important subsequent milestone was the publication of the keynote document, Delivering Better Government, two years later.

The brief foreword to that document encapsulates the spirit of this reform programme:

> Central to this programme is the delivery of the highest quality of service to the customers of the Civil Service at all levels. To achieve this, authority and responsibility will have to be devolved.... A more results and performance oriented Civil Service is essential. Rigorous systems of setting objectives and managing performance need to be put in place to support this. Civil Servants must be clearly rewarded for good performance and take responsibility for poor performance within a structure that emphasises teamwork within and between Departments.

The foreword also spoke of the essential requirement of "a flexible, effective and efficient Civil Service" and the task of "reforming our institutions to provide service, accountability, transparency and freedom of information".

Contrary to popular belief, the Irish public service is not frozen in aspic, impervious to change and modernisation. Under the influence of successive waves of reform, the public service has changed enormously, and mostly for the better, since the 1960s.

Under the auspices of the SMI, and in the spirit of "Delivering Better Government", an enormous volume of activity has occurred over the past decade or more, including countless meetings of committees and working groups, the publication of innumerable statements, reports and reviews, the institution of new practices and procedures, the installation of new systems and processes, the training and retraining of a virtual generation of public servants, and the enactment of several substantial pieces of legislation. If the appetite for reform was measured by related activity, the appetite of the Irish public service for reform would seem to be voracious if not insatiable. If activity were the measure of success, Ireland would surely have a public service that was a shining light to the rest of the world. However, activity is not to be confused with output or with superior outcomes. This is one of the key observations that animated the original impetus for public service reform and, perhaps ironically, it is equally applicable to the reform programme itself.

If activity were the measure of success, Ireland would surely have a public service that was a shining light to the rest of the world. However, activity is not to be confused with output or with superior outcomes.

In what follows, I examine three streams of reform within the current public service modernisation programme with a view to assessing the relationship between activity and output/outcomes. The picture that emerges is of a great deal of well-intentioned effort that is either carried out over an inordinately long gestation period, and/or has produced outcomes that are disproportionately modest and/or has struggled to embed the attitudinal and behavioural changes necessary for a transformation of performance.

The Management Information Framework (MIF)

According to the government website www.bettergov.ie, the public sector modernisation programme encompasses six major sub-programmes, one of which is financial management. A critical element in the achievement of better financial management for government departments is the implementation of an entirely new management information framework (MIF). The MIF is essentially a system of regular management reporting, comprehending both financial and non-financial data, designed to inform decision-making about the allocation and use of resources.

The time-line for the MIF arguably starts with the launch of the SMI in 1994, but it may be more reasonable to trace its origins to the 1996 Delivering Better Government report in which there was an explicit recognition that new financial management systems needed to be developed and deployed across the public service.

Three years were to pass before the proposals for the MIF were approved by government in July 1999, and it was March 2000 before the first MIF Project Plan was put together. This particular plan was mostly concerned with setting out a timetable for the installation of new financial systems across government departments. This was just one of many components of the overall project. Others included: the development of sets of indicators for monitoring and evaluating departments' performance; the design and roll-out of new management reports and the training of staff in the use of the new systems. Another element was to be the development of accruals accounting across government departments to replace or complement the existing cash accounting methodology.

Staff training is obviously critical to the successful roll-out of the MIF. A state of the art information system is of little benefit if people don't know how to use it. Judging from the audit trail in publicly available documents, it was February 2002 before the training piece was first addressed when the so-called MIF Project Management Subgroup adopted a proposal to develop an MIF training strategy. In due course thereafter, each department carried out detailed MIF training needs analysis, on the back of which suites of training courses were defined and designed. Delivery of the training courses took place over a timeframe that extended to the end of 2006.

In November 2004, another MIF Project Plan was launched. This one set out an indicative implementation timetable encompassing all nine streams of the project, together with final target dates for meeting key milestones and an overall project completion date of December 2006. My understanding is that the project was substantially completed at the end of 2006, although the development/refinement of performance indicators is still a work in progress (and will probably remain so for quite some time), and most of the planned work on accruals accounting (one of the original nine project workstreams) has not in fact been done.

... the management and delivery of big change projects require that an organisation be capable of gearing up to a significantly elevated pace of activity before reverting to business as usual.

The main purpose of the MIF example is to illustrate the very long timeline that characterises the project: 10 years, if we take Delivering Better Government as the point of origin; 7½ years if we date it from the approval of the relevant proposals by government. Of course, this was a very complex and multi-faceted piece of work and would have presented a stern challenge to any organisation. Still, 7 ½ to 10 years seems inordinately long, and much longer than execution of a similar project is likely to take in the private sector.

It's difficult to be definitive about the factors responsible for delay in this case, but some familiarity with private sector practice suggests a couple of candidate reasons. The first derives from the fact that the management and delivery of big change projects require that an organisation be capable of gearing up to a significantly elevated pace of activity before reverting to business as usual. Typically, this in turn requires flexibility in the mobilisation and deployment of resources and a willingness on the part of the organisation concerned, or a significant portion of it, to go on a 'war footing'. Public service organisations may be handicapped in these respects by overly rigid demarcation of duties and functions.

Second, there is the matter of project governance. The successful execution of a big change project requires not only clear ownership and accountabilities but also strong sponsorship. In the private sector, that sponsorship is typically provided by a senior management figure, if not the CEO, and is ultimately underpinned by the support of the board of directors. In the public service, the ultimate sponsor of a big change project is the relevant minister. If he/she doesn't demonstrate strong support, a sense of urgency will be hard to cultivate.

It is also worth mentioning that a project like the MIF is especially demanding of technical skills (systems design, quantitative analysis, accounting and so on). The successful and timely execution of such a project therefore requires an ability to mobilise significant numbers of specialists from within the organisation and/or recruit them where not available. Public service constraints on recruiting such resources may have been an impediment to speedy project delivery.

The Performance Management and Development System (PMDS)

Reference was made above to the six major components of the public sector modernisation programme of which one is financial management. Another is human resource management. One of the important elements within the human resource management area is the performance management and development system (PMDS).

The PMDS speaks to the objective of a results-oriented Civil Service envisioned by Delivering Better Government, and the need to put in place rigorous systems of setting objectives and managing performance that was articulated in that document.

The timeline for delivery of the PMDS therefore started in 1996. The following year, consultants were engaged to assist in the design of a system and in 1998 a sub-group of General Council – a forum for public service unions and management to discuss and resolve industrial relations issues – was convened to agree the design, development and implementation of a PMDS in each department.

In May 2000, General Council reached agreement on the introduction of PMDS, but with a number of significant caveats that effectively ruled out its use for Human Resources (HR) purposes. In fact, it was another five years before agreement was reached between management and unions on the integration of PMDS with HR strategy, with that agreement scheduled to take effect from January 2007.

The successful execution of a big change project requires not only clear ownership and accountabilities but also strong sponsorship. In the private sector, that sponsorship is typically provided by a senior management figure, if not the CEO, and is ultimately underpinned by the support of the board of directors. In the public service, the ultimate sponsor of a big change project is the relevant minister. If he/she doesn't demonstrate strong support, a sense of urgency will be hard to cultivate.

What all this means is that it has taken 11 years to arrive at a situation where a performance management system can be used for one of the (if not the) core purposes for which it was originally envisaged.

Even then, one has a strong sense of an elephant labouring to produce a mouse. What has actually been agreed at this stage is only a very pale shadow of a performance-related pay system. In the matter of pay, it has been agreed that the ratings produced by the PMDS are to be used only to determine if people can progress to the next point on their incremental scale. To better appreciate what is entailed here, it is worth briefly describing some of the nuts and bolts of the system.

The PMDS produces a uniform five-point scoring scale for individuals across all civil service grades, ranging from 5 ("outstanding") through 3 ("fully acceptable"), 2 ("needs improvement") to 1 "unacceptable"). What has been agreed is that a jobholder will qualify for payment of the next increment if he/she receives a rating of 2 or over. What this implies, inter alia, is that the outstanding performer will be treated in the same way as the person whose performance falls short of requirements and needs improvement.

The agreement incorporates a suggested rating distribution which, while not intended to be binding, is designed "to illustrate a broad pattern which could be expected at organisational level". This distribution envisages just 5 per cent of jobholders falling into the Grade 1 category.

So, it has taken eleven years to develop and deploy a performance management system that is pretty well pre-ordained to ensure that 95 per cent of the relevant civil service population will qualify for payment of the next increment. It is difficult to accept that this new system, painstakingly designed and patiently negotiated with staff interests through a labyrinthine process of engagement, represents much progress towards the Delivering Better Government objective of "clearly rewarding civil servants for good performance".

So, it has taken eleven years to develop and deploy a performance management system that is pretty well pre-ordained to ensure that 95 per cent of the relevant civil service population will qualify for payment of the next increment. It is difficult to accept that this new system, painstakingly designed and patiently negotiated with staff interests through a labyrinthine process of engagement, represents much progress towards the Delivering Better Government objective of "clearly rewarding civil servants for good performance".

Strategy Statements, Annual Reports and Expenditure Reviews

A key element in the public service modernisation programme is the building of robust and coherent links between the input of resources into government programmes at one end and the achievement of the objectives of those programmes at the other, together with effective feedback systems that signal the need for changes in prioritisation and resource re-allocation.

The Public Sector Management Act of 1997 spelled out the corresponding governance framework, in which three sets of documents were to play a critical role:

- Statements of Strategy, to be published by government departments every three years, the purpose of which was to identify and clarify the department's objectives and strategies, set out performance indicators, highlight spending priorities and resource allocation issues.
- Annual Reports, the essential purpose of which was to report on and assess progress in relation to strategy
- Expenditure Reviews, the purpose if which was to evaluate spending and thereby provide an important input into strategic decisions in relation to resource allocation and thereby into departmental strategy statements.

The Statements of Strategy and the Annual Reports that have been published by government departments have been the subject of an amount of critical scrutiny. The conclusions reached by Richard Boyle of the IPA, following his evaluation of annual progress reports, is not unrepresentative:

> In general, the reports do not provide a sufficiently balanced and informed picture of how departments and offices are progressing against agreed objectives and strategies. The widespread absence of data, and focus on activity reporting, makes assessment of performance difficult if not impossible in many cases.

Performance in respect of timeliness is perhaps the simplest and most eloquent testimony to how poorly embedded this governance framework is. As of mid-July, only eight out of fifteen government departments had published annual reports for 2006. In six cases the latest available annual report related to 2005 and, remarkably, the latest year for which the Department of Education and Science (budget: €8 billion plus) had published its annual report was 2004.

Not surprisingly, in the light of the deficiencies of the documents, there is little evidence to suggest that either strategy statements or annual progress reports play a significant role in the scrutiny of public spending by government or by the Dáil. Nor is there any evidence that these documents have helped to inform or raise the standard of public debate about spending allocations. On the contrary, the indications are that the preparation of these documents has for many departments become another box-ticking exercise.

Arguably, the way the expenditure review process has evolved, at least up to 2006, has been even more disappointing. A recent policy document by the two main opposition parties, The Buck Stops Here, published by Fine Gael and the Labour Party in March 2006, set out what was, even by the standards of adversarial politics, a savage indictment of the Expenditure Review Initiative, dismissing it as "a dismal failure" and in state of "almost entire collapse". Behind the perhaps politically-inspired hyperbole, some telling factual points were made:

- In 2005, just 13 expenditure reviews were carried out, representing just 0.5 per cent of total public spending.
- The Department of Health and Children was entirely exempted from the expenditure review process.
- The Steering Committee overseeing the process admitted that there was no evidence that any Expenditure Review that had been carried out had impacted on resource allocation decisions.

Since the FG-Labour document was published, the expenditure review process has been overhauled. Now re-labelled the Value for Money and Policy Review, its scope has been extended and the reports it generates are to be published and submitted to the Select Committees of the Oireachtas. It is intended that the new reviews process, in contrast to the one it has replaced, will focus on major areas of spending and will cover a minimum 10-15 per cent of each Department's spending in every three-year planning period.

On paper at least, the new process, together with the new annual Output Statements that each Department is now obliged to prepare and publish, promises to infuse fresh rigour into the evaluation and allocation of public spending. However, it is too soon to assess how well the new arrangements are working, although it is not too early to observe that already there has been a non-trivial amount of slippage. In the first twelve months under the new process, just 20 VFM reviews had been completed (34, if those "almost complete" are included). This compares with a target to complete 46 reviews in the first six months.

Conclusion

The examples analysed above suggest that the latest wave of public service reform in Ireland has been a slow process. Progress has been made, but sometimes elephantine effort (a great deal of it accounted for by negotiations with staff interests) yields apparently meagre results.

An important contributory factor to this state of affairs can perhaps be found in the distinction between the respective roles of passion and reason in reform programmes. In this context, passion is shorthand for the vision, principles and convictions that galvanise the effort and mobilise political support for reform; reason relates to the systems, procedures and mechanisms that convert the vision

The examples analysed above suggest that the latest wave of public service reform in Ireland has been a slow process. Progress has been made, but sometimes elephantine effort (a great deal of it accounted for by negotiations with staff interests) yields apparently meagre results.

and principles into practical implementation plans. The literature on reform strongly suggests that both passion and reason are necessary for successful reform. In more prosaic terms what this means is that efforts at reform don't succeed without political will.

In the Irish context, it is difficult to identify a strong political champion of public service reform. Certainly, there is nobody on the government side who has staked their political career on the transformation of the public service (although Mary Harney has staked her reputation on reforming the health services), and there doesn't appear to be anybody who is prepared to expend political energy and capital on injecting urgency and a sense of the imperative into the process.

There are not many reasons to suppose that this situation is about to change any time soon. For example, public service reform doesn't rate a mention amongst the 30 policy areas that provide the section headings in the new Programme for Government. It is perhaps unrealistic to expect a government, the dominant element of which has enjoyed uninterrupted power for over a decade now, to be animated by the need for public service reform. (How can we have done so well if reform were an urgent requirement?)

It is perhaps also unrealistic to expect strong impetus for reform to emerge in a governance model that places social partnership in a pivotal position and where the *raison d'etre* of one of the most powerful of the social partners is the protection of the advantages and privileges that attach to the status quo. I cannot help concluding that the slow pace of change in the Irish public service over the past decade and more, in part reflects the recalcitrance of public sector unions and the enhanced political leverage that social partnership confers on them.

I believe that this is immensely problematic as far as the development of the public sector is concerned. Public service reform is not just about improving the efficiency and effectiveness of expenditure programmes, although that is assuredly a big part of the motivation for reform. It is also about ensuring that the public service marches in step with the rest of society.

The public service may have a distinctive ethos, but there needs to be some degree of consonance between its culture and modus operandi and the culture and modus operandi of the wider society which it serves. At the very least, what the public service does and how it does it need to be susceptible to broadly acceptable explanation. In the words of one writer on the subject of public service reform: "In the last resort, governance has to attend to what ordinary citizens find just, appropriate or acceptable." Otherwise, the credibility and legitimacy of public sector organisations risks being eroded and with that, the willingness of taxpayers to finance their activities.

> ... public service reform doesn't rate a mention amongst the 30 policy areas that provide the section headings in the new Programme for Government. It is perhaps unrealistic to expect a government, the dominant element of which has enjoyed uninterrupted power for over a decade now, to be animated by the need for public service reform.

Peter McLoone

General Secretary of IMPACT, former President ICTU

Born in Donegal. Formerly psychiatric nurse. General Secretary of Ireland's largest public sector union, IMPACT, with over 46,000 members in health, local govt., education, the civil service, semi-state companies and the voluntary sector. President of ICTU 2005-7, he is a member of ICTU executive committee and its general purposes committee. He is also chairman of ICTU's influential public service committee. Played a key role in establishing the public service Benchmarking Body and was the main negotiator on benchmarking. Has been a member of the Labour Relations Commission since 2000.

Trade Unions Need to Become Advocates of Real Reform

During the recent General Elections, in both North and South, we witnessed an intensification of the debate among all the political parties about the efficiency and quality of public service. Among voters, shortcomings in public services were high on the agenda. Throughout the election campaign we also had accelerated criticism from sections of the media and some commentators. Despite what some earlier speakers said, I do not believe this debate will drop off the "agenda" simply because the elections are over.

I am convinced, that it's a debate that will continue in the coming months, and will intensify again with the publication of the Second Report from the Benchmarking Body on Public Service Pay at the end of 2007, and in the negotiations on the second pay module of "Towards 2016".

I believe the outcome of this debate will have a profound impact on those who depend on public services and those who deliver them. I have spoken on this topic at a number of trade union conferences this year, the most recent of which was at the Irish Congress of Trade Union's Conference in July in Bundoran.

I start from the premise that public service is what defines a society. It's what gives it humanity.

This morning, I simply want to share with you the issues I have raised and the points I have conveyed to an exclusively trade union audience over the last few months. I start from the premise that public service is what defines a society. It's what gives it humanity. I assert that campaigns in support of public services are essentially campaigns for a better, fairer, quality of life for all. You only have to consider the recent campaigns against, for example, the introduction of water charges, in Northern Ireland, the campaigns for proper cancer services in the South East and in the North West, campaigns

– 148 –

for reduced class sizes in schools, to recognise the validity of this argument.

I do not agree that private markets and the private sector should be seen as central to the improvement of the human condition. That is a view that is not ideological. It's a view primarily directed at areas of education, health, local government, the civil service and justice sectors. It doesn't include the commercial or all areas of the non-commercial state sector.

Remember also that in excess of 250,000 people are employed in the health, education, local government and civil service sectors. That constitutes one-eighth of the work force, who themselves represent a sizeable group of users of public services and who have the same vested interest as anybody else in ensuring that we provide the highest quality of public services.

My message to the union conferences included the following points:

- Public services are now under the spotlight and an increasingly critical spotlight as never before.

- The choice for unions, particularly public service unions, is to either let those who care more for private profit than for public service set the agenda or to boldly set it ourselves.

- I suggested that campaigns to defend public services must start from the premise that our strongest allies are the people we serve. I argued that there remains a strong culture of support for public provision throughout this island, where ordinary people have no stomach for the unfettered free market approach advocated by some critics.

- I asserted that unions have responsibility to genuinely engage with debates about the quality, more responsiveness and increased flexibility in service provision, if we are to retain public belief in our own bona fides. That means our campaigns must go beyond protecting the status quo and restating what we are against.

- I also suggested that we acknowledge that there are many shortcomings in the system, that we don't attempt to paint a picture of perfect services or uniformly high quality. Along with the people that use public services, public servants know better than anyone about the problems because they have to deal with them every single day.

- In my view, we must introduce some balance and objectivity into a debate that, too often, focuses on the occasional spectacular failure and then characterises all public services and all public servants on that basis. This I am convinced is critically important for

... there remains a strong culture of support for public provision throughout this island, where ordinary people have no stomach for the unfettered free market approach advocated by some critics.

the future of public services and the many people that depend on them. Because, if unchecked, the myth that public services are uniformly bad and incapable of reform will inevitably undermine any hope of developing equitable and high quality services, available to everyone in our society. I stressed that it was important that all unions work together to challenge the misconceptions about pay, staff numbers and performance, and tell the positive stories. I also emphasised that we need to go even further and become genuine advocates of real reform. We can no longer leave the task of defining the reform agenda to management or politicians. We need to come up with simple understandable reforms that meet public demands and embrace the involvement of citizens who want more say in how their money is spent and how we can achieve better outcomes.

We can no longer leave the task of defining the reform agenda to management or politicians. We need to come up with simple understandable reforms that meet public demands and embrace the involvement of citizens who want more say in how their money is spent and how we can achieve better outcomes.

- Although staff have undoubtedly delivered on the extensive changes required under the terms of recent National Agreements, "Sustaining Progress" and "Towards 2016", I believe we will have to change the way we link pay determination systems to better services if we are to rebuild public belief in both.

- It is a fact that in the negotiations on both Agreements, we left it to senior public service managers to draw up the so-called "modernisation" agenda for public services that we ultimately negotiated. It's now clear that the public perception is that this agenda has delivered little in terms of improved services on the ground. And you can count on one hand the number of managers or politicians who are now prepared to defend the outcome on the airwaves and elsewhere. In my experience, that difficult job has largely been left to us in the trade unions. This reluctance is evidence that not alone has the management agenda for change failed to relate to clients, customers and citizens, but they - the management - are not now prepared to come forward and defend it in public debates. I am totally convinced that in the future we have to put ourselves in the customers' or clients' shoes. Rather than solely developing elaborate new management systems and practices that reflect textbook theories, we also need to come up with simple, understandable reforms that meet public demands.

These reforms must:

- Make it simpler and easier to access public services and find your way around the system.

- Make it quicker to get your entitlements and easier to understand and appeal if you're told you have no entitlement.

- Make dealing with the public service generally a more pleasant experience.

- Strengthen a "value for money" culture at all levels of the public service, but without reverting to complicated IT solutions or management systems that take years to develop, but which seldom deliver.
- Place respect for the service-user and the taxpayer at the centre of everything we do.
- Bring staff along, by explaining our objectives, valuing their experience and ideas and developing their skills and potential.

The Problem

At this point you could reach the conclusion that if unions accepted this message from someone like myself then unions and management are already on the same wavelength – because the approach I have used to advocate how trade unions should adapt to reform is no different to the approach to reform advocated by the political system. For example, let's compare my view with what the Taoiseach said when he spoke to the ICTU Conference in July.

> Another reason for confidence is that we have a good public service but we can – and must – make it better.
>
> I am proud to be, and to have been, all my working life, a public servant. I am proud of the traditions and achievements of the Irish Public Service. But I know, as you know, tha=t the people expect, and are paying for, a service that puts the public first. It is no longer enough – if it ever was – to offer the public a service that simply suits the provider. The private sector stands or falls on the goods and services it delivers and the way it delivers them. The public service faces a similar test because, if it fails to deliver, the taxpayer – the electorate – will simply look elsewhere for service; and there is no shortage of people willing to take up the slack.
>
> Despite real progress, major investment and the efforts of very many people in the front line, I do not think anyone who campaigned during the recent General Election could say that, for example, the health service is working as well as it should. Earlier this year, I established a Forum on the Health Sector, on foot of a proposal from Congress.
>
> The Forum is aimed at engaging the problem solving capacity of social partnership in addressing the challenges facing the health service in a concerted way, similar to the approach adopted to the boarder economy in 1978. It could provide, for the first time, the opportunity for the people who deliver

... the people expect, and are paying for, a service that puts the public first. It is no longer enough – if it ever was – to offer the public a service that simply suits the provider.

the service to help to put this right through a process of open dialogue. I would strongly urge all stakeholders in the health system to seize the day on this one.

In order to move the modernisation of the public service to the next level, earlier this year, the Government invited the OECD to undertake a major review of our public service as a whole.

The OECD will tell us how the Irish public service compares with the best in the world and it will make recommendations on future directions for reform. There may be some stark messages for us arising from this review, but we should be prepared for them and be prepared to make the hard decisions that reforms often require.

The Real Challenge

Language is not always the route to a common understanding of our respective positions, particularly when we talk about public service reform. If someone like myself argues trenchantly that unions have a proven track record of commitment to "Quality Public Service" I would do so in reality from a background of campaigns to defend jobs and protect services. If the trade union movement finds itself more often than not at opposite ends of the debate on change and re-form it is because reform is frequently presented/perceived by union members as something that is a threat – driven solely by management – who are in turn driven entirely by pressures to reduce expenditure and effect greater controls on finance and the numbers employed. It follows that trade unions have traditionally been slow to take the ini-tiative on reform in a practical and pro-active way. So, let's reflect on why and what we have to do to change the approach.

Reform is, more often than not, seen solely as a management function or prerogative. "Getting it through" the unions is seen as a major barrier to overcome.

Reform is, more often than not, seen solely as a management function or prerogative. "Getting it through" the unions is seen as a major barrier to overcome. As a result, reform is usually seen as something that, at worst, is not owned by staff and, at best, is im-posed from above. A key element of any reform project must be to involve the staff at every level – not just as objects of reform but as active participants.

There are, in fact, many many examples of success that I could go in to if we had more time. In fairness, there have been major im-provements in both the prison service and the courts services. The Revenue Commissioners has improved its services dramatically in the last decade. In agriculture and food, not alone has there been re-forms but our response to the foot and mouth crisis some years ago was second to none.

So let's consider one example of the problems that are of major public concern. Top of the list is undoubtedly the Health Service and the questions we are currently engaged with are, "What is wrong with the entire delivery system?", "What needs to be done to fix it?", "Who and what has to change?", "How do we bring this about?".

There is in fact quite a lot of reform currently under discussion in Health. We have, for example, complex separate negotiations on the consultants' contract, NCHD working hours, nurses' working hours and practices, up-skilling of non-nursing staff – the outcome of each is critical to providing real solutions to the public debate about providing better access to services, better utilisation of a highly skilled workforce and, more importantly, making the patient journey through the health system easier. Recently the Government agreed to a proposal from the Irish Congress of Trade Unions to establish a National Health Forum. This will bring all of the major groups and Government departments together, focused, for the first time, in working collectively to bring about the changes and the investment that should deliver the type of health service that we all aspire to and which every citizen deserves.

Conclusion

I believe that in any debate on public service reform the involvement and empowerment of front-line staff is one of the keys to better quality service, the reduction of waste and better value for money, that building trust and confidence are crucial and essential building blocks. When it comes to reform in the public service, public service unions do represent a "vested" interest. Public servants have a vested interest in ensuring that the quality of the services we provide is second to none. As I said earlier, the same people who provide a service in local government, the civil service or health also depend on schools, hospitals, roads, and environmental services and so on. Their needs as citizens and the needs of their families are no different from the rest of us. As Dermot McCarthy, the Secretary General in the Taoiseach's Department said recently, "What ultimately matters most is the commitment to a culture of change and reform, empowering public servants, in all the various roles which they occupy to take the initiative to make changes that make sense".

> When it comes to reform in the public service, public service unions do represent a "vested" interest. Public servants have a vested interest in ensuring that the quality of the services we provide is second to none.

Cormac Lucey

Former Special Advisor to Minister for Justice,
Equality & Law Reform

*Brought up in Banbridge, Co. Down and Castlebar, Co. Mayo. A chartered
accountant and business consultant, he is a graduate of UCD where he
was Auditor of the Literary and Historical Society and Chairman of the
Students' Club. He qualified as an accountant with Craig Gardner (now
PriceWaterhouseCoopers). He worked as Special Advisor to Michael McDowell
TD, Minister for Justice, Equality & Law Reform 2003-7.*

Rationality, Reality and Unreasonableness

While I may have spent most of my career in the private sector, I'm
not here to lecture the public sector from a position of superiority. I
am here, like many of you, to grapple with a problem of major importance to all of us – the effective management of the public service.

It is my firm belief that the problems of the public service are not
a result of the people in the public service but the result of the system
under which the public service operates and, in particular, the moti-
vations which operate in the public service. It was the apostle of the
free market, Warren Buffet, who stated:

> When a management with a reputation for brilliance tackles
> a business with a reputation for bad economics, it is the
> reputation of the business that remains intact.

I am of the view that the public service is a business with bad economics rather than bad managers.

**I am of the
view that the
public service
is a business
with bad
economics
rather than bad
managers.**

Public Service Reform – The Official Record

When we look back over the last decade or so, we can see a long list
of reports and initiatives designed to reform the Irish public service.
Here is an incomplete list of these items:

- In 1995, the National Economic and Social Forum published a document titled "Quality Delivery of Social Services".
- In 1996, the paper "Delivering Better Government" expanded on
  the Strategic Management Initiative (SMI) that had been launched
  in 1994. A similar strategic approach for the delivery of local authority services was initiated in 1996 with the publication that year
  of "Better Local Government – A Programme for Change".

- In 1997, the Quality Customer Service (QCS) Initiative was promulgated setting out a series of nine principles for dealing with the public. Departments were asked to draw up two-year Customer Action Plans based on these principles.

- The Freedom of Information Act 1997 and the Public Service Management Act 1997 both facilitated change towards more open and accountable governance. Under the latter act, each government department is required to publish a strategy statement.

- The Implementation Group of Secretaries General was established in July 1997 with a mandate to drive forward the reform process within the Civil Service. Performance Management Development was introduced. The Management Information network was established. Risk Management was introduced as was the Regulatory Impact Assessment.

> **The Freedom of Information Act 1997 and the Public Service Management Act 1997 both facilitated change towards more open and accountable governance.**

- In July 2000, a revised set of 12 QCS principles was approved by the Government and Departments were asked to draw up customer action plans for the years 2001–2004 based on these principles. The three new principles added were: Equality/Diversity; Official Languages Equality and the Internal Customer.

- PA Consulting completed an independent evaluation of the Strategic Management Initiative in 2002.

- In 2003, the Government asked all departments to publish Customer Charters guaranteeing service levels of members of the public. A review of this process is currently being finalised and is expected to be published at the end of July.

- In 2005 the Department of the Environment commenced the publication of the key performance indicators of our local authorities.

- Last year, the Government asked the OECD to carry out a review of the Irish Public Service. Their report is expected by the end of this year.

So there has been no shortage of official initiatives in the area of public service reform. But do these initiatives add up to whole lot?

Public Service Reform – The Unofficial Record

There is a list which one can recite which reflects less well on the Irish public service. It is a list of clear failures and disasters. Consider the following:

- The breakdown in discipline in the Garda Síochána in County Donegal that occurred in the 1990s – this resulted in innocent people being oppressed and even falsely imprisoned for lengthy terms. When the Morris Tribunal looked into the causes of this they found a breakdown in management in local command in Donegal and between Dublin and Donegal. They also found a culture of gross dishonesty among elements of the ordinary ranks.

- PPARs – the HSE recently decided to abandon plans to roll out the PPARS system (personnel, payroll and related systems). It is believed that about €130 million has been spent on the project to date. It is clear that the whole project was mis-specified from its inception. It is also clear that external contractors were grievously under-managed during the project's development. And it is clear that – under the old Health Boards – a multitude of varying local agreements on pay and conditions had developed which any system would have difficulties accurately capturing.

- Failure to collect DIRT – the investigations of the Committee of Public Accounts into the failure of people to pay their DIRT (Deposit Interest Retention Tax) uncovered systemic failure by the Revenue Commissioners to use data available to them to ensure collection of amounts owing to the State.

- Illegal nursing home charges case – monies were collected from pensioners resident in state nursing homes even though there was no legal basis for doing so.

- Blood Transfusion Service Board (BTSB) supplied infected blood thereby poisoning many people and giving them Hepatitis C. A number of public inquiries were held into this matter. One was established in 1996 and the other in 1999.

What can we learn from these failures? The first item which I would draw to your attention is the fact that the Donegal, PPARs, DIRT and BTSB failures resulted from the failures of unelected public officials. They did not result from the failure of elected public officials or of public representatives.

Only in the case of the nursing home charges "scandal" could the blame for what happened be possibly laid at the feet of elected public representatives. It is clear that proposals to legislate for the practice of deducting from home residents' pensions had been considered and rejected by the 1987-1989 Haughey Government. That Government's failure to deal with the problem was then compounded by the decision five years ago to extend free medical cards to the over-70s. But when Minister Mary Harney attempted to identify what had happened it was reported that the then Secretary-General of the Department of Health and Children had "deliberately withheld information from her".[1]

So, while the Nursing Home Charges case could possibly be blamed on elected public officials (and even that is questionable when one considers that the key departmental files have gone miss-

... it is clear that – under the old Health Boards – a multitude of varying local agreements on pay and conditions had developed which any system would have difficulties accurately capturing.

ing) in the other cases – Donegal Gardaí, PPARs, DIRT, BTSB – it is clear that unelected public officials were responsible.

Media Coverage of Public Service

Yet, when we consider most media coverage of public service matters it seems to focus almost entirely on elected public officials and it overlooks the actions of unelected public officials.

We know the names of the Justice Ministers who were in office when scandalous wrongdoings were practiced by the Gardaí in Donegal. But do we know the name of the person who headed up the Gardaí in Donegal at the time under whose watch this all happened? Do we know the identity of the chairperson of the committee responsible for managing the PPARs project? Do we know who headed up the activities of the Revenue Commissioners in collecting DIRT? In the public eye, it was Mary Harney who was responsible for the Nursing Home Charges matter while few would be able to name the Secretary-General moved from his position.

During the recent general election, the leader of the Labour Party, Pat Rabbitte TD, was asked by Marc Coleman (then of *The Irish Times*) whether public servants found guilty of incompetence should be sacked. His answer was honest and unequivocal: "I do not agree with the proposition that what is required is the sacking of incompetent public servants". Justifying the answer, Rabbitte spoke of the "long traditions" of the public service (traditions whereby ministers took ultimate responsibility for the mistakes of public servants). This is an absurd and potentially destabilising position. In addition to being paid more than people in the private sector, in addition to having far better pension deals than in the private sector, public servants should not be sacked, even if incompetent, according to the Labour leader.

The editor of *The Irish Times*, Geraldine Kennedy was interviewed recently on RTE by Eamon Dunphy. In the course of that interview she stated that *The Irish Times* is "anti-establishment". I don't think that it is nearly anti-establishment enough. That paper and our media in general seem to prefer to hold to account elected and accountable public officials who flit in and out of ministries than unelected and barely accountable public officials who are there permanently. Consider two recent cases.

Consider the recent Miss D case. A 17-year-old in the care of the HSE found that she was pregnant. But an ultrasound showed that her baby was suffering from anencephaly and had no head. Miss D sought an abortion. The HSE then sought to prevent her travelling to Britain to get one. Then, when the matter went to the High Court, the

> In addition to being paid more than people in the private sector, in addition to having far better pension deals than in the private sector, public servants should not be sacked, even if incompetent, according to the Labour leader.

HSE suddenly decided that it was OK for Miss D to travel to Britain. The court decided she could go.

To what end and for what purpose was this case brought at all, one might ask. The High Court judge who ruled on the matter, Liam MacKechnie, criticised the HSE for taking the action. Yet in all of the coverage on the matter was there any focus on who within the HSE had taken the decision to go to court to prevent Miss D from travelling? Who was that official and what were they playing at? And why is our "anti-establishment" media so little interested in such questions?

Consider a request to the Chief Justice John Murray, by the then Justice Minister Michael McDowell, for observations on proposals for regulating and disciplining judges. These proposals received a fresh impetus when the case of Judge Brian Curtin, who was arrested on suspicion of viewing child pornography on his computer, came to light. Michael McDowell sent his letter to John Murray in January 2005. By the time of Michael McDowell leaving office, in June 2007 – some 29 months later – John Murray had not replied. I am open to correction on this point, but only the *Sunday Business Post* has followed up on the matter. Why is our "anti-establishment" media so little interested in the question of whether our judiciary is willing to countenance a practical proposal for their accountability?

Instead this week we get a report from the Irish Council for Civil Liberties. That report cited an anonymous Judge of the Superior Courts quoted in the report saying:

> I think the public demand accountability from judges. It only takes a couple of high profile cases to increase the need for it....
> I cannot understand how every other jurisdiction can have a Judicial Council, and this jurisdiction seems to have such a great difficulty in putting one in place.

That comment takes my breath away. As does the comment of the ICCL that it is "calling upon the new Government to introduce a Judicial Council Bill at the earliest possible opportunity" when there is a draft bill sitting in the Chief Justice's in-tray for two and a half years. This report will be commented upon by "specialist correspondents" who frequently seem to act as unpaid lobbyists for – rather than objective observers of – the sector they are supposed to report on. My real fear is that our media and upper middle classes secretly despise our politicians. As Oscar Wilde put it:

> Morality is simply the attitude we adopt to people whom we personally dislike.

Why is our "anti-establishment" media so little interested in the question of whether our judiciary is willing to countenance a practical proposal for their accountability?

Whereas the media adopts a moralising attitude towards our elected public official it does no such thing to our unelected public officials be they judges or permanent civil servants. Recently in *The Guardian*, Polly Toynbee made a passing comment on the candidacy of Boris Johnson for Mayor of London:

> The danger is that politics is so despised and politicians are so loathed that anyone who manages to seem "not one of them" starts ahead of serious contenders.

It is taken for granted across the western world that our politicians are despised. And if our media and upper classes despise our politicians how can they not effectively despise our politics? How can they not despise, what is after all, the only collective method we have as a society to direct our affairs?

Why is Politics So Despised?

And why is politics so despised? We may all have our opinions but in my view the very messiness of politics stands in stark counterpoint to the objective of all good members of the middle class: to insulate themselves from the messiness of life so as to better secure an orderly existence for themselves.

One of the advantages of modern Irish life is that more and more people are able to experience third-level education. But that development comes at a cost. There is an obvious financial cost. But there is also a cost in terms of peoples' life views. Academics spend their lives putting an intellectually rigorous gloss on a life which the rest of us spend muddling through from day to day. As more and more of us go through higher education we become more impatient of the mess we came from and we keep our eyes on that neat little spot in life where we're headed to. As George Bernard Shaw put it:

> A learned man is an idler who kills time with study. Beware of his false knowledge, it is more dangerous than ignorance.

Politics is the realm where society's conflicting demands must somehow be reconciled. Promise hits reality. Disappointment is nearly always the result. That is an affront to the neat and orderly minds being increasingly churned out by our institutions of higher education. To quote Shaw again:

> Democracy is a device which ensures that we shall be no better governed than we deserve.

I can see some truth in that, especially when I consider that Michael McDowell lost his seat at the last election while Michael Lowry secured 12,919 votes in a three-seater!

It is taken for granted across the western world that our politicians are despised. And if our media and upper classes despise our politicians how can they not effectively despise our politics? How can they not despise, what is after all, the only collective method we have as a society to direct our affairs?

The Harsh Reality

In addition to the problems of entrenched public servants reluctant to reform, "independent" lobby groups who act as media cheerleaders for insider interests and a public which wants others to do the heavy lifting in life, we have a host of other obstacles to public service reform:

- Part-time ministers. If a department is governed by a minister from outside the Dublin commuter belt, that minister is unlikely to be in Dublin from Thursday evening to Tuesday morning. Much of the three days when the minister is up in town will be taken up with cabinet and parliamentary business. So, the amount of time which the head of the department can devote to departmental affairs is actually quite small.

- Effectively no dismissals. The All-Ireland football and hurling championships are in full flight at present. Imagine how different they would look if, at the start of each period of a few years, the team coaches had to select their team and they weren't allowed change their selection. Imagine if they weren't able to switch players, drop players who were out of form, elevate squad members who were in form. Yet that is the system which effectively operates within the civil service. It is absurd and it gives rise to significant injustice within the civil service.

- Entrenched interests. Whereas a minister will be in office for an average of about three years, officials and the beneficiaries of a department's employment or spending will be there much, much longer. Clever Ministers may just sit out problems hoping the roof doesn't collapse on them and escape from "Angola" asap. Their successors may commission reports as a therapeutic alternative to action. It takes a brave minister to take firm and resolute action.

Conclusion

As a country we should not be competing with Britain or with Sweden. We should be competing with Singapore, Hong Kong and Switzerland. These countries don't have lengthy debates about public service reform. Rather, they keep their public services small and inexpensive. So should we.

But our politics is too dominated by the beggar-my-neighbour attitude of sectional and local interests competing to suck at the teats of government. The dominant ideology is that of Huey Long: "don't tax you, don't tax me, tax the guy behind the tree."

I want to finish with another quote from George Bernard Shaw:

> As a country we should not be competing with Britain or with Sweden. We should be competing with Singapore, Hong Kong and Switzerland. These countries don't have lengthy debates about public service reform. Rather, they keep their public services small and inexpensive. So should we.

The reasonable man adapts himself to the conditions that surround him.... The unreasonable man adapts surrounding conditions to himself.... All progress depends on the unreasonable man.

In the final analysis the government will remain committed to public service reform. But that commitment is likely to be little more than a rhetorical commitment while we continue to enjoy unprecedented levels of material prosperity. Real reform won't take place as a result of rhetoric; it will take place because of crisis. It will take guts, courage and unreasonableness. And it will require political leaders with the measured unreasonableness of people like Ray MacSharry, Charlie McCreevy and Mary Harney. In such people lies the real hope for public service reform.

Real reform won't take place as a result of rhetoric; it will take place because of crisis. It will take guts, courage and unreasonableness.

Endnote

[1] *Sunday Business Post*, 4 February 2007

Colm McCarthy

School of Economics, University College Dublin

Born in Dublin. Founding partner of the economic consultancy group, Davy, Kelleher McCarthy (DKM). Previously worked at the Economic and Social Research Institute (ESRI) and at the Central Bank. Has served on the boards of ESB and Bord Gáis Éireann (BGE) and has undertaken assignments for the EU Commission and the World Bank. Has published extensively in Irish and international journals on applied economics.

The Need for Reform in Economic Policymaking

1. The Concerns of Policy have Shifted

The concerns of policy shift over time, and the machinery of Government must adjust too. But the architecture of economic policymaking in Ireland has failed to keep pace with rapid changes in the policy-making agenda. Until roughly the mid-1990s, the critical issues were macroeconomic: what to do about unemployment, the debt mountain, interest rates, exchange rate policy. The two decades preceding that transition had seen successive governments struggle, unsuccessfully in the main, with the dilemmas of macro-management in a small open economy, in an international context of inflation, low growth, and high unemployment. Honohan and Walsh (2002) contains an extended review. Both the economic policy debate and the research agenda of the dismal science, until the mid-1990s, were understandably dominated by macroeconomic concerns.

The new policy agenda is dominated by microeconomic issues, many of them exceedingly complex, and the policymaking machinery has struggled to keep pace.

These problems have either been solved, at least for the time being, or taken out of our hands through membership of the eurozone. Ireland no longer has an exchange rate to worry about, the European Central Bank fixes interest rates, and fiscal policy is conducted within the narrow parameters of the Stability and Growth Pact, adherence to which is a condition of eurozone membership. The new policy agenda is dominated by microeconomic issues, many of them exceedingly complex, and the policymaking machinery has struggled to keep pace.

For example, the period since the mid-1980s has seen the dismantling of State monopolies in most Western countries, and their replacement with competitive industrial structures. Former state-owned firms have been privatised and new entrants encouraged. This has happened in sectors such as transport, energy, telecoms, broadcasting and financial services. The result has been a challenging new agenda for policymakers. How should liberalised markets in these sectors be structured? How many competitors is enough? Will there be a need to regulate the new markets? How should state assets be valued, and how should they be disposed of? A specific example: Ireland has consistently chosen to dispose of state assets such as radio and TV licences, and the spectrum necessary for telecoms services, through beauty contest rather than through sale to the highest bidder, the route preferred in many other countries. No basis for this policy position has ever been brought forward, notwithstanding the evident perils of the beauty contest route (McCarthy, 2003).

The economic growth spurt over the last fifteen years has placed enormous pressures on Irish infrastructure in areas such as transport and water services. The response has taken the form of a substantial increase in the volume of public capital spending, but there have been controversies over cost estimates, budget over-runs and the selection of priorities. Policymakers have not been able to rely on a comprehensive body of policy research in areas like transport, resorting instead to ad-hoc consultancy studies and opaque project selection procedures.

Countries with substantially greater policymaking resources than Ireland have struggled with these issues. For example, the regulation of energy industries in the USA has been accident-prone, bedevilled by split responsibilities between the states and the federal government. In the United Kingdom, there have been successive rounds of re-regulation in several sectors, acknowledged as an error-learning process. At European Union level, there have been successes and failures. The airline industry liberalisation is regularly cited as an example of a policy success, while even the EU's admirers have been critical of its failures in the energy sector.

It is important to understand that this new microeconomic policy agenda posed unfamiliar challenges for economic analysis. The economics of regulation, for example, barely existed as a subject for empirical inquiry outside the United States until relatively recently. In Ireland, the issues which now dominate the policy agenda have not traditionally been priorities for economic researchers. The creation of policymaking capacity in the face of these changing priorities has not been addressed systematically, with consequent risk of hurried decisions and expensive mistakes.

2. The Response in Ireland has been Sluggish

You can't make bricks without straw, and you can't address microeconomic policy issues adequately without the necessary analytic

Policymakers have not been able to rely on a comprehensive body of policy research in areas like transport, resorting instead to ad-hoc consultancy studies and opaque project selection procedures.

apparatus. The Minister for Communications, Energy and Natural Resources, Eamon Ryan, called recently for a policy debate on nuclear energy, notwithstanding his personal reservations on the matter. This is commendable: whether Ireland should have nuclear power generation is a serious policy choice, but also a difficult and technical matter, raising complex economic and engineering issues. Last October, the Government released a Green Paper on Energy Policy, followed in March 2007 by a White Paper (Department of Communications, Marine and Natural Resources (2006, 2007). These documents dismissed the nuclear option in categorical terms.

> The Government will maintain the statutory prohibition on nuclear generation in Ireland. The Government believes that for reasons of security, safety, economic feasibility and system operation, nuclear generation is not an appropriate choice for this country. (White Paper, page 25).

And that's it, folks. No analysis on any of these issues is offered in either the Green or White Papers, nor is there any reference to background studies dealing with these questions. Had such studies been undertaken, as they have been in many countries reviewing their nuclear policies, they might well have supported the Government's conclusion. It is not self-evident that Ireland should choose the nuclear power option, but it is absurd, even irresponsible, to dismiss it without serious consideration.

The US review of nuclear policy has been informed by, for example, a comprehensive Massachusetts Institute of Technology study of the economic and engineering issues, including operating safety and waste disposal (MIT (2003)). The study concluded that, for the United States, the nuclear option should be preserved. A study along similar lines for Ireland should logically have preceded the Green Paper (what are Green Papers for, if not for thinking out loud?) and Minister Ryan seems to have acknowledged this.

However, to call for a public debate on issues of this kind in Ireland is not enough. An informed public debate requires analytic input, and only the Government in a small country has the resources to finance basic research. We don't have universities and research institutes with lavish endowment funds ready and able, like MIT, to identify and study the emerging policy priorities. It is unrealistic to pretend that an informed public debate can be whistled up in Ireland in the absence of a publicly-funded programme of research. Whether an Irish study along the lines of the MIT report would come to the same conclusion is impossible to say, but ultimately that is the reason for doing it.

The same Green and White papers on energy policy commit the Government to ambitious targets for power generation from renew-

However, to call for a public debate on issues of this kind in Ireland is not enough. An informed public debate requires analytic input, and only the Government in a small country has the resources to finance basic research.

ables, targets which imply high levels of wind penetration. While the potential of wind generation in Ireland is well established, it needs to be understood that high levels of wind penetration eventually run up against increasing cost, since conventional thermal stations must be available as back-up and will face rising costs due to intermittent running. Wind also gives rise to heavy transmission costs. The targets in the Green and White papers are not based on system-wide cost studies, and, to that extent at least, the renewables targets are a shot in the dark. We cannot be sure, in the absence of such studies, that the strategy proposed represents the best-value plan to reduce emissions, or that the target penetration levels correspond to the least-cost abatement strategy. Without a systematic framework that seeks to identify the least-cost abatement strategy for greenhouse gas emissions, this is policymaking on the hoof.

3. "You Can Get away with Anything if You Call it Capital" (Anon.)

In popular discussion of economic policy in Ireland, there is a conception that capital investment is somehow good, and current spending somehow less good. Communications wizards employed by Government departments and agencies peddle this line in constant descriptions of current spending as "investment", as in "investment in the health services". They mean current spending on health, not capital spending, and we have entered Orwellian territory. If current spending on health requires a mis-description by way of justification, the wizards and their employers are treading water. But the abuse of language is revealing: capital spending by Governments is perceived as less suspect than current spending, presumed to be more public-spirited and less driven by base motives such as (perish the thought) vote-buying. Profligacy, it is being presumed, never manifests itself in the form of a large capital budget, and the recent surge in Ireland's public capital programme is perceived as a political badge of honour. But there is plentiful scope for wasting money on capital projects, and there can be no presumption that capital spending deserves an exemption from scrutiny on the value-for-money issue.

A series of reports analysing the National Development Plans has been commissioned from the ESRI by the Department of Finance over the last decade, the most recent released last year (FitzGerald and Morgenroth (2006)). A recurring theme in these reports has been the weak process of project appraisal which underlies the selection of priorities for the public capital programme. The ESRI has recommended (ad nauseam) that a rigorous regime of ex ante cost-benefit appraisal should be applied by a central Government agency, pref-

In popular discussion of economic policy in Ireland, there is a conception that capital investment is somehow good, and current spending somehow less good. Communications wizards employed by Government departments and agencies peddle this line in constant descriptions of current spending as "investment", as in "investment in the health services". They mean current spending on health, not capital spending, and we have entered Orwellian territory.

erably the Department of Finance, to all significant capital projects. This is not happening: to the extent that cost-benefit studies are being conducted at all, they are commissioned from consultants, not by the Department of Finance, but by the Department or agency promoting the project in question. Routinely, these studies are commissioned after the responsible Minister has committed publicly to the project. Not surprisingly, the cost-benefit appraisals, some of which are not even made available for external scrutiny, tend to be positive. There have been exceptions. Lawlor et al. (2007) conducted an ex-post study which found mixed results for the water infrastructure programme, for example, and it should be acknowledged that some studies are better than others, but the ESRI have concluded that the manner in which capital project appraisal is organised in Ireland is flawed: the structure is wrong.

... cost-benefit analysis has come to be seen by many public officials in Ireland as a branch of the public relations industry, which is a pity. It is difficult to squeeze maximum value for money from the public capital programme, but quite impossible if project appraisal is neglected.

As a result, cost-benefit analysis has come to be seen by many public officials in Ireland as a branch of the public relations industry, which is a pity. It is difficult to squeeze maximum value for money from the public capital programme, but quite impossible if project appraisal is neglected. On a charitable view, the practice of delegating project appraisal to sponsoring departments and agencies is a removal of the dead hand of Finance, and a vote of confidence in the capacity of the spending departments. A less charitable view is that there has been an abdication of responsibility, and consequent waste, in the capital budget. Two reforms suggest themselves:

• Project appraisals should be conducted before the event, and

• The appraisals should be done by an agency other than the project promoter, or at least reviewed rigorously by some such agency.

Whether sponsoring departments and agencies should be involved at all is a moot point. At minimum, one of the central departments, preferably Finance, should develop in-house expertise in this area, to conduct project appraisals directly or at least to assess the competence of work carried out by project promoters. This kind of reform is particularly urgent when there is a large capital programme, and correspondingly large opportunities for waste. It would help if Ministers could refrain from the endorsement of capital projects until the project appraisals have been completed.

4. The Economic Policy Industry Needs a Make-over

Outside the civil service, the principal sources of input to policy analysis are research institutes and think tanks, universities, consulting firms, ad hoc commissions and committees of inquiry and specialist State bodies, including the regulatory agencies. In Ireland, the most important of the research institutes is the ESRI, routinely described in the press as "the Government's think tank". It is in fact a private company limited by guarantee, and direct government subvention represents less than one-third of the Institute's income. In round figures, the ESRI spends about €10 million per annum, of which about €3 million is direct subvention. Most of the rest comes from commissioned research, which means that the Institute must hustle in the consultancy market for once-off projects. In practice, the Institute's clients include many of its natural prey, the spending departments and their agencies.

This is not an ideal funding model. It is unrealistic to expect Government departments in the Irish political culture to finance the type of vigorous policy re-appraisal that is often needed, and it would be far better if the Department of Finance subvention covered the Institute's full costs, as it used to do in the early years of the Institute's existence. Apart from ESRI, there are no non-university research institutes or think tanks operating on any significant scale in the economics area in Ireland. It would be nice if private donors would finance more think tanks, but in the meantime the ESRI's funding model should be reviewed.

Apart from ESRI, there are no non-university research institutes or think tanks operating on any significant scale in the economics area in Ireland.

In the mainstream university economics departments, the choice of research topics is a matter for individual academics, and policy-relevant applied work is not everyone's cup of tea. There is scope for central Government departments to fund applied research programmes in the Irish universities, and to influence the pattern of work undertaken. Some of the universities have begun to locate economic and social science research programmes in dedicated, on-campus institutes, such as the IIIS in Trinity and the Geary Institute in UCD.

Government departments are regularly berated for excessive reliance on consultants, but relatively little of the total spend is on policy work proper. It is in effect out-sourcing of executive functions, including IT and other once-off projects. Some of what does get spent is on reviews of policy commissioned by departments whose Minister is publicly committed to the policy in question. An intensification of existing policy, not surprisingly, is a popular theme in the recommendations of these reports.

Political parties, in Ireland as elsewhere, are not a substantial source of policy initiatives. The party or parties in Government tend to become absorbed in the civil service machine, and parties in opposition lack resources. A Canadian writer phrased it thus:

> The Pulp and Paper Association has more capacity to do strategic analytical work than the Liberal and Progressive Conservative parties combined (Savoie, 2003).

A more exceptional feature of the Irish system is the modest input from parliamentary committees. In both the United States and the United Kingdom, parliamentary committees have become a major conduit of policy analysis, and have substantial staffs and research budgets.

The capacity to develop and appraise economic policy is a critical resource. It would be a worthwhile exercise for central Government, perhaps through the Taoiseach's department, to compile an inventory of existing capacity in Ireland. I have no doubt that such an exercise would identify weaknesses across a wide range of micro-policy areas.

5. And So Does the Civil Service

I would like to finish with a few unconnected thoughts about civil service reform, from the standpoint of economic policy capacity.

The establishment of numerous executive agencies and regulatory bodies in recent years has had the unintended side-effect of hollowing out some of the central Government departments. Quite simply, some of the most knowledgeable people have left for careers, not in the private sector, but for pastures new within the public service. **It is important that the key Government departments have sufficient in-house expertise to supervise their own offspring, without excessive reliance on consultants, as well as to undertake their other policy development functions.** This implies an aggressive graduate recruitment programme, as well as further opening up of civil service promotional appointments to all-comers. The only large organisations left in Ireland which promote predominantly from within are the public service and the church.

Mobility between the private sector and the civil service is greatly inhibited by the structure, and not just the perceived generosity, of the civil service pension arrangements. Some form of conversion option to a defined contribution formula should be available to junior and mid-career civil servants, with a corresponding arrangement for people transferring into the service from the private sector.

Finally the Department of Finance is inevitably the central player in economic policy. In hard times (say from 1922 to about 1998!) the traditional Treasury function of seeking to secure value for money in public spending could be pursued in large degree by simply pointing out that the kitty was empty, and that the worthy proposals from spending Departments could wait. But in times of economic plenty, the traditional response is not believable. This makes things harder for the Department of Finance. Instead of saying that the Minister's proposal is fine and dandy, it's just that we don't have the resources, you have to argue that the Minister's proposal is not worthwhile, or that the objective could be better achieved some other way, and at less cost. This is a far more difficult assignment. There is justification here for an increased payroll budget in Finance.

References

Department of Communications, Marine and Natural Resources (2006): Towards a Sustainable Energy Future for Ireland, Green Paper, October.

Department of Communications, Marine and Natural Resources (2007): Delivering a Sustainable Energy Future for Ireland, White Paper, March.

FitzGerald, J., and E. Morgenroth (eds) (2006): Ex Ante Evaluation of the Investment Priorities for the National Development Plan 2007-2013, Economic and Social Research Institute, Dublin, October.

Honohan, Patrick and Brendan Walsh (2002): "Catching up with the Leaders: the Irish Hare", Brookings Papers on Economic Activity, pp. 1-77.

Lawlor, J., C. McCarthy and S. Scott (2007): "Investment in Water Infrastructure: Findings from an Economic Analysis of a National Programme", *Journal of Environmental Planning and Management*, January.

Massachusetts Institute of Technology (2003): The Future of Nuclear Power, downloadable at web.mit.edu/nuclearpower/pdf/nuclearpower-full.pdf.

McCarthy, Colm (2003): "Political Corruption in Ireland: Policy Design as a Countermeasure", Economic and Social Research Institute Quarterly Economic Commentary, September.

Savoie, Donald J. (2003): *Breaking the Bargain: Public Servants, Ministers and Parliament*, University of Toronto Press.

Mary Hanafin TD, Minister for Education & Science

Prof John Hegarty, Provost
of Trinity College Dublin

Prof Tom Collins, Head of Education
Department, NUI Maynooth

Chapter 7

Investing in Education

Education is Key to Ireland's Economic Transition
MARY HANAFIN TD
Minister for Education & Science

Ireland's Universities Must Rank with the Best
PROF JOHN HEGARTY
Provost of Trinity College Dublin

Schools Must Create Knowledge, Not Just Deliver It
PROF TOM COLLINS
Head of Education Department, NUI Maynooth

Mary Hanafin TD

Minister for Education & Science

Born in Tipperary and educated at Presentation Convent, Thurles, St. Patrick's College, Maynooth (BA, HdipEd) and Dublin Institute of Technology. Formerly secondary school teacher, first elected to Dáil Éireann 1997. Minister of State at Depts. of Health & Children, Justice and Education & Science 2000-2. Minister of State at Dept. of An Taoiseach (Chief Whip) and at Dept. of Defence 2002-4. Appointed Minister for Education & Science 2004 and reappointed to the portfolio in June 2007. Joint Hon. Treasurer of Fianna Fáil since 1993. Member of Dublin City Council 1985-91

Education is Key to Ireland's Economic Transition

Irish society continues to attach a premium to education that reflects its central role in the lives of our citizens and communities. For the individual, initial educational attainment has a broad-ranging impact on many aspects of life, from personal development to civic engagement and economic well-being. For society, education provides a potential, unmatched by any other public policy instrument, for addressing the root causes of social exclusion, for promoting good citizenship and for enriching culture. And of course in terms of our economy, policy developments in education over the past four decades have been responsible for developing the human capital to which we owe Ireland's Celtic Tiger success.

Exciting and Challenging Times in Irish Education

These are both exciting and challenging times in Irish education. They are exciting because the opportunities available to our young people today are not only way beyond the dreams of previous generations in this country, they are also considerably ahead of those available in other many other OECD countries.

This year, 7 out of every 10 students that sit the Leaving Cert exams will go on to third level courses. Many thousands more will avail of the increased opportunities in the PLC colleges or opt to pursue apprenticeships. And with the strength of the Irish economy, the prospects for all young people after education have never been better.

But these are also immensely challenging times for Irish education as our schools and colleges try to respond to the emerging and evolving needs of our society and our economy and as we intensify

This year, 7 out of every 10 students that sit the Leaving Cert exams will go on to third level courses. Many thousands more will avail of the increased opportunities in the PLC colleges or opt to pursue apprenticeships.

our work to ensure that all our people get an opportunity to reach their full potential.

Changing Shape of Society

By any analysis, Irish society has undergone an incredible transformation in recent times. The impact that this has had on our schools in particular is quite pronounced. There are now more than 150 different languages spoken by our schoolchildren. While this new diversity has enriched our classrooms, language barriers are presenting new teaching and learning challenges and are impacting on parent-teacher relationships.

The fact that our young people are more confident and more outspoken than ever before, while positive in so many ways, can make it more difficult for teachers to maintain order in the classroom. And, while levels of freedom and opportunity have grown, the pressures on young people have also become more intense. They are under pressure to act a lot older than they are, to conform to narrow stereotypes, to succumb to consumerism and to experiment with alcohol and drugs.

Our schools face major challenges in responding to the direct impact of these and other changes. More than that, they have a central role in influencing our broader collective response to such changes and in helping to shape the vision and the values on which we want to move forward as a community.

For example, a true appreciation of social, cultural and ethnic diversity, that can be developed and facilitated in the school environment, is critical in strengthening and sustaining cohesion in our increasingly multi-ethnic society. Through initiatives such as links with local community groups, schools can help our young people to become caring, socially aware and active citizens. For while our schools are microcosms of the society of today, they also have considerable influence on the nature and values of that of tomorrow. This is a weighty responsibility.

> Through initiatives such as links with local community groups, schools can help our young people to become caring, socially aware and active citizens.

Evolving Economic Needs

The changing needs of our economy have also brought new challenges for the Irish education system. As the nature of the global economy evolves, the role of education in safeguarding our future prosperity has become more pronounced. Rapid advances in technology and information are now the main drivers of economic growth and success. Knowledge and skills will be our key sources of competitive advantage in the twenty-first century.

There will be a demand for an increasing breadth of knowledge, greater numbers of skilled graduates, particularly in the science and technology areas, an increased output of PhDs and an emphasis on the importance of continuing learning over the career life-cycle.

Analysis by Forfás indicates that the Irish economy in 2020 will require significantly enhanced skills. They project that our workforce will grow in size by more than 20 per cent over the next 15 years. This will require the entry of 948,000 new workers into the labour force, sourced from a combination of the education system and inward migration. The profile of the economy will continue to change with a growth in the importance of the services sectors, a reduced reliance on traditional manufacturing and an increasing emphasis on higher value activities – particularly in the emerging high technology sectors of the economy. There will be a demand for an increasing breadth of knowledge, greater numbers of skilled graduates, particularly in the science and technology areas, an increased output of PhDs and an emphasis on the importance of continuing learning over the career life-cycle.

The role of education at first, second and third levels, together with the development of our research capacity at fourth level, clearly holds the key to Ireland's ability to successfully chart the economic transition that lies ahead.

Priorities for the Next Five Years

Turning back to the theme of this week's MacGill Summer School, what must our priorities be in education over the next five years if we are to meet the needs of the individual, of our society and of our economy?

Meaningful Participation for All

Firstly, our overriding priority must be to provide for meaningful participation for all. This means ensuring that we not only improve our rates of school completion and third level participation, but that we ensure that the education available at all levels enables students to reach their full potential – whatever their needs or abilities. Improving the level of supports available to students with special needs, those from disadvantaged areas and those whose first language is not English are important factors here.

Special education is an area that has undergone immense change in recent years and one in which major improvements are planned for the next five years. There is no doubt that the record of the State over decades in providing for children with special needs was very poor and that we are still playing catch up. But significant advances have been made in recent years, improving the lives of children with special needs and their families.

There are now in the region of 17,000 adults in our mainstream schools working solely with children with special needs – compared to just a fraction of this a few years back. Over €820 million is being provided for special education in 2007 – €180 million, or nearly 30 per cent, more than last year's provision.

But we know that we are still not where we want to be in terms of support for children with special needs. Over the next five years, there will be an emphasis on providing early assessment, expanding pre-school provision, giving each child the right to an Individual Education Plan and ensuring better training for teachers. Improvements in services for children and young people will be built upon through better provision in the adult and further education and third level sectors.

Delivering equality of educational opportunity at all levels for students from economically and socially disadvantaged areas is also a major priority for the next five years. Key elements of our action plan in this area include an emphasis on high-quality pre-school education for such children and a focus on tackling literacy and numeracy difficulties at an early age before they become entrenched. Extra investment is also being provided for increased staffing in disadvantaged schools, school meals, summer camps, home-work clubs and school libraries.

Over the next five years, there will be an increased emphasis on partnership and integration of services between Government departments and agencies that work with families at risk. Many of the barriers to the educational progress of children and young people are caused by issues outside the education system. These barriers can be financial, social or cultural. They may relate to the educational experiences and expectations of a young person's parents, peers or community. The challenge for the education system is to work, in partnership with others, in seeking to overcome as many of these barriers as possible. Working with parents and communities is absolutely vital in that respect.

We are determined to dramatically improve the educational attainment of young people from disadvantaged areas. This means achieving much higher rates of school completion in these areas and expanding out-of-school opportunities such as Youthreach and other second chance options. It also means investing in our PLC colleges and opening up new routes of access from the further education sector to the third level sector. And it means an increased focus by our third level colleges on ensuring much greater levels of access, participation and attainment by young people from disadvantaged areas.

While the challenge of ensuring real equality for students from all backgrounds is considerable, there is evidence that measures put in place in recent years are making a difference. For while the overall increase in third level education between 1998 and 2004 is impressive, what gives me most satisfaction is the substantial increases in areas like Finglas, Ballymun and Darndale where the number of young people making it to college doubled during the period. Increasing these rates much further is a major priority for the next five years.

There will also continue to be a major focus on adults whose educational opportunities were limited in the past. The number of places on adult literacy programmes and the Back to Education Initiative will be increased and there will be an emphasis on workplace learning, on up-skilling. A new system of means-tested free fees for approved part-time courses will also be introduced. Together with incentives for colleges to offer more flexible and diverse course structures, this will enable more people with work or family commitments to avail of opportunities at third level.

As Irish society becomes better educated as a whole, it is absolutely imperative that we do all we can to tackle the obstacles and inequalities that have for too long limited the opportunities available to those from less well-off backgrounds.

Another group of children and young people who need extra support to enable them to succeed at school are the increasing number of students whose first language is not English. The number of language support teachers in our schools has risen dramatically from just about 250 in 2002 to more than 1,400 this year. The Government is committed to increasing this further to 1,800 language teachers by 2009. This is a relatively new area for Irish education but one which it is imperative we get right if we are to ensure the successful integration of immigrants and their families into Irish society. As well as extra teachers, other priorities in this area for the next five years include promoting home-school links and providing access to English language classes for adult immigrants.

A School Curriculum in Tune with Social and Economic Needs

Another key priority for the next five years is ensuring that our young people get an education that prepares them well for the society and economy not just of today, but of 20–30–40 years from now. And so, building on the new primary curriculum that has been phased in since 1999, we are committed to curriculum change at second level that builds on the strengths of our existing system, while responding to emerging needs. We know that there are particular issues in relation to Irish and Maths and so we have prioritised these areas.

For students starting first year in 2007, 40 per cent of the marks available for Leaving Cert Irish will be for the oral exam. We want to make sure that our young people learn Irish in a way that is interesting and relevant. And we believe that increasing the emphasis on the spoken language in our schools can achieve this.

Another key priority for the next five years is ensuring that our young people get an education that prepares them well for the society and economy not just of today, but of 20–30–40 years from now.

Just as Irish is central to our heritage and culture, Maths is crucial to our economic future since it underpins many other disciplines, including science and technology. There is a need not only to improve the uptake of higher level Maths for the Leaving Cert, but also to ensure that all young people leave school with good mathematical skills. This means reforming our Maths courses to place a much greater focus on problem-solving and on applying mathematical logic to real-life situations.

The National Council for Curriculum and Assessment, of which Professor Collins is the Chair, is working on detailed proposals for the reform of post-primary mathematics education. One proposal they are developing that I am very interested in is the potential for two options for those pursuing Higher Level Maths for the Leaving Cert – one of these to be aimed at students who intend to pursue careers in science, technology or engineering. This would ensure that the Maths that our young people are learning can be more relevant to their future plans.

Of course strong science education is also crucial for Ireland's future economic success, and here too changes are being made. The new Junior Cert level science curriculum – which has a greatly increased emphasis on hands-on student investigative work – was examined for the first time this year. This, too, will be built upon by changes to the senior cycle curriculum that are being developed by the NCCA at present.

New Leaving Cert syllabi in Technology and Design and Communication Graphics are being introduced this September. We are also investing in ICT, with broadband having been brought to every school over the past year and provision in the new NDP of €252 million for schools' ICT over the lifetime of the plan. Over the next five years, new curricula in Leaving Cert engineering, architectural technology, economics, agricultural science and art will also be implemented.

The NCCA are also involved in a full review of senior cycle education aimed at ensuring that our school programmes are up to date and can enable students with different abilities and interests to reach their full potential. The ability of our schools to prepare young people for lifelong learning is also a central consideration.

The Government is also anxious to encourage more schools to offer alternative curricula such as the Junior Certificate Schools' Programme and the Leaving Certificate Applied course, both of which, in my view, do not always get the recognition they deserve. At the same time, we recognise that school is not necessarily suited to the needs of all young people and we are committed to improvements in apprenticeship education and other areas that may be more relevant for some students.

The NCCA are also involved in a full review of senior cycle education aimed at ensuring that our school programmes are up to date and can enable students with different abilities and interests to reach their full potential. The ability of our schools to prepare young people for lifelong learning is also a central consideration.

Developing World-Class Third and Fourth Level Education

Moving on now to third level education, our key priorities for this sector over the next five years are to widen participation, to reform and modernise programme delivery and to achieve truly world-class quality at all levels from undergraduate education to advanced research.

In responding to the challenges of recent decades, I think it is fair to say that Ireland's higher education system has not so much evolved as revolutionised. The extraordinary growth in participation levels over the past twenty years is the most obvious manifestation of that. Within the space of a single generation we have gone from elite to mass provision.

Beyond those dramatic changes in participation levels, there is evidence of wider and deeper change and development across a broad range of activity in the sector. It can be seen for example:

- in the response of the sector in recent years to the critical skills needs of our rapidly growing economy;
- in the development of cutting edge infrastructure on campuses across the country through a combination of both public and private investment;
- in the level of successful internal organisational reform; and
- through increasing inter-institutional collaboration.

In recognising these achievements, we know that the new challenges facing Ireland's higher education system are greater than ever. Developing more flexible, innovative and student-centred approaches to the delivery of programmes will be one such challenge. This is vital if our higher education institutions are to successfully meet the needs not just of the school-leaving cohort, but also those of traditionally under-represented groups such as adult learners, students with disabilities and students from socio-economically disadvantaged areas. I appreciate that the challenge of becoming more inclusive while also enhancing quality is a considerable one and I assure the sector of the Government's determination to support them in meeting it.

Equally, we are committed to working with our higher education institutions to create a new fourth level of advanced research education that will play a vital role in driving Ireland's future economic development.

The global economy is changing rapidly, shaped by exciting new advances in knowledge and technology. Ireland's future success will depend on the strength of our research and development base and its ability to produce new and better products and technologies. It will also depend on the continued availability of highly educated, creative people to fill jobs in the ICT, biotechnology and pharmaceutical

... we are committed to working with our higher education institutions to create a new fourth level of advanced research education that will play a vital role in driving Ireland's future economic development.

industries and to attract further foreign investment in these areas.

The transformation of the research landscape in Ireland has already been dramatic. In 1998, one of my predecessors announced a £5 million investment in research. The new National Development Plan published earlier this year provides no less than €3.5 billion for higher education research. Today there are dozens of world-class research facilities on campuses across the country and a range of schemes are supporting thousands of student and staff researchers. For the first time there is a real alternative to going abroad for the individual who wants to pursue advanced research.

But as a Government, we have now set ourselves even more ambitious plans to build on this progress and to develop a new "fourth level education" research system that will provide an engine for innovation and shape future economic success as we look to safeguard our national prosperity for the next generation. This will involve doubling the number of PhD students by 2013, while also maintaining a very high quality of research. One of the ways in which this will be promoted is through the establishment of graduate schools to achieve structured quality PhD training and enhanced postgraduate skills. There will be an emphasis on developing flexible and attractive career paths for researchers and on enhanced industry/academia collaboration to benefit business and secure growth.

The Strategy for Science, Technology and Innovation and the National Development Plan have set ambitious targets for growing the research capacity of our higher education institutions. But we have no doubt that the sector is more than up to the challenge and I believe that the next five years will be a very exciting period for higher education in this country.

Conclusion

To conclude, the agenda of education is an extremely large one covering so many areas. I hope I have succeeded in giving a broad outline of the type of improvements that the Government intends to focus on over the next five years.

We believe that in these times of considerable social and economic change, it is now more important than ever to prioritise education. To ensure that it is at the heart of public policy and our drive for a better Ireland. And to work with all the partners in education – students, teachers, parents, management bodies, third level colleges and others – to ensure that every individual gets the opportunity to reach their full potential.

We believe that in these times of considerable social and economic change, it is now more important than ever to prioritise education.

Prof John Hegarty

Provost of Trinity College Dublin

Born in Claremorris and educated at St. Patrick's College, Maynooth, UCG (Ph.D) and Post-doctoral Fellow University of Wisconsin. Research fellow, Bell Laboratories, New Jersey 1975-86. Professor of Laser Physics at TCD 1986-2001. Head of Dept. of Physics 1992-5. Adjunct professor, University of Georgia (USA) 1990-5. Visiting professor University of Tokyo and Sony Corporation 1995. Dean of Research TCD 1995-2000. Appointed provost TCD in 2001. Member of Royal Irish Academy, the American Physical Society, the American Optical Society, the Institute of Electronic and Electrical Engineers and Fellow of TCD. Has published extensively on laser physics in national and international journals.

Ireland's Universities Must Rank with the Best

Although Ireland's economic success has been the result of many factors, it is now generally recognised that education has been the most pivotal. The intense interest in education by parents across the country coupled, since the 1960s, with critical policy developments by the government - and the willingness of the educational system itself to respond - has helped to leverage the economic success we have achieved to date. A number of key milestones are worth noting.

The introduction of free second-level education in the 1960s was a pivotal development. Today, 80 per cent of young people complete second level education, a figure that should be increased further. Recent initiatives by the Minister for Education at second level demonstrate a willingness to help achieve this goal.

The expansion of the third level sector from the 1970s was the next major milestone in education. After three decades of uninterrupted growth, 55 per cent of all 18-year-olds now go on to third level. The policy driving this development has been wise, as the new graduates have fed the labour market very effectively, especially over the last decade.

From the 1980s, a number of special skills initiatives were funded by the government to address the particular needs of the information technology sector. And from the 1990s onwards, increasing emphasis was placed on broadening access to the third level to hitherto excluded disadvantaged young people.

The situation currently is that the number of 18-year olds is decreasing year by year and we have passed beyond the need to fill quotas. In fact, the number of Leaving Certificate students is the low-

> The expansion of the third level sector from the 1970s was the next major milestone in education. After three decades of uninterrupted growth, 55 per cent of all 18-year-olds now go on to third level.

est for 20 years at 50,021. So, for the moment, we have overcome the need to focus merely on numbers at undergraduate level.

The Story from the Late 1990s

One of the more critical landmark shifts in policy came in the late 1990s when investment by the government in research experienced a quantum leap, much of it in the university sector and involving collaboration within and between institutions and between institutions and industry. The National Development Plan 2000-2006, principally through PRTLI (Programme for Research in Third Level Institutions) and SFI (Science Foundation Ireland) investments, devoted some €2.5 billion to Higher Education research. From this point on, the universities in particular began to develop the characteristics of leading universities in other countries – a balance between education and research and between undergraduate and postgraduate education – that have a proven and fundamental long- term impact on the welfare of those countries. It is important to note this link, and we ignore it at our peril. Universities, with this profile, I would contend, are at the heart of the transition to a new Ireland.

Looking to the Future

Looking to the future, the country faces new challenges. The first and most obvious is the sustainability of our success in the context of intense global competition. We are at one with the UK, US, Sweden and Switzerland in contending with newly-developing major societies like China and India. In the past, cheap labour and a growing skills base served us well. Continued success in a new knowledge society will depend more critically than ever before on the creativity, imagination and ideas of our people and on the creation, transmission and best use of new knowledge. This is the very stuff of education, and more particularly of Higher Education. There is no escaping the fact now that to survive at this level Ireland must be as good as its new peer-countries. Our Higher Education institutions must be able to compare favourably with their institutions. Most importantly, Ireland's universities must be able to compete with their best universities as the international benchmarks become the norm. A whole new challenge awaits Higher Education and especially our universities.

There is no escaping the fact now that to survive at this level Ireland must be as good as its new peer-countries. Our Higher Education institutions must be able to compare favourably with their institutions.

The system of universities, institutes of technology and other providers will have to deliver on all of the needs of Irish society – lifelong learning, including non-traditional students, and full access to those still suffering disadvantage. Regional development will have to be a focus. World class research will have to be produced with an increase in PhD numbers; the new knowledge from scholarship and research will have to be put to good use in industry, services, and public policy – all contributing to the development of a civil and wise society, a society of which we may be proud. No one institution can deliver all the complex needs to be addressed, hence the need for diversity of mission. Each institution should decide its own distinctive mix of activities based on its history, strengths and location.

It is a very positive sign that the significance of the role of Higher Education to Ireland, and especially the growing importance of postgraduate education, was reflected in the 2005 budget speech of the Minister for Finance. Minister Cowen announced funding to enable higher education institutions adapt to changing conditions – the Strategic Innovation Fund under the remit of the Minister for Education, Mary Hanafin. It was also heartening last year to hear of the new Strategy for Science, Technology and Innovation (SSTI) 2006-2013. Under this initiative, some €5 billion was suggested for research in Higher Education. The strategy also articulates a very specific vision for university-based research. That vision is centred round the building up of world-class research teams, the doubling of PhDs and the transfer of the knowledge generated for social and economic progress.

Role of the University

I should point out that research can be done without education and education can be delivered without research. But it is the combination of the two elements in a powerful university that resources both well – recognising their synergy – that Ireland needs.

I would like to come back to the role of the university in particular since there is much debate nationally and internationally on the topic. The university is a unique institution in today's world since it embodies both education and research in a holistic way. The great universities of the world have always been powerhouses of learning and knowledge creation. The Irish monasteries were such powerhouses in their own way. Today, this intimate combination of learning and the exploration of new knowledge through research within a living community is not just at the heart of culture, it is the driving force of the world economy. So it is for modern Ireland. This knowledge can transform society by creating and sustaining new enterprises and jobs. Student learning at all levels is precisely about the exploration of knowledge – of existing domains in the case of undergraduate students and of new knowledge in the case of postgraduate research students. In a university, research enriches education and vice versa. I should point out that research can be done without education and education can be delivered without research. But it is the combination of the two elements in a powerful university that resources both well – recognising their synergy – that Ireland needs. Ireland's universities must be as good as the best in its peer group of countries. Nothing less suffices in today's competitive global environment.

Comparisons between Universities Globally

So how do Ireland's universities compare with those universities? There are some indicators. For example, there are a number of international university league tables involving Ireland's universities for the first time. While you might argue about the basis of the tables, you cannot deny their existence or their impact. They are watched closely by the huge number of international students interested in studying abroad, and even Irish students who are increasingly looking to universities overseas for a good education. They are also monitored by our potential academic staff and by international business leaders. In the world university rankings compiled by the Times Higher Education Supplement in 2006, only one Irish university featured in the top 200. This surely must be a worry. In separate rankings compiled by the Shanghai Jiao Tong University in China, no Irish university featured in the top 200. Both rankings have different criteria but what is evident is that the widely accepted best universities in the world feature at the top of both.

To demonstrate a more meaningful comparison with universities in other countries, I have selected three European universities for which comparable data is available from the Royal Irish Academy Study, "Cumhacht Feasa" 2004. They do not include the obvious universities like Oxford and Cambridge who are in the top 10 by any ranking but which unfortunately are far outside our league of resources. The universities rank close to the Irish university in the Times Higher Education Supplement.

The table shows total student and staff numbers, student staff ratios and budgets for Edinburgh and Copenhagen Universities, the ETH in Zurich, and the Irish university. The most striking feature of the comparison is the student/staff ratio. The ratios of staff to students is almost twice that that in the Irish university sample, a rather worrying statistic. This holds true across the Irish university system. It translates into much higher levels of investment per student than Ireland is currently providing.

Why is the student/staff ratio so important? A low ratio means a greater personal interaction between staff and student with learning in both directions, and more time for high quality research involving students to PhD level. This translates into the ability to achieve excellence which in turn attracts the best academic minds from across the world as teacher/scholars. World class teacher/scholars in turn create a better student learning experience and so on in an ever-improving cycle. One can argue about what is an optimum student/staff ratio but the average in Irish universities is certainly far from optimal.

> The most striking feature of the comparison is the student/staff ratio. The ratios of staff to students is almost twice that that in the Irish university sample, a rather worrying statistic.

Comparison of Leading European Universities				
	ETH Zurich	Edinburgh	Copenhagen	Irish University
THES Rank 2004 (in Europe)	3	13	19	28
Student Numbers (FTE)	12,626	18,347	16,493	12,492
Teaching Staff (FTE)	1,926	2,430	2,576	749
Operating Budget Per Student (FTE) (€'000)	40.3	26.1	29.3	15.2
Student/Staff Ratio	6.6	7.5	6.4	16.6

Source: *Royal Irish Academy Report on Higher Education: Cumhacht Feasa*

It is fair to say that the Irish universities are performing superbly relative to the resources available to them – but that resource level is far out of line with the good universities internationally.

What Do We Do?

Unfortunately, we have to catch up in a much more compressed timeframe than we might like. What we need is not tinkering round the edges but a quantum shift.

We must recognise the fact that the countries whose peers we aim to be are in a different situation to us. They have decades – if not centuries – of economic success and associated infrastructural and social spending behind them. The foundations of Ireland's success are far less deep, less stable and more recent. Unfortunately, we have to catch up in a much more compressed timeframe than we might like. What we need is not tinkering round the edges but a quantum shift.

How Are Universities Responding?

Firstly, I would like to say that my colleagues in the university sector really do accept the role that the universities must play to sustain and develop a successful economy and civil society. They are fully aware that universities must be creative with the curriculum, responding to demand, yet balancing short term and long term needs. The style of teaching and learning must evolve, balancing again the intensely personal nature of learning with the power of technology to deliver information in new ways. They also understand that they will be key to delivering the national goals of doubling PhD numbers. They are committed to ensuring that new knowledge is used well for the benefit of society through technology transfer, involvement in policy formation, engagement in public debate and so on.

All institutions are undergoing internal change in terms of organisation and management - as you might expect, given the change in the environment. These shifts in institutional culture are not without controversy! We need to reconnect disciplines in new ways to counter the fragmentation that has occurred over several generations. We also need to manage our affairs well. Good management is often seen as anathema in an academic community. Good management, however, empowers the university to focus on its intellectual mission with minimum bureaucracy. Structures must continually change to suit the needs and complexities of the time.

Universities recognise that the quality of performance in all areas has to be benchmarked internationally rather than nationally, but the level of investment that they need to make is vastly greater than the resources currently available to them.

Budgets – Going Backwards Will Not Produce a Quantum Shift

My colleagues and I are painfully aware that while investment in research from public funds has been phenomenal, this investment only covers the marginal costs of the research: the core academic staff, all aspects of teaching and learning, and the infrastructure that supports both teaching and research are largely paid for from the annual government allocation to the universities. Ironically, the investment in the core operation of teaching and learning and in the infrastructural fabric of the universities has been going in the opposite direction to that of research in recent years. Taken in real terms, the budget for the Irish Universities has been cut for several years in a row and has remained static over the last two years. It is estimated that to restore the universities in real terms to where they were a decade ago would require some €120 million per annum. This figure does not take account of the vastly increased complexity of today's university and the need to be internationally competitive as outlined. Similarly, playing catch-up in undergraduate facilities we estimate to cost in the region of €1.7 billion.

In financial terms, therefore, there is a scale of investment required which is significantly beyond the scope of what has been envisaged in the recently launched National Development Plan. There is a serious risk that even as research funding has increased, the underlying fabric of the universities may not be able to sustain it. This is a serious disconnect in overall funding policy.

> Good management is often seen as anathema in an academic community. Good management, however, empowers the university to focus on its intellectual mission with minimum bureaucracy. Structures must continually change to suit the needs and complexities of the time.

Quantum Policy Leap Needed

We need a huge leap of imagination to grasp the scale of our needs; it takes imagination to shape the future. As Henry Ford said, the automobile would never have been developed in a society whose vision was limited to wanting faster horses ...

I believe that the country now needs the new government to recognise the new and more challenging role that its universities must play. An overarching strategic vision and policy for all of Higher Education is necessary which addresses each of the elements in a holistic, and not a piecemeal way. Research, teaching and learning, knowledge transfer, and the interface with society, cannot be pursued in isolation from one another. Neither can the different types of institutions be considered under separate policies.

> The policy should state firmly what level of investment would make the universities internationally competitive with some of the best in the world. Following from this, a fundamental review is necessary to determine how much of this investment can be afforded from public funds, and how much should be contributed by those most to gain – the students.

The policy should state firmly what level of investment would make the universities internationally competitive with some of the best in the world. Following from this, a fundamental review is necessary to determine how much of this investment can be afforded from public funds, and how much should be contributed by those most to gain – the students.

Grasping the Funding Nettle

I do not see any inclination on the part of government to meet this overall need through public funding alone. If this is the case, the clear issue to be addressed is the private contribution – whether it be termed "fees" or not. It is noteworthy in this context to see how Tony Blair addressed the deep concern about the competitiveness of the universities in his country. This was through a new partnership of the student and the state via top-up fees. The complementarity of public/personal investment is releasing very significant resources for universities which are, by and large, already better funded than Irish universities. For a university of 10,000 students, his new policy could generate an additional €40 million income!

Other sources of funding must be considered as part of overall policy. Recruitment of non-EU students is good for education and generates income through fees. However, the international market is very competitive and care must be taken to deliver high quality education to these students - and to charge enough so that they are not a drain on existing tight funding.

Philanthropy is a potentially new source of funding given the current wealth in Ireland. Ironically, it is clear that philanthropists will only give to excellence – even if that means giving to institutions in other countries. If our institutions are not performing at a world class level, they will get little sympathy from the philanthropic world. Nor do philanthropists see it as their role to substitute for public funding in the situation where the state has reserved to itself the right to control the funding of universities. Nevertheless, the cause of philanthropy in Ireland would be greatly helped by a clear public policy on higher education and by providing clear incentives for giving.

I will sum up by making reference to Charles Handy's book, *The Age of Unreason.*

> The future is not inevitable. We can influence it if we know what we want it to be. We can and should be in charge of our destinies in a time of change.

I have attempted to illustrate today that the leaders of Ireland's universities have a clear sense of direction and a perspicacity as to what needs to be done to ensure that our universities play a full role in building a cultured, sustainable, progressive Ireland. It requires that we maintain a strongly outward focus as befits a cosmopolitan trading nation. It requires that we see ourselves as part of a global ecosystem in which there is strong competition for intellectual capital and that we benchmark ourselves against some of the best in that ecosystem. It requires that we embrace change and the consequences. It requires that we are realistic about the scale of resources that achieving excellence requires.

We have arguably made this type of big-scale shift twice before in the last century. One was the introduction of universal free secondary education and the second was the introduction of a progressive tax regime. Both were spectacular successes. The time for an equally big and brave step for Third Level Education is … NOW.

… the cause of philanthropy in Ireland would be greatly helped by a clear public policy on higher education and by providing clear incentives for giving.

Prof Tom Collins

Head of Education Department, NUI Maynooth

Formerly Director of the Dundalk Institute of Technology, he is also Dean of the Faculty of Social Sciences in NUI Maynooth. In March 2006, he was appointed to the chair of the National Council for Curriculum and Assessment by the Minister for Education. He is a member of the Board of Pobal, the Irish local development agency and is chairperson of the National Rural Water Monitoring Committee. He has written extensively on issues in education and on the theme of participatory development.

Schools Must Create Knowledge, Not Just Deliver It

I used to point out to the students that when they were born their parents could not possibly have imagined the kind of world that they as young graduates were now entering. It is useful for us to think about the kind of world our children are going to emerge into and basically to say that we invest because we try to protect and create a future for them and that is why the topic of education is so important.

It seems to me that education has a number of purposes but the main purpose is that if the home and the community could do it you would not ask schools to do it. That appears to me to be a simple enough conclusion. Schooling emerged into the world because the home and community were not able to train kids for the industrial revolution. They were not able to teach them to read and to write because parents themselves did not know how to read and write and children were, at least in this sense, always better educated than the parental generation. They had to be. First of all, everyone understands that education is about intellectual development, that it is about teaching people to know things, ranging from literacy, from being able to read, being able to write, being able to do computation to the very highest level of expertise to the post-graduate studies in the best universities in Ireland and abroad. But there are other things that we expect, and increasingly need, schools to do.

The world now recognises that we need people who have interpersonal skills, who can operate socially, who are able to influence people. The whole business of politics, for example, is hugely reliant on these kinds of training and skill development. It seems to me that the cultural and the aesthetic are an increasingly important part of the world of education. Our children should know what beauty means. They should be able to distinguish between what is beautiful and

> The world now recognises that we need people who have interpersonal skills, who can operate socially, who are able to influence people. The whole business of politics, for example, is hugely reliant on these kinds of training and skill development. It seems to me that the cultural and the aesthetic are an increasingly important part of the world of education.

what is not beautiful. They should be led into worlds and into imaginative neighbourhoods that they have never ever thought of. I am often struck by the fairy tales and probably one of the great fairytales is Beauty and the Beast. Beauty and the Beast is a theme that runs through Western philosophy, certainly since time of the great Greek philosophers. It contrasts ugliness with beauty and demonstrates that when ugliness encounters beauty it can itself become beautiful, and when the princess kisses the beast she unleashes his beauty. It seems to me that when the child encounters education, education should be about releasing that child's capabilities to be completely delighted by the possibilities of their imagination and by their creative powers. That means being exposed to story, to music, to song, to dance, to art, to literature. It seems to me that education must also deal with the physical development of the child.

We now know that children spend so long sitting down every day that the best possible investment that the Irish state could make in the world of education is that every child would be safe enough to walk to school, a two-mile trip perhaps through the countryside or through their city, and in that two-mile trip they might meet people, they might pick berries, they might experience what it is like to have rain falling on their faces. They might know what it means to have the wind blowing in their hair, and they might know the joy of running. I believe that physical well-being and of course the manual dexterity which the child learns through many senses are a crucially important part of the child's learning.

And, of course, education must teach moral development. One of the really interesting things, it seems, about the growth of knowledge is that as we grow knowledge it does not necessarily mean that we improve morally. I would even say that there is a great distrust in the literature of people who think that if they grab all the knowledge they somehow become a force for bettering society. The great story of Genesis where Adam ate the apple of knowledge was in a sense the first great tragedy of humanity. If we have knowledge without restraint, without learning responsibility to the group, we become dangerous. I often wonder whether the nuclear physicists who developed the atomic bomb ever wondered about their moral position. It seems to me that humanity, and if we are to believe Darwin we are at the top of the evolutionary chain, are the supreme predators, destroys better than all other species. If we do not, as a community, learn what it means to have communal responsibility, to have responsibility to the group then, I think, knowledge becomes dangerous, and we are increasingly seeing the dangers of knowledge if applied in an unrestrained way. I believe that these are the challenges children are going to face in 20 years' time. I think they

It seems to me that when the child encounters education, education should be about releasing that child's capabilities to be completely delighted by the possibilities of their imagination and by their creative powers.

are going to face huge challenges of environment and energy.

They are going to have to live without oil and maybe that's a good thing, but we haven't figured out yet what we are going to re-place it with. They are not only going to have to live without oil; they are going to have to live with the consequences of all the oil we have used. Again, if we think of that tank of petrol that we used coming here today, it took 10,000 years at least to get that tank of petrol into my car and in two hours and twenty-five minutes I released 10,000 years of work out into the atmosphere. So, cleaning up that mess is going to be some challenge for the next generation.

I think increasingly that living with difference is going to become a massive global challenge. We have never been good at it in Ireland and that is why we create myths about ourselves such as the "Ireland of the Welcomes". This is a nonsense. I have lived and worked in America, and I know what "welcome" means and that the Ameri-cans give it. I live on a road in Co. Meath with eight or nine neigh-bours whom I have known for the last 20 years. I would say that in that time I have been in three houses. We celebrate parting much better. We have wonderful rituals of waking, but actually welcom-ing people in is not something we have ever done well. We are now having to do it and probably the great task, and I would say the great achievement, of Irish education has been how well it has managed the process in which about 10 per cent to 12 per cent of the popula-tion of primary schools are now born either outside of Ireland or to parents who were born outside of Ireland. That has been a phenom-enal achievement on the part of the entire ministerial, administrative and teaching staff in Irish social life over the past 10 years. But I do think that it is going to be a huge issue in the future.

I believe we need to nourish the soul and accept that our children are growing up in a context which is not enriching for them. They are spending 17 hours a week looking at television. If you think all childhood activity is about preparing for adulthood we are spending 17 hours a week preparing them to do nothing.

I believe we need to nourish the soul and accept that our children are growing up in a context which is not enriching for them. They are spending 17 hours a week looking at television. If you think all childhood activity is about preparing for adulthood we are spending 17 hours a week preparing them to do nothing. I have this image of Plato's cave. Plato proposed the idea that if men were in a cave and they were locked in a position and they couldn't turn their heads left or right and you lit a fire behind them, or the sun shone and their shadows appeared on the wall of the cave, they would never know that life is anything other than shadows. According to Plato, they would not be able to distinguish between reality and virtual reality. Oddly enough, it seems that the TV and the computer screen are teh equivalent of Plato's cave and I think that children need to learn to appreciate the civic.

We are living in a society where returning to the communal, as opposed to the individual, is becoming increasingly difficult. I will always take issue with the politician who says that we are proposing low taxes because the money is yours and we are only giving it back to you. I have never been in favour of a low taxation policy. In Sweden, in Denmark and in several countries in Europe people readily pay tax, up to 45 per cent of their income, but they expect a return on it. They know that if they contribute to the communal then the communal will give back to them.

I think the experience of childhood in Ireland is increasingly diminishing or depleting. I really think that education is about giving childhood back to children. I think the homes are failing to do this and they are looking to schools to do it and, most particularly, to the primary sector. This country is so lucky in the people who are running those schools and contributing to them. There is a huge depletion in the roles of family and neighbourhood in the education of children, in simply talking to them, in inserting them in the story of their community, in placing children as part of the next generation. There is an overwhelming presence of the media. It has some positive attributes but I think that the problem for children is that it reduces them to passivity. I came across a report recently which talked about parents buying their three-year-old child an exercise bike and placing the child in front of a video. The video showed outside spaces, so that the child could imagine he was cycling through outside spaces. I have seen myself, and many teachers will vouch for this, that if you ask children in school today how many of them play football they will all put up their hands, and then when you qualify it and ask how many of them play in a field, two of them perhaps will put up their hands. I have to say that the children I meet are universally wonderful so how they are managing in this environment is amazing.

Generally, primary school has changed massively. There were three great powerhouses, other than the pub, in rural Ireland where I grew up. One was the parish priest, the second was the guard, and the third was the schoolmaster. You knew what power meant when you came up against that trio. That has changed and women are now the great majority of new entrants to the teaching profession. I think that has feminised the profession and made it gentler. The syllabus is far more child-centred and child nurturing though maybe it does not always work like that. It is developmental in focus especially in primary. It is not terribly concerned about what you are going to be when you are grown up. That was the great line we always got: "you better work now or you might end up etc. etc." Nowadays, I think that would be an unacceptable kind of statement to make to a child, because the curriculum is developmental, it is focused on where he or she is now. The seven-year-old child is concerned with being seven; he or she is not hugely concerned with being seventeen.

I think the experience of childhood in Ireland is increasingly diminishing or depleting. I really think that education is increasingly about giving childhood back to children. I think the homes are failing to do this and they are looking to schools to do it and, most particularly, to the primary sector.

There has been a lot of change in the syllabus in second level, but the dominant pedagogical, organisational models persist and are largely driven by the Leaving Certificate and the points system. Everybody in secondary school – principals, teachers, students – are all in a sense prisoners of that.

Lastly, there is a great concern with integration. This is challenging, not only from the point of view of the multicultural aspect, but also in the case of children with special needs. This is a very big challenge that the schooling system has taken on in recent years. The second level experience is a tougher one for children and, for a variety of reasons, I don't think that it works as well. About 18 per cent don't complete it, and another 10 per cent barely manage to scrape through, which is about 30 per cent of the cohort for whom it doesn't really work. The key point is that it is at second level, I think, that disenchantment begins and not only at second level, but specifically in second year. There has been a lot of change in the syllabus in second level, but the dominant pedagogical, organisational models persist and are largely driven by the Leaving Certificate and the points system. Everybody in secondary school – principals, teachers, students – are all in a sense prisoners of that. There is one very notable exception, I believe, which is Transition Year where in fact children do actually say: "We'll pull off this motorway for a while and we'll develop." The problem is that, coming back on the first of September the following year, they are brought into the principal's office and told that "the fun" is over and that the real work starts now. Where things are not working well in secondary school and there is a low level of comfort with the school, you have poor performance, retention issues, low motivation among staff and students, low self-esteem among students, poor staff morale and often staff management-related issues. These are problems that happen in every organisation, but it particularly affects the secondary school.

At third level the big challenge is to deal with mass education. In the 1830s we developed mass primary education, in the 1970s mass second level education and now we are moving up to a national target of 70 per cent participation in third level. This poses a challenge to keep up standards. As we move into a mass agenda in third level, there will be variation in motivation, in ability, in supports. I think the long-term impact of selection based on points is something this country needs to look at now. The points system has been applied in Ireland for 35 years. That is a whole generation. So, if you think about it, there are very few doctors now who have gotten into medicine with less than 580 points in their Leaving. There are a few still hanging out there who managed it before the points system. I think other professions had a much more democratic mix. The points system has actually streamlined all of that. You could easily look at some professions and it is like the gene pool weakening as the aptitude mix begins to actually disappear. I think that is beginning to happen now in some of the areas that I work in in the university and I think it will tell in the way this country manages itself into the future.

I would say, finally, that I think there is a huge challenge to traditional approaches to teaching and learning as we move away from a chalk and talk-based model to a much more interactive one. From prescription to negotiation is what I have called it here. I think schools will need to focus much less on preparation for the future than on the current developmental challenges of the child, on the understanding that all people now have to actually learn for life. That is the best way to plan for the future. The most important thing that a school can give a child is a love for learning. What they know when they come out of it is largely irrelevant, so long as they know that they are talented and capable. That is really all they need to know. Increasingly, second level teachers have said to me: "You're in the third level – it must be wonderful for you that we are solving all the problems for you, we are filtering out all the people who couldn't make it and giving you our best." I always say to them that this is not what I want. What I actually want are students who want to learn, that's all I want, students who love it and who are capable of taking it on. For that to happen schools, I think, must increasingly create knowledge rather than just deliver it. That means going about exploring things, working in teams, collectively discovering the world which surely is what learning is always about. It means we adapt systems, not people. We should learn from special needs education. I do think that a teacher trained in special needs will probably be able to teach in any context and this is something we should look at. I think we should look as well at learning from the outside. I watch children in sport – teacher friends tell me that, even around suburban Dublin, the single most important organisation in the lives of children is the GAA. It provides an anchor for them, it involves them physically, it engages them socially, it links them with adults, it creates a life around them. I think most sports do that and we probably should be doing an awful lot more of it.

We need to focus very heavily on staff development in teaching. Teaching is an attritional job, it is a tough job. Secondary teaching is a hugely demanding job and, because it is, it wears people out. We can only do so much in the pre-service training of teachers. I think that is true of most professions. Most professions learn best in the doing, and in reflecting on the doing, so we need, I think, to ensure that we continue to nurture a culture of enthusiasm and engagement in teaching staff. In Maynooth, I see young teachers heading out into schools with the most unbelievable levels of dedication and commitment. They love it. I think maybe it's because, unlike previous generations of teachers, they haven't fallen into it but they've opted for it. It is so important, it seems to me, to continue to nurture and nourish that idealism.

The most important thing that a school can give a child is a love for learning. What they know when they come out of it is largely irrelevant, so long as they know that they are talented and capable.

Brian Lenihan TD, Minister for Justice, Equality & Law Reform

Chapter 8

Tackling Crime

Making Ireland a Fairer, Safer Place
Brian Lenihan TD
Minister for Justice, Equality & Law Reform

Brian Lenihan TD

Minister for Justice, Equality & Law Reform

Born in Dublin and educated at Belvedere College, TCD, University of Cambridge and Kings Inns. Formerly barrister, first elected to Dáil Éireann in 1996 to succeed his father, Brian, in the constituency of Dublin West. Appointed Minister of State in 2002 with responsibility for children at the Depts. of Health and Children and Justice, Equality & Law Reform. Appointed Minister for Justice, Equality & Law Reform in June 2007 following the general election.

Making Ireland a Fairer, Safer Place

British Prime Minister, Tony Blair, famously said at a Party Conference in Brighton in 1993: "Labour is the party of law and order in Britain today – tough on crime and tough on the causes of crime". To his detractors it might seem like policy making by sound byte – though even they would have to recognise that it is a very good sound byte. In fact, it summarises an essentially sound approach and one about which, in its generality, I don't think there would be much disagreement.

But in a way that phrase hides more than it reveals because while we all know what crime is – the law tells us – the question of what causes crime is a much more complex one. The conundrum at the centre of this can be demonstrated by a simple – and regrettable – fact: the murder rate in Ireland is running now at a multiple of what it was in the 1960s.

How has that come to be? Nobody could deny that in material terms we are disproportionately far better off now than we were then. Yet, we cannot overlook the fact that young men in general and certain socially-deprived areas and groups are still over represented in our prison population and this suggests a link between relative social disadvantage and crime. There is, though, a difference between a link and a cause. How is it that some people brought up in almost identical environments – even in the same family – go on to lead worthwhile lives in the community while others get involved in a life of crime? There is the danger, too, that in overemphasising social factors in the commission of crime this might be interpreted as absolving people from their responsibilities for their actions. An unfortunate truth is that it is often those suffering from similar disadvantage to the offenders themselves that are their victims.

We could have a very interesting discussion here on the nature of good and evil and on whether, when that apple was eaten in the

> **Yet, we cannot overlook the fact that young men in general and certain socially deprived areas and groups are still over represented in our prison population and this suggests a link between relative social disadvantage and crime.**

Garden of Eden, an inevitable consequence was a proliferation of busy Departments of Justice. I suspect, however, that people would be more comfortable with a Minister for Justice who has to deal with transgressions in the here and now setting out in practical terms what is being done and what will be done about the crime problem.

That said, as a Government we have to be conscious that a range of decisions we make on social issues can have implications as to the likely extent of our crime problem. Improving the lot of people and their opportunities to thrive is not only right in itself; it also can also have a substantial bearing on the nature and extent of our crime problem.

The reality is that as a society we have to build prisons and build schools but it is hard not to have sympathy with the view expressed by Eliza Cook in "A Song for the Ragged Schools" when she said:

> Better build schoolrooms for the "boy"
> Than cells and gibbets for the "man"

Patrick MacGill – in whose honour we meet – entitled one of his earliest works, "Children of the Dead End" and, while the context and circumstances are different from our own, we have to give priority to how we deal with what can be, perhaps, our children of the dead end when they get in trouble with the law and, indeed, hopefully , before that happens.

That is why, as Minister for Children, I was anxious to put our approach to youth justice issues on a proper footing. Thankfully, we have made substantial progress and I am confident that with the implementation of the Children Act and the establishment in particular of the new Youth Justice Service we at long last have proper structures in place to deal with offending by young people. This is an area in which we must heavily invest. And it is an investment – not least because it provides us with a chance to tackle criminal behaviour by young people on a relatively minor scale and do what we can to prevent their throwing their lives away and becoming involved in serious crime later on.

It is no disrespect to those who were involved in this area previously to say that the State's overall approach in this area lacked coherence. It is vital that youth justice is no longer regarded as the Cinderella of our system and as Justice Minister I will be fully supportive of the work of the Youth Justice Service and others working in this area. For example, the new Programme for Government commits us to doubling the number of Garda Youth Diversion Projects – projects that have, in a low-key way, been invaluable in keeping young people out of trouble. These projects, too, are examples of successful partnerships with the local communities – which is a

Improving the lot of people and their opportunities to thrive is not only right in itself; it also can also have a substantial bearing on the nature and extent of our crime problem.

theme of what I will be saying this afternoon. I am glad to note as well that the Probation Service has been resourced and restructured in the context of the full implementation of the Children Act.

I want to deal now with the wider criminal justice system and its response to the problems it must tackle. I do not intend to dazzle you with a blizzard of international crime statistics – many of which show Ireland in a favourable light. It is indeed cold comfort to a victim of any crime to show that statistically the chances of it happening were low. Crime statistics taken over time are the best indications of trends we have. However, we cannot forget that behind every crime statistic is a story. Distinctions are traditionally made between crimes against people and crimes against property. But it is very hard to say to someone whose house has been burgled and the victim is suffering from feelings of distress, fear and sheer frustration that the offence doesn't amount in reality to a serious crime against people. The larceny of a pedal cycle might sound trivial to some but it's not trivial, for example, to a young person who has worked hard part-time to buy a bike and then has it stolen.

My job as Minister for Justice, put simply, is to help protect and vindicate people's rights. For whatever reason, discussions of human rights issues often concentrate on the individual and the State as antagonists. What can tend to be forgotten is that it is a fundamental duty of the State to vindicate people's rights not to be subject to attack by others and to have peaceable enjoyment of their property. I am not suggesting for a moment that persons accused of crime are not entitled to due process. Of course they are and we must defend that vigorously if we are not to cheapen the very basis of our society. What I am putting forward is the proposition that it is a blinkered approach to see the vindication of human rights as being irrelevant to the protection of people from crime. To see human rights as something a democratic state is inherently disposed to undermine rather than protect is, in my view, a fundamentally flawed analysis.

Day in, day out, week in, week out, people who have been involved in crime are successfully brought to justice. That is a reality that in the white heat of a particular "controversy du jour" can be overlooked. It is unfair to all those working in the criminal justice system to ignore that. What I hope to do is to build on those successes.

It is probably fair to say that social partnership has been the mainstay of building our successful economy. What I am anxious to do as Minister for Justice is to develop partnerships with communities as a mainstay of our efforts to tackle crime. Preventing or detecting crime cannot be done by agencies of the criminal justice system alone; they need the active help of communities. At the same time as part of that

... it is a fundamental duty of the State to vindicate people's rights not to be subject to attack by others and to have peaceable enjoyment of their property.

partnership, the work of those agencies must be responsive to the needs of communities.

Joint Policing Committees provide a forum where members of a local authority, the senior Garda officers responsible for policing the area, with the participation of Oireachtas members and community and voluntary interests, can consult, discuss and make recommendations on matters affecting the policing of the area. Twenty-two of these Committees have been established on a pilot basis with a further seven being established. I believe that these Committees can form a cornerstone of the sort of partnership arrangements I want to see. I am working with Minister John Gormley to see that we finish a review of the pilot project quickly and that these Committees are established in all 114 local authority areas by early next year.

I have no doubt that a key issue that will be aired at these Committees will be anti-social behaviour. The phrase "anti-social behaviour" can cover a multitude. We should be in no doubt that in some areas behaviour of that kind is making people's lives a misery. It has to be tackled effectively and the people who engage in it will have to come to appreciate – one way or another – that it is simply not acceptable and it will have to stop. Of course, high jinks that spill over into disorderliness can be dealt with without necessarily turning it into a federal case. It is a different matter where people persistently indulge in behaviour that is adversely affecting the lives of members of their community.

People have to pay a price for that type of behaviour and, to underscore the type of partnership approach I am talking about, I have asked my Department to look at the question of what the Programme for Government refers to as Community Payback. This involves people who have transgressed providing real services for the communities they have damaged. It is the case that community service orders already mean that some offenders make reparation to society generally but what we will be looking at is whether it is possible to make a more direct connection between the offence and reparation to a particular community.

A key to any successful partnership is the relationship between the parties involved. Of its nature, one of the most important relationships in the Criminal Justice system is that between the Gardaí and the community they serve.

There is no point in pretending – particularly here in Donegal – that the past few years have not been troubled ones for the Garda Síochána. At a time when the crime problems they have had to face in the front line have become more difficult, they have had to live in the shadow of what has emerged – and will continue to emerge – at the Morris Tribunal. It is in the interests of no one – except the crimi-

Joint Policing Committees provide a forum where members of a local authority, the senior Garda officers responsible for policing the area, with the participation of Oireachtas members and community and voluntary interests, can consult, discuss and make recommendations on matters affecting the policing of the area. Twenty-two of these Committees have been established on a pilot basis with a further seven being established.

nals – for us to have a demoralised police force. By the same token, we have to take fully on board the lessons which can be learned from what happened in Donegal. Many reforms have been made to the Garda Síochána, under the leadership of Commissioner Noel Conroy, and that programme of reform will continue. We have had the establishment, as well, of the Garda Síochána Ombudsman Commission and the Garda Inspectorate. Those reforms arise not just because of what happened in Donegal but as part of the changes which are necessary to ensure that An Garda Síochána, while maintaining its exemplary and proud tradition, is properly equipped to do its work in an ever-changing society.

The activities engaged in by some Gardaí in Donegal not only were inherently wrong in themselves but did the gravest of disservice to their honourable and dedicated colleagues. It imperilled the high esteem in which the force is held by the community. Thankfully, I believe that the vast majority of the community still have the greatest respect for the Gardaí but the Gardaí know that respect is earned. The interaction between the Gardaí and members of the public is the bedrock on which the partnership between the Gardaí and the community is maintained. This is one of the reasons why I am proceeding with an extensive programme of civilianisation in the Force so as to free up Gardaí for the frontline duties for which they were trained and enable them to be visible in the communities in which they serve.

> **Thankfully, I believe that the vast majority of the community still have the greatest respect for the Gardaí but the Gardaí know that respect is earned.**

My first official function as Justice Minister was to attend a passing-out parade of members of the Garda Reserve. The enthusiasm which those people showed underlined both the high respect they had for the Garda Síochána and their willingness to give something back to their community. It is a true partnership between the Gardaí and members of the community. I do not intend to recount here the industrial relations difficulties surrounding the introduction of the Reserve. If there were reservations on the part of some that the introduction of the Reserve was intended to get around taking on the number of full-time Gardaí that were needed then I think that matter is well and truly put to rest at this stage. As well as meeting the commitment to bring the strength of An Garda Síochána up to 14,000, the new Programme for Government pledges that we will complete the current expansion of Garda numbers to 15,000 by 2010 and 16,000 by 2012. I have no doubt that members of An Garda Síochána, against that background, would not for a moment spurn the help of those in the community who want to support them in a practical way.

Another important way of underpinning partnership with the community is through the expansion of Garda and Community Closed Circuit Television. This can play an important role in supporting the work of the Gardaí in deterring criminal and anti-social behaviour. CCTV is not intended to be – nor could it be – an alternative to Gardaí on frontline duties; but it can function as an effective aid to policing, assisting the work of Gardaí in communities.

We should never forget that fear of crime – rather than being an actual victim of crime – can deeply impair the quality of people's lives. CCTV plays a valuable role in reassuring people. The Community CCTV scheme has the added benefit of providing a forum for partnership with local communities of exactly the kind I want to encourage. That is why I will be attaching particular priority to the roll out of this type of scheme. There are some who have reservations that use of these cameras represents the intrusion of technology into privacy, but I would suggest that it is far more sensible to see them as akin to a benign and helpful big brother rather than an Orwellian one.

Before I leave the issue of partnership, I want to make the general point that in my approach to my job as Minister for Justice, I do not operate on the basis that the font of all knowledge and wisdom on how to tackle crime lies in some repository on St. Stephen's Green. I believe that the Programme for Government provides a sound basis for us to proceed, but I have both an open door and an open mind in considering any constructive proposals for tackling these issues.

It would be unthinkable, in dealing with the issue of crime generally, not to talk about the plight of the victim. The effect of crime on victims is bad enough; but for victims to feel then that they have been ill-served by the criminal justice system can literally compound a felony. The sad fact is that victims can feel that they are the forgotten part of the criminal justice system. In saying that I am not at all to be taken as impugning the good work that has been done by all the agencies in the criminal justice system to improve how they look after the needs of victims. I want to commend in particular the work of the Commission for the Support of Victims of Crime. Nevertheless, one of my first acts as Minister was to direct that we should move ahead as quickly as possible to get a Victims Support Agency up and running. One of its functions will be to provide a voice for those who often feel that their concerns are not being heard. That agency too will form part of the type of partnership I want to encourage in tackling crime.

There can be no doubt but that the activities of gangs in Dublin, Limerick and elsewhere pose – to use an American phrase – a clear and present danger. Their activities are by and large inextricably linked with the market in illegal drugs.

I want to deal first of all with what I regard as the fanciful argument that if illicit drugs were legalised we could, at a stroke, eliminate much of this crime. If you accept the proposition that harmful drugs should be freely available that analysis may have some superficial attractions. I do not believe it is a proposition that would be accepted by the vast majority of people. The fact is that as long as you attempt to control the distribution of drugs – in other words that they are not freely available to anyone who wants them – an illicit market will exist with all its attendant criminality. Decriminalisation would be a recipe for vastly increased dependency on drugs and the harm that would be done by going down that road would far exceed any benefits that might be gained from it. It would be a nonsense too to think Ireland could take such a step while drugs remained controlled in other jurisdictions. People who make the argument for decriminalisation rarely seem to carry its logic to its conclusion and say that if people stopped using illicit drugs then the crime associated with supply would also disappear.

> It is a cruel irony that while the use of what would be regarded as hard drugs was once confined to areas of deprivation there is evidence now that in many cases the use of hard drugs is the product of affluence.

There are real issues which we as a society have to address about demand for illicit drugs. It is a cruel irony that while the use of what would be regarded as hard drugs was once confined to areas of deprivation there is evidence now that in many cases the use of hard drugs is the product of affluence.

The value of human life has been set at nought by members of the gangs at the centre of this pernicious trade. We have seen a spate of savage killings. Sometimes they happen because of rows that take place related to the drugs trade. Other times the killings relate to feuds. Anyone who has any doubt about the dangers of illicit drugs and the corrosive effect they have on society just has to take a look at the savagery with which often "coked up" young men take each others' lives.

There is no point in underestimating the difficulties which the Gardaí face in trying to bring these killings to an end. They have launched – and will continue to undertake – countless operations aimed at saving the lives of those involved. They get absolutely no help from the people they are trying to protect and when killings take place they get no cooperation either. In my view, to condemn these killings as in some way a failure on the part of the Gardaí - or, indeed, the Government - flies in the face of the harsh realities involved.

It is no consolation that the vast majority of these killings take place among members of criminal gangs. To take that view would be to share their disregard of human life. Tragically, it has been the case that their activities too have spilled over into the law abiding community. The truth is that the fight against the activities of these gangs is going to be long and has to be relentless. I am satisfied that the Gardaí have the resources – and are using them – to take all reasonable steps which are open to them to counteract this deadly menace.

They now have the benefit too of the Criminal Justice Act which was enacted by the last Dáil. Of their nature, the effect of those provisions will take some time to fully work through.

I would say to members of those gangs who fear for their lives that they should break out of the vicious circle they find themselves in and talk to the Gardaí. I have told the Garda Commissioner that there is no limit to the funding that will be available under the Witness Protection Programme.

It is simply not possible in a democratic state to take the type of measures which would absolutely guarantee that shootings of this kind will not take place. To resort to those measures would be to hand a perverse victory to the members of the gangs involved. To pretend otherwise is no help to anyone. As Minister I will promise that no resource or effort will be spared within the full rigours of the law to bring everyone involved in these activities to justice.

To return to the criminal justice system generally, it is hardly rocket science to say that the key to the effective operation of the agencies in the criminal justice system is that they be properly resourced and effectively managed. It is not special pleading on my part to say that that is what has been happening in recent years and what I hope to continue.

It is, of course, the case that it is not simply financial resources that are at issue. We have to ensure that all the agencies have the resource of a proper legal framework in which they operate. There is no doubt that recent years – indeed, decades – have seen a vast amount of criminal law reform. That said, I will be bringing forward a series of legislative measures in the sphere of the criminal law. My priorities include Bills dealing with forensic evidence and people trafficking. I also regard the work of the Balance in the Criminal Law Group, chaired by Dr. Gerard Hogan, as a sound basis for taking forward the complex issues which they were asked to examine.

My ambition as Justice Minister is as simple to set out as it is daunting to achieve: I want, in partnership with the people I serve, to help make Ireland a fairer, safer place.

> **I would say to members of those gangs who fear for their lives that they should break out of the vicious circle they find themselves in and talk to the Gardaí. I have told the Garda Commissioner that there is no limit to the funding that will be available under the Witness Protection Programme.**

John Gormley TD, Minister for the Environment,
Heritage & Local Government

Dr John Sweeney, Department of Geography,
NUI Maynooth

Eamon Gilmore TD, Leader of the Labour Party

Chapter 9

Saving Our Environment

Global Warming Threatens Our Survival
JOHN GORMLEY **TD**
Minister for the Environment, Heritage & Local Government

A Revision of Our Attitudes towards the Natural World is Required
DR JOHN SWEENEY
Department of Geography, NUI Maynooth

We Need a National Forum on Climate Change
EAMON GILMORE **TD**
Leader of the Labour Party

John Gormley TD

Minister for the Environment, Heritage & Local Government

Born in Dublin and educated at St. Munchin's College, Limerick, UCD and Freiburg University in Germany. Formerly Director of Languages College. First elected to Dáil Éireann for Dublin South-East in 1997. Elected to Dublin City Council in 1991 and was Lord Mayor 1994-5. First Chairman of the Green Party. Elected leader to succeed Trevor Sargent in July 2007. Following the 2007 general election, was a member of the Green Party negotiating team in the talks with Fianna Fáil to draw up a Programme for Government. Author of The Green Guide for Ireland.

Global Warming Threatens Our Survival

The walk across the floor of the Dáil to the Government benches may be a short distance in physical terms but it's an enormous step in political terms and one which I'm very glad that the Green Party has taken. Having achieved that ambition, I don't see things any differently – the principles and issues that were important to me in opposition remain important to me in government. What is different, of course, is that responsibility for progressing the environmental agenda and delivering on the specific commitments in the Programme for Government now rests with me; progress is the yardstick on which my time in government will be judged, not least by myself.

The theme for this year's school, "Priorities for Government for the Next Five Years", is therefore particularly appropriate. It's a topic on which I claim an intimate familiarity in the wake of the negotiations on the Programme for Government.

> Despite what many in the commentariat have said and written in recent weeks, Green party principles, ideals and policies are at the very heart of the Programme for Government.

Despite what many in the commentariat have said and written in recent weeks, Green party principles, ideals and policies are at the very heart of the Programme for Government. To this end, the Government will introduce and implement an extensive set of measures over a broad range of areas, especially in relation to the environment:

- Measures such as a reform of waste management, to reduce waste levels and ensure that incineration is no longer the cornerstone of our waste management policy.

- Measures such as a review of the Environmental Protection Agency, so as to ensure the Agency can address the ever-increasing pressures on the natural environment.

- Measures such as a review of the current levels of fines and sentences for environmental crime, to improve enforcement of our environment laws.

In my role as Minister for the Environment, Heritage and Local Government, there are further priorities. The litter problem in this country continues to astound me, and I strongly suspect I'm not alone on this point. We will intensify our efforts to make real and visible progress on litter and I will be announcing a series of new initiatives on this in the near future.

The protection of precious water resources in the country will also be a priority for me. Access to clean drinking water is a fundamental right but one which some people in this country do not experience. Upgrading local group-water schemes and improved enforcement measures against councils and schemes that fall below high standards will be a priority.

Finally, on our built heritage, the Government will work on an all-island basis to protect our shared archaeological heritage. I have ordered a fundamental review of archaeological procedures and practices to improve this.

These priority areas, like almost all environmental issues, have a direct bearing on our "quality of life" and the "quality of life" of future generations. But there is one priority for the Greens, one which we believe to be fundamental to the future of mankind. That priority is climate change. It is the Green's single biggest priority and the reason we are in government today. Indeed, every single major environmental issue here in Ireland, from planning to transport, can be linked back to climate change.

Let me be very clear on what I believe. Global warming threatens not just our "quality of life" but the very survival of this planet and we who live on it. If global warming is allowed to continue unchecked, the sheer scale of potential disruption and destruction of people and the environment is almost beyond comprehension. We cannot tackle climate change until we recognise the true extent of the problem.

It is the biggest issue facing humanity. It is a global problem which requires a global response. Such is the gravity of the situation that I believe it can only be addressed by recognising now that we have a global emergency. For anyone with a sceptical view about the evidence or the impact of global warming, they might read the fourth assessment report by the Intergovernmental Panel on Climate Change, a body incorporating the foremost experts on meterology and climate change in the world.

In their report last April on the impact of climate change, the sci-

> **The protection of precious water resources in the country will also be a priority for me. Access to clean drinking water is a fundamental right but one which some people in this country do not experience.**

entists gathered information from 29,000 sources in relation to the natural world, from habitats in the Arctic to the leafing of trees in Europe. Ninety per cent of the evidence pointed one way: climate change had already begun to impact on the earth. In addition, the report concluded it was almost certain that the climate change was caused by man's impact on the environment.

Here in Ireland, scientists are gathering similar information. Consider the following:

- Mean annual temperatures in Ireland rose by over 0.7°C between 1890 and 2004; more than half of that increase, or 0.42°C, has taken place since 1980

- Six of the ten warmest years in Ireland have occurred since 1995; the last decade has been the warmest on record; and last year was the second warmest year on record.

- Projections for the future continue along a similar record-breaking vein. The EPA report, Implications of the EU Climate Protection Target for Ireland, shows that we can expect significant changes in Ireland's climate even if the international efforts were successful in limiting the increase in average global temperature to not more than 2°C above pre-industrial levels. The fact of the matter is that Ireland will experience significant impacts even within this limited temperature increase, and we have already reached a stage where many of those changes are unavoidable.

- Widespread negative impacts are projected for the agricultural and marine environments, for plant and animal and for water resources. Sea level rise will negatively impact on certain coastal areas due to increased inundation and erosion.

But the most profound impacts of climate change, if unchecked, will be in other countries. Again the IPCC report from last April concluded that it would be the poorest people living in the poorest regions who will suffer most. In other words those who have contributed least to the problem will bear the brunt of the consequences. Dry areas, such as those in sub-Saharan Africa, will become up to 30 per cent drier, resulting in food shortages and increased levels of illness. Low-lying areas with high rainfall, like the Bay of Bengal, will become up to 30 per cent wetter. People living in these low-lying areas, again many of them living below the poverty line, will be very prone to flooding. Not only may they lose their homes but their drinking water is likely to become contaminated with salt water.

There are those who believe that a little bit of global warming in Ireland would be no bad thing. That viewpoint has no doubt become more popular of late, given our recent summer weather. But that view fundamentally misunderstands the global impact of climate change

Widespread negative impacts are projected for the agricultural and marine environments, for plant and animal and for water resources. Sea level rise will negatively impact on certain coastal areas due to increased inundation and erosion.

from which Ireland will not escape.

These probable events, though thousands of miles away, will have profound impacts on Ireland too. This vista of famine, flood and pestilence will lead to the displacement of more than one billion people by the end of the century, possibly more. The ramifications of such numbers of refugees are barely comprehensible.

The other view is that there is nothing we can do here in Ireland to tackle climate change. It is another viewpoint which I utterly reject. This argument says that Ireland is so small that any reductions in greenhouse gases will have a minimal effect on the global average. To those people I like to quote the Chinese proverb, used notably by Amnesty International: It is better to light a candle than to curse the dark.

Ireland's record on reducing its greenhouse gas emissions has been poor in the past. Indeed some climatologists, like Dr John Sweeney of NUI Maynooth, who is one of the contributors to this publication, has called Ireland a "delinquent nation". It is a sentiment I share. But if a small, developed and prospering nation like Ireland could manage to break the link between prosperity and greenhouse gas emissions then we would show true leadership in the area of tackling climate change.

Fundamentally, however, climate change is a global problem that requires a global response. The European Union has set a target of minimising global warming to three degrees or less. This will, it is hoped, allow the world to avoid the worst effects of climate change. That is why the Government supports, and will continue to support, the strongly proactive EU position on an ambitous and binding international agreement to succeed the Kyoto Protocol from the beginning of 2013.

Following this year's Spring meeting of the European Council, the EU sent a strong signal on its expectations of a post-2012 agreement. Using 1990 as the base year, Heads of State and Governments agreed to reduce total greenhouse gas emissions in the EU by at least 20 per cent by 2020. They also signalled a willingness to reduce emissions even further – up to 30 per cent – if other developed countries committed themselves to comparable emission reductions and economically more advanced developing countries contributed to the process in terms compatible with their responsibilities and respective capabilities.

I am hopeful that the meetings of the parties to the UN convention on climate change and the Kyoto Protocol later this year will see movement by our international partners, particularly the United States. The outcome of the recent G8 meeting in Heiligendamm was a welcome step in the right direction and we must and we will con-

But if a small, developed and prospering nation like Ireland could manage to break the link between prosperity and greenhouse gas emissions then we would show true leadership in the area of tackling climate change.

tinue to press our case for final agreement on a comprehensive post-2012 treaty to be reached no later than the scheduled meetings of the parties in Copenhagen in 2009.

My personal belief is that, such is the gravity of the situation, it can only be addressed by recognising now that we have a global emergency and that emergencies require emergency responses.

I believe passionately that meeting our national duty on climate change provides us with a chance to address many of the downsides we have experienced during this period of economic growth. It also provides business with an opportunity to cut costs and become more competitive internationally. What is now seen as progress does not equate with better quality of life for many families in this country. Being stuck on the M50 for hours on a daily basis is not progress by any yardstick. A long commute home after a nine hour work day to pick up your kids from childcare, if you're lucky, is not progress either. Nor is it helping our greenhouse gas emissions. We know that over-reliance on the car is driving up our CO_2 emissions. The transport sector represents the biggest challenge in terms of greenhouse gas reduction in this country. Investment in quality public transport, combined with proper planning, where facilities are close to communties, is real progress. And that would indeed mean a better quality of life and a reduction in our emissions.

> **Being stuck on the M50 for hours on a daily basis is not progress by any yardstick. A long commute home after a nine hour work day to pick up your kids from childcare, if you're lucky, is not progress either. Nor is it helping our greenhouse gas emissions.**

Our Programme for Government will begin this process. It will mean better-planned communities, with schools located close by, with better public transport links, better-insulated houses and, as a result, a reduction in our CO_2 emissions.

This isn't just about the environment. I've mentioned transport. But what about agriculture? What about planning and housing? What about industry? What about the public service itself? We all have a huge responsibility and because this is an emergency, we can no longer depend on an altruistic or voluntary impulse. We're now at the stage where each of us has an obligation and this requires a legislative response.

The Programme for Government emphasises the Government's commitment to take the necessary action. In addition to the full implementation of the National Climate Change Strategy, the Government intends to agree an all-party approach on climate change targets and, in advance of this, to set a challenging target of a 3 per cent reduction per year on average in our greenhouse gas emissions. Reform of energy markets, ambitious targets for renewables, record investment in public transport will all play their part in Ireland reducing its greenhouse gas emissions.

The measures in the Programme for Government are comprehensive but will take time to be fully effective. Meanwhile, compliance with our Kyoto target will be measured over the 2008-2012 period and our starting position is that we're more than 10 per cent above the target level of emissions. While carbon credits are a second-best solution, they do have a role to play and, along with most other EU member states, we will have to avail of them.

My absolute priority will be to ensure that we meet our Kyoto target; failure to do so would seriously damage the post-2012 agenda and undermine our credibility as a nation committed to sustainable development. In the short to medium term, my department and the Government will introduce a series of initiatives aimed at tackling climate change. These will include an environmental levy on low-efficiency bulbs. We have set an ambitious target to reduce energy consumption in the public sector by 33 per cent. There will be greatly increased energy efficiency in heating and lighting public buildings and in fueling public sector fleets. The Government will also introduce a carbon offsetting scheme for all ministerial and official air travel. The scheme will be ready for implementation by the end of this year.

> While carbon credits are a second-best solution, they do have a role to play and, along with most other EU member states, we will have to avail of them.

I expect that the Government will be in a position shortly to proceed with the establishment of the new Climate Change Commission. We will be inviting a small group of highly-accomplished people who will constitute the Commission to observe and comment on issues of relevance to Ireland in the context of a progressive global transition to a low-carbon society. On the issue of awareness, the Government is preparing a major national climate change campaign which is going out to tender. A budget of €15 million over five years has been earmarked for the project. From past experience we know that targeted information campaigns can bring about a real difference in behaviour.

In conclusion, I believe that we have reached a milestone in the international climate change agenda – a milestone with profound implications for the developed world. We have ten years to get it right. It is a small window of opportunity, but one we have to grab, for mankind's sake. Climate change is not something the Government, or the Green Party can be left to tackle alone. It is down to every individual, every person to play their part, to take action, to become part of the solution.

It is no longer an option therefore for those of us who live in developed countries to continue as before. Changing our lifestyles has become essential for our very survival.

Dr John Sweeney

Department of Geography, NUI Maynooth

Born in Glasgow and educated there, he holds a First Class Hons. B.Sc from the University of Glasgow where he also completed his Ph.D. in 1980 on The Meteorology and Climatology of Air Pollution in the Glasgow Basin. He has taught at NUI Maynooth since 1978 and has also taught at a number of universities in North America and Africa. He has also been involved in course design and curriculum development matters at second and third levels. He has served as President of the Irish Meteorological Society 1996-9, Secretary and Editor of the Geographical Society of Ireland 1984-96, Treasurer of the Irish Quaternary Assoc. 1982-5 and chairman of the RIA's Irish Committee on Climate Change 2001-4. Dr. Sweeney has written extensively on climate change and is a contributing author and review editor on the recent Intergovernmental Panel on Climate Change's Fourth Assessment Report.

A Revision of Our Attitudes towards the Natural World is Required

1. Introduction: Climate Change and the Issue Attention Cycle

From being a rather abstract academic concept as recently as a decade ago, climate change has now become an issue which has gripped the attention of society and mobilised the energies of the young. For them it has replaced the fear of nuclear conflagration which dominated the issue attention cycle of the last generation. As with all major environmental issues, a schism exists between the idealism of the young and the pragmatism, some would say cynicism, of their elders. In his book *Global Warming: the Complete Briefing*, Sir John Houghton (2004) reports on a conversation with a senior administrator in the United States who is reported as saying: "We cannot change our lifestyle because of the possibility of climate change; we just need to fix the biosphere." In some ways, this comment epitomises the conviction of many that we can always repair damage done to the environment by some, as yet to be discovered, technological "fix". Nuclear fusion, deep geological storage of greenhouse gases, the hydrogen cell – all offer panaceas in the long term to the problems we have created in the short term and with some justification. Certainly, human development has historically been characterised by an ability to develop

> As with all major environmental issues, a schism exists between the idealism of the young and the pragmatism, some would say cynicism, of their elders.

technological solutions to problems as and when needed. Stone tools, iron weapons, the water wheel, the steam engine, medical break-throughs, transportation innovations, computer technologies – all have provided platforms for addressing and overcoming particular limitations to human achievement and endeavour. For climate change, however, the lesson of history is that the past is not always the key to the future. People were historically prisoners of climate through its life supporting determination of the annual harvest surplus on which economic, cultural and intellectual advancement depended. Today, climate is at the mercy of people and blind faith that a technological solution is just around the corner is not enough on which to base our present social well-being. Strong leadership from those we elect to represent our concerns is of paramount importance.

2. Global Dimensions of the Problem

In the Fourth Assessment Report of the Intergovernmental Panel on Climate Change (IPCC, 2007a), a picture of accelerating problems associated with human misuse of the atmosphere is presented. Un-equivocal evidence of warming and a 90 per cent level of confidence that the loading of greenhouse gases on the atmosphere to concentra-tions not experienced for over 650,000 years, is the main driver of re-cent changes is reported from a synthesis of research from across the peer-reviewed literature over the past seven years (IPCC, 2007a). To-gether with almost all the nations of the world, the Irish Government have signed off and sanctioned the findings of this report. Among the more significant findings indicative of the quickening pace of global climate change are the following:

- The second half of the twentieth century was the warmest in at least the last 1300 years in the Northern Hemisphere. Temperature extremes have significantly increased in many parts of the world. The oceans have warmed to a depth of 3 kilometres.

- Acceleration in the rate of sea-level rise, melting of glaciers, and re-ductions in snow cover are now apparent. Summer sea ice extent is reducing by 7.4 per cent per decade and may well disappear in the Arctic by mid century with serious consequences for ecosystems dependent on it.

- Precipitation increases in many temperate regions are now occur-ring while droughts have become more frequent and more intense in many parts of the tropics.

These observed changes are consistent with model projections and provide confidence that the latter are reliable ways of looking into the future. Inevitably, looking into the future is a risky business and for

Today, climate is at the mercy of people and blind faith that a technological solution is just around the corner is not enough on which to base our present social well-being. Strong leadership from those we elect to represent our concerns is of paramount importance.

climate change projections this is even more so. It must be acknowledged that uncertainties regarding population, economic and energy
growth in the years ahead will always mean that climate change scenarios cannot ever be taken as absolute certainties. Nonetheless, this
is not an excuse for inaction since serious impacts are likely in a wide
range of areas and sectors (IPCC, 2007b).

• While water availability is likely to increase in high latitude areas,
  and in some parts of the wet tropics, many of the presently water-
  stressed areas of Africa are likely to become more drought-prone,
  seriously compromising their development potential.

• 20-30 per cent of plant and animal species will face a high risk
  of extinction if global temperature increases above pre-industrial
  levels go beyond –2°C.

• While food production may increase globally in the medium term
  due to the fertilising effect of higher CO^2 concentrations in the atmosphere, once temperature increases exceed about 3°C, yields are
  likely to start declining. In dry parts of Africa this will commence
  sooner, with any rise above present levels raising the spectre of
  widespread hunger during drought events.

• Hundreds of millions of people in the densely populated delta
  regions of the developing world will become more vulnerable to
  floods and tropical storms. Small island states, especially low ly-
  ing tropical islands, will also be highly vulnerable.

• Outside of the temperate regions, adverse health effects will be apparent from heat waves, storms, floods, fire and drought as well as
  changes in water and vector borne diseases. These will more than
  counterbalance any improvements due to warmer winters in high
  latitudes.

As with all environmental problems, the burden of climate change falls inequitably on those least able to bear it. It is also evident that the developing world will suffer for a problem not primarily of their making.

As with all environmental problems, the burden of climate change
falls inequitably on those least able to bear it. It is also evident that
the developing world will suffer for a problem not primarily of their
making. Richer countries will, in the medium term at least, have the
financial and organisational resources to better adapt to the problem
though, even in areas such as Ireland, significant changes in climate
will be observed.

3. Climate Change Impacts on Ireland

As a result of the work carried out at NUI Maynooth, it can be concluded that July mean temperatures will increase by 2.5°C by 2055
with a further increase of 1.0°C by 2075. Mean maximum July temperatures in the order of 22.5°C will prevail generally with areas
in the central Midlands experiencing mean maxima up to 24.5°C.

Overall increases of 11 per cent in precipitation are predicted for the winter months of December–February. The greatest increases are suggested for the north-west, where increases of approximately 20 per cent are suggested by mid-century. Little change is indicated for the east coast and in the eastern part of the Central Plain. Marked decreases in rainfall during the summer and early autumn months across eastern and central Ireland are predicted. Nationally, these are of the order of 25 per cent with decreases of over 40 per cent in some parts of the east.

These scenarios will have impacts on several aspects of Irish life, though not all of them are adverse. Only two sectors are briefly discussed here.

Agriculture

- For livestock production, the expectation of more frequent summer droughts will require supplementation of grazed grass. Although warmer temperatures would be expected to result in shorter winter housing times for livestock, a trend towards wetter winters may result in problems of poaching and soil damage which may negate this. The balance of grazing season length against winter rainfall will dictate the stored feed requirement, and the actual climate will dictate the choice of forage crops grown. Opportunities to spread slurry or dirty water in winter will be further reduced and increased slurry storage requirements are likely to be needed.

- Maize silage is increasingly likely to replace grass silage, potentially increasing grazing land areas. At the same time, increased production of grain maize is expected. Grain maize yields are expected to increase dramatically in western areas by more than 150 per cent on today's national average value.

- Spring barley yield increases of approximately 25 per cent are likely by 2055 with harvesting time earlier than today.

- For potato, drought stress will be the most important limiting factor determining its viability and it is likely that potatoes may cease to be a commercially viable crop over much of Ireland, though should survive in wetter parts of Donegal.

Water Resources

- A widespread reduction in annual runoff, most marked in the east of the country. All areas will experience a major decrease in summer runoff, particularly in the east of the country. These reduc-

Marked decreases in rainfall during the summer and early autumn months across eastern and central Ireland are predicted. Nationally, these are of the order of 25 per cent with decreases of over 40 per cent in some parts of the east.

tions are likely to average approximately 30 per cent over large parts of eastern Ireland by mid-century.

- Winter runoff is predicted to increase. The magnitude and frequency of individual flood events will probably increase in the western half of the country. Seasonal flooding may occur over a larger area and persist for longer periods of time. Areas such as the Shannon basin and turloughs in the west will be vulnerable to these changes

- During the summer months, long-term deficits in soil moisture, aquifers, lakes and reservoirs are likely to develop. It is likely that the frequency and duration of low flows will also increase substantially in many areas. Water supply infrastructure is expected to come under growing pressure particularly in the Greater Dublin Area and the strategic implications of this are profound for a number of areas, particularly spatial settlement strategy. The projected changes in water availability pose potential problems for the dilution of water-borne effluent. With a greater frequency of low flow conditions, additional precautions will be required to ensure that concentrations of water pollutants do not give rise to acute effects.

4. The Environment in the Programme for Government

An impressive menu for action in the area of environment is provided in the Programme for Government (Appendix 1). Only a few are capable of being addressed here though as with all environmental issues, overlapping and hopelessly intertwined issues arise.

- In advance of agreeing an all-party approach on climate change targets, the Government will set a target for this administration of a reduction of 3 per cent per year on average in our greenhouse gas emissions and mandate the Department of Environment, Heritage and Local Government to publish an Annual Report setting out progress on meeting climate change targets.

As one of the world's top greenhouse gas polluters on a per capita basis, Ireland has a responsibility to play its part in addressing the problem. Thus far it has failed to do so, and the radical measures necessary have not been forthcoming.

As one of the world's top greenhouse gas polluters on a per capita basis, Ireland has a responsibility to play its part in addressing the problem. Thus far it has failed to do so, and the radical measures necessary have not been forthcoming. The political will to make the necessary policy changes in how Irish society is organised has not yet been demonstrated. These Carbon Budget proposals are a welcome development. "Business as Usual" has characterised Irish greenhouse gas emissions growth over recent years and globally it appears that we are committed to a likely increase of 3°C as atmospheric concentrations double, probably towards the latter half of the present century. Such an increase is beyond the value of 2°C deemed by the EU as constituting "Dangerous Climate Change". This is where the next big crunch comes. At this point the climate system may become dangerously unstable with non linear increases in impacts, especially in the poorer parts of the world (Figure 2). Large scale events such as the collapse of the West Antarctic ice sheet, the long-term melting of the Greenland ice sheet, the destabilising of the thermohaline circulation and the release of methane clathrates become more probable events, difficult to reverse over timescales of centuries (McElwain and Sweeney, 2007). The prospect becomes bleak, not least for Ireland.

- Make clear provision in Development Plans for environmentally sustainable transport methods.
- Implement all aspects of Transport 21 so that the use of public transport becomes a real option for more and more people.

Transport emissions are the most intractable aspects of the problem and the recent Census results make unpalatable reading. In 1992 Ireland had 227 cars per 1000 people. Today the figure is over 400. CO_2 emissions from road transport have doubled over this period and are likely to rise close to the same level as that projected for carbon credit purchases. Fifty-six per cent of commuters in the Dublin Region now drive to work. Eighty per cent less schoolchildren cycle to school in the Dublin area than in 1991. Even one in three school pupils who live less than a mile from school is driven each day. Small wonder that average bus speeds in Dublin have dropped below 13kph, with comparable figures for London being 26kph, Stockholm 28kph, and Copenhagen 24kph.

Fifty-six per cent of commuters in the Dublin Region now drive to work. Eighty per cent less schoolchildren cycle to school in the Dublin area than in 1991. Even one in three school pupils who live less than a mile from school is driven each day.

- Ensure all County Development Plans are "sustainability proofed".

Tackling this problem requires a determined assault on sprawl. A fundamental review of the land use planning practices is required. Regional Planning Guidelines/Strategic Planning Guidelines have failed to stem the rezoning frenzy and the planning profession has, in my opinion, been demoralised by a lack of support from both within and without the local authority system. The proper implementation of the Strategic Environmental Assessment Directive will go some way towards helping this by forcing plans, programmes and policies to be scrutinised for their resource consumption dimensions more scrupulously. In this context, however, it is perplexing to note that the most important plan of all, the National Development Plan, was not submitted for SEA, a matter on which the EU may yet have the last word.

- Introduce a National Landscape Strategy.

We must move to the implementation of the concept of stewardship in legal terms, hard as that may be for some to swallow. The Irish environment belongs to us all and we all have an interest in its stewardship, especially as taxpayers.

Private gain versus public and community good is a familiar issue for those seeking to manage environmental resources of all kinds. The Irish Constitution excessively enshrines the right of private property to the detriment of the common good. Land ownership does not imbue the right to do with it what the owner likes any more than ownership of a river bank gives the right to pollute at will. We must move to the implementation of the concept of stewardship in legal terms, hard as that may be for some to swallow. The Irish environment belongs to us all and we all have an interest in its stewardship, especially as taxpayers. Since we do we have an ethical responsibility to leave the earth for future generations in at least as good a state as we inherited it from our forefathers, by not acting now we reduce options for those who come after us and bequeath them damaged goods. This is why sustainable development needs to move from a nebulous concept to a reality in decision makers' minds.

5. Humans as "Subduers" of the Earth

Throughout recorded history, humans have exploited their environment to create an anthropocentric world fashioned to suit their needs for food, shelter, transport and technology. Driving wild game by setting fires undoubtedly helped create and maintain the grassland biomes. Deforestation, for example in Ireland, associated with the medieval monastic settlements, or to remove cover for rebels, or to supply timber needs for Elizabethan naval vessels, was instrumental in the creation of the treeless landscape of much of the island. Only Iceland has less forested area in Europe. Canals, railways, roads, mines, reservoirs, dams and farms fashioned a landscape designed for supporting better the dominant animal of the biosphere. Once part of nature, struggling to overcome its vicissitudes and caprices, technologically advanced humans increasingly became exploiters and dominators of a natural world increasingly geared to meeting their material needs. Nature was tamed.

Most of the earth's resources have been privatised. Utilisation of a resource involves either paying an access cost or conforming to regulatory requirements such as licensing. Water, for so long thought of as part of our birthright, has now been commoditised in most parts of the world. Resistance to the process has been marked – witness the hostile reaction to water charges in Ireland. The atmosphere however remains largely an open access resource. For greenhouse gases, it is effectively a global commons. As with all resources, common resources provide a facility and, if no utilisation cost is involved, tend to get overexploited. This is the root problem of atmospheric pollution either by industrial emissions such as sulphur dioxide or greenhouse gases. Regulation of the atmosphere for greenhouse gas emissions is as yet in its infancy with only the United Nations Framework Convention on Climate Change and more recently the Kyoto Treaty providing the first steps towards restricting access and the European Emissions Trading Scheme creating a market in utilisation costs. Still however, the resource provides an individual incentive for most of the world's countries to spread their damage costs over the whole global community.

In tackling the problem of climate change clearly a revision of our deeply ingrained attitudes towards the natural world is required. The anthropocentric view of the natural world has blinded humanity to the obvious fact that far from being above nature we are as dependent on it today as the Neanderthals, though the relationship is more complex. Scientific advances have given us answers to fundamental questions of earth functioning. But these often come in an ethical and religious vacuum. Perhaps the non anthropocentric view of humankind as humble components of a natural web, as espoused by Francis of Assisi, offers an alternative perspective. Humans as stewards of the earth is perhaps the ideology which needs to be inculcated in all of us if we are to have success in tackling the environmental problems facing us, especially that of climate change.

The anthropocentric view of the natural world has blinded humanity to the obvious fact that far from being above nature we are as dependent on it today as the Neanderthals, though the relationship is more complex.

References

Fealy, R and Sweeney, J. (2007) "Climate Scenarios for Ireland," in, Sweeney et al, *Climate Change in Ireland: Refining the Impacts*. Environmental Protection Agency, Johnstown Castle, Wexford (In Press).

Houghton, J. (2004) *Global Warming: The Complete Briefing*, 3rd Edition, Cambridge University Press, Cambridge.

Intergovernmental Panel on Climate Change (IPCC) (2007a) *Climate Change 2007: The Physical Science Basis. Contribution of Working Group 1 to the Fourth Assessment Report of the Intergovernmental Panel on Climate Change*. Cambridge University Press, UK. (In Press).

Intergovernmental Panel on Climate Change (IPCC) (2007b) *Climate Change 2007: Impacts, Adaptation and Vulnerability. Contribution of Working Group II to the Fourth Assessment Report of the Intergovernmental Panel on Climate Change*. Cambridge University Press, UK. (In Press).

McElwain, L. and Sweeney, J. (2007) Implications of the EU Climate Protection Target for Ireland. Environmental Protection Agency, Johnstown Castle, Wexford, 25 pp.

Meinshausen, M. (2005) On the risk of overshooting 2°C. Paper presented at Scientific Symposium Avoiding Dangerous Climate Change. UK Meteorological Office, Exeter, 1-3 February 2005.

Parry, M.L., Arnell, N., McMichael, T., Nicholls, R., Martens, P., Kovats,

S., Livermore, M., Rosenzweig, C., Iglesias, A. And Fischer, G. (2001) "Millions at risk: Defining critical climate change", *Global Environmental Change*, 11(3), 181-183.

Tuan, Y. (1968) "Discrepancies between environmental attitude and behaviour: Examples from Europe and China", *Canadian Geographer* XII(3), 176-191.

White, L. (1967) "The Historical Roots of our Ecologic Crisis", *Science* 155 (3767), 1203-1207.

Appendix 1: Extract from the Programme for Government

Climate Change: A Challenge for the Whole World

As a developed country, as a Member State of the EU, and as a responsible nation in the wider international community, Ireland must play its part in meeting the most important environmental issue facing the world today.Meeting our obligations to the future generations requires all sectors in society to play their part. To ensure this Government will implement a comprehensive range of measures as set out in the new National Climate Change Strategy. This Government believes in the need to commit to a clean and renewable energy future and we commit ourselves to a Green Energy Revolution.

In particular, we will:

- Agree an all-party approach on climate change targets.
- In advance of agreeing such targets, the Government will set a target for this administration of a reduction of 3 per cent per year on average in our greenhouse gas emissions.
- Mandate the Department of Environment, Heritage and Local Government to publish an Annual Report setting out progress on meeting climate change targets.
- Increase the use of alternative energies for generating power in order to ensure that one-third of electricity consumed in Ireland comes from renewable sources by 2020.
- Create new opportunities for our farmers by moving agriculture to a new dual system of food and power production.
- Facilitate the establishment of a new bio-fuel industry in Ireland on the back of this new agricultural production.
- Improve the energy efficiency of new Irish homes by up to 40 per cent or more.
- Introduce a minimum requirement for the use of bio-fuels in State-owned and public transport vehicles. Dublin Bus and Bus Éireann will move their existing fleet to a 5 per cent bio-diesel blend and

will achieve a 30 per cent bio-diesel blend in their new buses.

- Make clear provision in Development Plans for environmentally sustainable transport methods.

- Continue to use the taxation system to encourage good environmental behaviour and discourage poor practice, e.g. through re-balancing the VRT and Motor Tax system to reward the purchase of greener cars.

- Complete the phasing out of incandescent light bulbs in favour of more energy efficient compact fluorescent bulbs to reduce our carbon emissions and save on electricity costs.

- Require the public sector to lead the way on energy efficiency with a mandatory programme of efficiency measures including the sole use of energy efficient lighting and heating in offices, schools and hospitals and other public buildings to produce 33 per cent energy savings by 2020.

- Require all street lighting and traffic lighting systems to be energy efficient and replace inefficient systems.

- Require carbon offsetting of all official air travel in support of urban forests.

- Require the mandatory use of bio-fuel mixes in transport fuels and ensure that there is a nationwide bio-fuel distribution network.

- Ensure that the development of renewable energy heating systems is encouraged through targeted grant schemes and facilitated by appropriate planning exemptions.

- Introduce smart electricity meters and ensure that energy produced in the home and at work can be sold back into the national grid.

- Implement all aspects of Transport 21 to so that the use of public transport becomes a real option for more and more people.

- Establish a high level Commission on Climate Change to oversee implementation of the Climate Change Strategy.

Figure 1: Projected temperature changes for Ireland

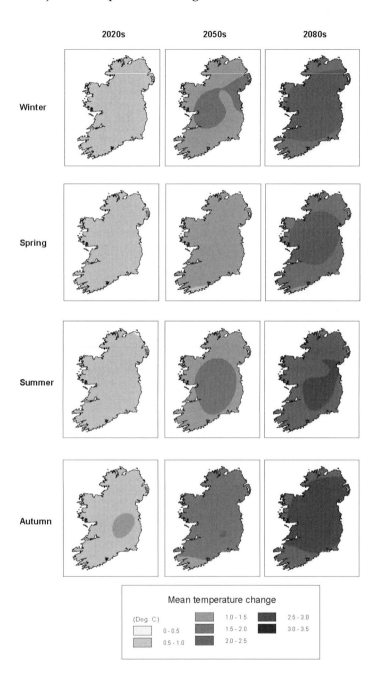

Figure 2. Millions at risk from various hazards in the 2080s as a result of global climate change

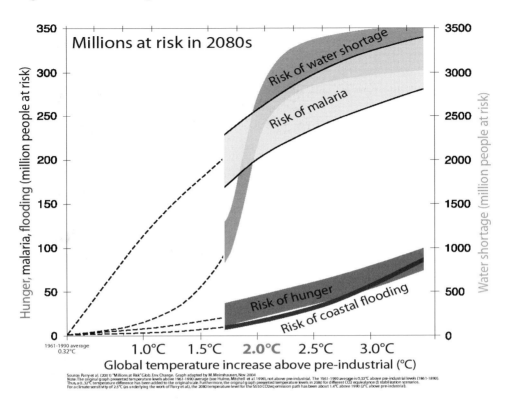

Eamon Gilmore TD

Leader of the Labour Party

*Born in Galway and educated at Garbally College, Ballinasloe and UCG (BA).
Former trade union official, former President of USI 1976-8. First elected to
Dáil Éireann for Dun Laoghaire 1989. One of the six Workers' Party deputies in
the 26th Dáil who formed a new party, Democratic Left. Minister of State at the
Dept. of the Marine 1994-1997. He was Labour spokesperson on Communications
and Natural Resources 2002-2004 and spokesperson on Environment and Local
Govt. since 2004 until his uncontested election to the leadership of the Labour
Party in Sept. 2007.*

We Need a National Forum on Climate Change

The appointment of a Green Party Minister for the Environment is
a great opportunity to make progress on the environmental agenda.
The Labour Party shares the policy objectives of the Greens on the
environment and, over the life of this Government, Labour will take
a very positive approach to the environment commitments in the
Programme for Government, and towards those issues and initiatives which need to go beyond the Programme itself. Labour will
support Minister Gormley, where he is taking action to protect the
environment. When we have to be critical, we will, I hope, not be
motivated by political opportunism, but by the genuine interest in
our environment, which we share with the Green movement. I hope
that Labour will find itself more often on John Gormley's side than
on his back!

The next five years will be dominated by the global challenge of climate change and by the domestic measures necessary to meet it. Climate change is one of the greatest challenges facing humanity.

The next five years will be dominated by the global challenge of
climate change and by the domestic measures necessary to meet it.
Climate change is one of the greatest challenges facing humanity.
Without urgent and decisive action within the next decade we are
likely to experience flooding affecting one sixth of the global population, drought and famine for 200 million of the world's poorest citizens, extinction of up to 40 per cent of all species and more extreme
weather patterns threatening lives and livelihoods over the coming
decades. The cost to the global economy could be up to 10 per cent of
GDP per annum. The human and environmental costs are unquan-
tifiable.

The international consensus on the need for radical action to
avoid serious climate change has been growing steadily since the
Kyoto Protocol was negotiated in 1997. The British Government has
indicated its intention to achieve a CO_2 reduction of 60 per cent be-

low 1990 levels by 2050. Germany and France have signalled their intention to push climate change up the European agenda, and Sweden is on track to being an oil-free economy by 2020.

Ireland has had ten years to prepare for our first-round commitments under the Kyoto Protocol, commencing on 1 January 2008. Despite this, Ireland is set to overshoot its target by 7.2 million tonnes of CO^2 a year for each of the next five years. The last Government has already sanctioned the purchase of €270 million worth of carbon credits (or "clean air") from abroad to compensate for its failure to meet our domestic target. However, this figure assumes that global demand for carbon credits will remain reasonably static. The truth is that the direct cost of failing to meet our CO^2 reduction target could be up to €750 million for the first Kyoto period alone.

Ireland needs to take serious action now to meet our Kyoto commitments and to position ourselves for a medium to long-term economic climate where energy and environmental issues will dominate. The message of the recent Stern report for the British chancellor is clear: early action to avoid runaway global warming far outweighs the costs. Decisions taken over coming decades will be crucial in determining success or failure in the fight against climate change.

This Government, and Minister Gormley in particular, will have responsibility for negotiating Ireland's second Kyoto commitment, and for putting policies in place between 2008 and 2012 to achieve that target. The EU has already agreed to cut emissions within the member states to 20 per cent below 1990 levels, by the year 2020. Ireland supported this cut and, according to John Gormley's predecessor, it did so in the belief that Ireland would be be able to negotiate a burden sharing arrangement similar to the first round, when an overall EU reduction of 7 per cent on 1990 levels meant Ireland was permitted an increase of 13 per cent on 1990 levels.

The new minister's first challenge therefore is to set out Ireland's negotiating position for the EU burden sharing discussions. Is a Green Party minister going to seek to minimise the carbon reductions which will be sought from Ireland by our European partners and can we realistically expect as generous a share as was agreed a decade ago, given the enlargement of the Union, the increased urgency on climate change and not least our own lamentable record over the past decade?

All of that, of course, is negotiating the regime for the post 2012 period. More immediately, however, is the need to get Ireland into line with its existing international obligation to reduce carbon emissions from our current 26 per cent above 1990 levels to 13 per cent above and to do so by 2012.

The Programme for Government seeks an "all-party approach on

Ireland needs to take serious action now to meet our Kyoto commitments and to position ourselves for a medium to long-term economic climate where energy and environmental issues will dominate.

climate change targets". Labour will co-operate with such an all-party approach. We welcome the commitment in the Programme to reduce greenhouse gas emissions by an average of 3 per cent per annum during this administration, and we can broadly agree to the range of measures set out in the environment, energy, transport, housing and agriculture sections of the programme, which are aimed at achieving the target.

There are, however, a few things in the Programme, (or perhaps more accurately, omissions from it) which are surprising. The first is the absence of any mention of a climate change bill, which would enshrine in law the 3 per cent annual carbon reduction. The environmental NGOs have sought (and published) a draft of such a bill. Both Labour and the Green Party gave pre-election commitments that carbon reduction targets would be statutorily based, in a climate change bill, similar to that being introduced by the Labour Government in the UK. If there is to be all-party agreement on the targets, then what is the apparent reluctance to the bill?

The second surprise relates to transport policy and to the National Development Plan. The major reductions in Ireland's greenhouse gas emissions must come primarily from the energy and transport sectors. While the Programme for Government appears to be clear on the measures to be taken in Energy, it effectively signs up for the transport and infrastructure strategies of the pre-May 18th Government. "We believe that the full implementation of the NDP must be the first priority of the next administration" declares page 3 of the Programme for Government, while page 10 tells us that "we are committed to the implementation of Transport 21 on time and on budget". The Green Party had previously criticised both the NDP and Transport 21 for putting a disproportionate emphasis on road building and private cars. How is this now to be reconciled with the measures which will be necessary to reduce carbon emissions from transport sources?

The third area, which is more vague than surprising, relates to carbon taxation. There is a fairly clear indication of intent to rebalance VRT and motor taxation. But the destination of motor tax is now a little unclear. Until now, motor tax was ring fenced and allocated by the Minister for the Environment to local authorities in the form of general purposes grants and allocations for non-national roads. In the re-allocation of departmental responsibilities, which was announced by the Taoiseach on the evening the Government was formed, responsibility for non-national roads was transferred from the Department of Environment to Transport. So who will now allocate roads money to the councils and, just as interesting, how much of motor taxation will now go to roads and how much will go to the general

> The major reductions in Ireland's greenhouse gas emissions must come primarily from the energy and transport sectors.

Local Government Fund, and who will decide this?

The general issue of carbon taxation is even less clear. One reference in the PFG says, "appropriate fiscal instruments, including a carbon levy, will be phased in on a revenue-neutral basis over the lifetime of this Government". A second reference is contained in the section of the PFG which promises to establish a Commission on Taxation, which will "investigate fiscal measures to protect and enhance the environment including the introduction of a carbon tax". Is the afore-mentioned "carbon levy" the same thing as the carbon tax, which presumably is subject to initial consideration by the Commission on Taxation? Or are we to get both carbon levies and a carbon tax?

I look forward to having all of these issues considered in the all-party context promised by the Government. However, I believe that the "parties" to be involved should be wider than just the political parties. There is now, I believe, some general appreciation of the scale and consequences of climate change. But there is not, as yet, a sufficient public understanding of the scale of the measures which will be required to firstly meet our existing Kyoto commitments, and then to prepare for the even more demanding challenges of its successor. Neither is there an appreciation of the enormous cost to the taxpayer and to the economy of continuing failure to reduce carbon emissions.

Even with a generous burden-sharing arrangement, Ireland will be required to cut its carbon emissions within the next 10 years by the equivalent of the entire current emissions from the transport sector, including every car, truck, train and plane in the country. And if we don't, the cost to the taxpayer could be over a billion euro every year!

It is essential, therefore, that the main players in the economy and in society are brought together with the political process to work out a national consensus on the steps needed to secure significant carbon reductions between now and 2020. To achieve this, I am proposing that the Government should establish a National Forum on Climate Change, representative of economic, governmental and non-governmental interests to consider, and hopefully agree, the practical steps which will be necessary to cut down on carbon. This goes beyond the Government's idea of some kind of all-party committee, and crucially will engage with those very sectors of the economy and of society who will have to carry the burden!

I am also making this proposal, because the idea of adding an environmental pillar to the social partnership process appears to have been successfully resisted by Fianna Fáil in the Programme for Government. The environment movement has been seeking a status in social partnership, similar to the social pillar with which Fr. Sean Healy is most associated. I was disappointed that the only concession to it in the PFG was to "consider arrangements for representation of environmental issues in social partnership will be considered in the course of the review of T16". As that review will not take place until well into next year at the earliest, a separate process will be necessary to address climate change.

On its own, climate change would probably justify a single stand-alone ministry. Indeed, the Labour Party had proposed the creation of a new Department of Environment, Energy and Climate Change, with the responsibility for Local Government and Infrastructure being given to a separate department. Given the rapid pace of development in Ireland, it is difficult for an individual minister to lead simultaneously on both the provision of infrastructure, and on protecting the environment. John Gormley encountered this conflict on his very first day in office when he found that the drive to build the M3 took precedence over his instinct to protect the heritage of Tara. And he had barely drawn his breath from that baptism of fire when the conflict surfaced again, in his own constituency, where the City Council, for which he has ministerial responsibility, wants to build an incinerator which has major environmental consequences.

While, probably, there will be some political synergy between John Gormley's responsibilities and Eamon Ryan's Energy portfolio, it is a pity that Energy and Environment were not consolidated into a single powerful department, with a clear focus on the environment.

The present Department of Environment, Heritage and Local Government is enormous, with responsibilities covering housing, planning, local government, the provision of infrastructure such as water and sanitary services, the fire service and the licensing regime that goes with it, waste management, and our electoral system, including the care of the now discredited electronic voting machines.

Housing is entering a new phase, both as a market and as an issue for Government. For the first time in over ten years, it appears that recent house purchasers may be exposed to negative equity, caught in a new pincer between rising interest rates and possibly declining property values. Secondly, housing construction appears to be slowing, with considerable consequences for employment, the exchequer and the economy. Thirdly, there is a continuing unfulfilled housing need, made up of record numbers on social housing lists, thousands of disappointed applicants for affordable housing and many who can not afford to buy or, at least, cannot afford to live in the area of their choice and need.

On its own, climate change would probably justify a single stand-alone ministry. Indeed, the Labour Party had proposed the creation of a new Department of Environment, Energy and Climate Change with the responsibility for Local Government and Infrastructure being given to a separate department.

There is no simple solution for this complex housing dilemma. The Government will need to handle the situation with great delicacy in order to protect from financial hardship and possible repossession those who have already bought; to provide housing at an affordable price for those who need it and to support the residential construction industry and those whose livelihoods depend on it.

State housing policy in Ireland needs to change. In many respects, our system of housing supports condemns people to continuing poverty. Take the rent supplement scheme. Approximately 60,000 households are on rent supplement, at a cost to the taxpayer of over 400 million euro per year. To qualify, one has to be on a social welfare payment, and if one takes up an offer of regular employment one loses it. Take two tenants in similar accommodation in the same apartment block. The tenant on social welfare has most of the rent paid for by the State, but the tenant who is working has to pay all the rent himself or herself.

I believe that State housing policy needs to be recast to encourage and support the maximum number of people to buy their own homes and to be self-sufficient in housing. Labour's "Begin to Buy" scheme meets those needs.

Among the Housing commitments in the Programme for Government is this one, which I welcome: "Legislation will be brought forward on foot of the recommendations of the All Party Committee on the Constitution on Property Rights". This refers to the report published three years ago, which effectively updates the old Kenny Report on Building Land and provides for the compulsory purchase of land at little more than "existing use value". I look forward to the publication of this legislation and I will be enquiring about its preparation when the Dáil returns in the autumn.

Closely related to housing is planning. Over the past ten years, almost one-third of Ireland's entire housing stock has been built. And the planning system has been adapted to facilitate this record level of construction.

New legislation was introduced to fast-track infrastructure projects. New Residential Density Guidelines were adopted to allow the kind of suburban apartment development that is typically to be found on the Stillorgan Road. Tax incentives were allowed which enabled investors to buy a cheap urban renewal property in Ballymahon and then be able to claim tax relief on every other rented property owned by the same investor. The planning laws were rewritten to give the advantage to developers and to make it as difficult as possible for local communities to control developments in their neighbourhoods.

State housing policy in Ireland needs to change. In many respects, our system of housing supports condemns people to continuing poverty.

People's frustration with the planning process is at the heart of the local environment movement. There is a sense that most developments are developer-led; that the planning authorities are on the side of the developer rather than the local community; that the law is skewed in favour of the developer; that the tent at the Galway Races is doing great business, notwithstanding the lessons of the tribunals.

One would have expected therefore that reform of the planning system would have been at the heart of a concord between the Green Party and Fianna Fáil. The Programme for Government is a big disappointment in this area. No abolition of the 20 euro fee to make a planning objection. No reversal of the legislation on infrastructure. No change in the restricted way in which City and County development plans are now made. No change in the law which allows developers to have private meetings with planners while making it increasingly difficult for local communities to have any such access to officialdom.

The failure on planning is repeated in waste management. The first and second Fianna Fáil/Ahern Governments transferred to City and County Managers the power to make waste management plans and to levy waste charges. No change is proposed in this arrangement. This means that the decision to locate an incinerator or a major waste dump will rest with the County Manager and not with the councillors who have been elected by the people.

> **This means that the decision to locate an incinerator or a major waste dump will rest with the County Manager and not with the councillors who have been elected by the people.**

It would appear from the Programme for Government that the pass has been sold on incineration. Firstly, there is no mention of any change in Government policy on incineration. This gives the green light, in every sense, to An Bord Pleanála to approve the Poolbeg incinerator. The absence of any reference to the planned incinerators for Carranstown, Co, Meath, and Ringaskiddy in Cork means that these facilities are to go ahead. Indeed, it is also likely that the, as yet unidentified, incinerator for the South-East will also proceed because, while the Programme for Government comes down strongly against landfill, there is no such option taken against burning waste.

All of this brings us to the sad state of local government in Ireland. Last week, Minister Gormley announced a consultative process on local government reform, with particular reference to the proposal to directly elect a City Mayor for Dublin. Consultation is always welcome, although in this case the subject matter has been well trawled in previous reports and initiatives on local government reform.

What is really curious about the Government's plans on this occasion is the timing. We are told that the Government "will introduce a directly elected Mayor for Dublin with executive powers by 2011". Why 2011? The local elections are scheduled for the summer of 2009 and they are now fixed, by law, at five yearly intervals. So, are we to have a separate election in 2011, which would put the term of office of the mayor out of line with the election of the councils or will the necessary legislation be introduced by 2011, with the actual election not then taking place until 2014?

Labour supports the introduction of directly elected mayors into our local government system, but it needs to be done now. Minister Gormley should accelerate the process and have the directly elected mayor for Dublin elected at the 2009 local elections.

Minister Gormley should accelerate the process and have the directly elected mayor for Dublin elected at the 2009 local elections.

Liz McManus TD, Labour Party
Spokesperson on Health

Prof Orla Hardiman, Consultant
Neurologist, Beaumont Hospital

Brian Hayes TD, Fine Gael Spokesperson on
Health and Children

Michael Scanlan, Secretary-General,
Department of Health and Children

Chapter 10

Reforming the Health Service

Health: The Debate is Over, the Debate Begins
Liz McManus TD
Labour Party Spokesperson on Health

We Should Be Cautious about Embracing Privatisation
Prof Orla Hardiman
Consultant Neurologist, Beaumont Hospital

No Thorough Analysis of Co-location
Brian Hayes TD
Fine Gael Spokesperson on Health and Children

Extra Investment in the Health Service is Not the Panacea
Michael Scanlan
Secretary-General, Department of Health and Children

Liz McManus TD

Labour Party Spokesperson on Health

Born in Montreal, Canada and educated at Holy Child Convent, Killiney and UCD (B.Arch). Formerly architect, first elected to Dáil Éireann for Wicklow in 1992. Minister of State at Dept. of Environment in "Rainbow" Coalition Govt. 1994-7. Has served on Wicklow Co. Council and Bray UDC. Founder of Bray Women's Refuge. Has been Labour Party spokesperson on Health since 2002 when she was elected Deputy Leader of the party. An accomplished writer, has won the Hennessy New Irish Writing Award, the Listowel Award and the Irish P.E.N. Award for her fiction. Published her first novel, Acts of Subversion, *in 1980.*

Health: The Debate is Over, the Debate Begins

The argument about co-location is over. The decision to sell off public lands to developers to build "for-profit" hospitals has now been made. We have the return of Mary Harney as Minister for Health. In fact, we have the return of the same Government albeit with minor changes. That is the context in which we are debating the future of health care. In my view, the real debate is only starting.

There is a need to provide about 2,300 extra hospital beds. Although this has been disputed by Professor Drumm, I believe that, as our population continues to grow and age, the case for additional capacity is irrefutable. The Labour Party has consistently argued that expanding capacity within the health service should be accompanied by fundamental reform of how health care is delivered.

The Government has decided to develop capacity using the developer-led approach of co-locating for-profit hospitals on public grounds. There are flaws to this approach which I will return to later. But, more than anything, it is an approach that creates an imperative to reform and – indeed to transform – the way that the health service is funded.

We are now facing a landscape of healthcare provision where public, voluntary and for-profit hospitals will be providing services. Unless we change the financial relationship between patients and these providers, market forces will inevitably determine that private patients will have better and speedier access to healthcare to an even more marked degree than currently pertains.

Last week it was revealed that 22,000 public patients are waiting for surgery or medical treatment in our hospitals. This is despite a promise in 2001 to eliminate waiting lists. The fact that 7,226 public

> Unless we change the financial relationship between patients and these providers, market forces will inevitably determine that private patients will have better and speedier access to healthcare to an even more marked degree than currently pertains.

patients have been waiting a year or more for treatment, a rise of 10 per cent in just eight months, is particularly shocking.

These are not just statistics. Each individual is someone who is sick, in some cases very seriously so, who cannot access the treatment they need. These patients wait while the health service that they have paid for struggles to keep up with the demands placed on it. In the main, the same does not hold for private patients.

A major health survey was carried out by the Labour Party at the beginning of the year. We found that a private patient is almost three times more likely than a public patient to be seen by a consultant within three months of referral.

- 84 per cent of private patients are seen within three months, compared to just 30 per cent of public patients.
- 98 per cent of private patients – virtually all – are seen within six months, compared to 58 per cent of public patients.

These statistics do translate into individual tragedies.

Most of us are no doubt familiar with the tragic circumstances of "Rosie". "Rosie" is a woman aged 40, terminally ill with bowel cancer, who has young children and who courageously went on radio to talk about her experience of a seven month delay before she had a colonoscopy which found a tumour. By then the cancer had spread. The day before she appeared on Liveline, she was getting chemotherapy alongside a man with the same diagnosis. He, too, had bowel cancer but had got his colonoscopy within three days of seeing his GP. He was a private patient. Like almost half of the Irish population, Rosie did not have health insurance.

The HSE has radio ads directed at alerting people to the early signs of colon cancer: "Early diagnosis can save lives," the radio ad says. But early diagnosis can only save lives if the services are there. Rosie, along with two million other Irish people, is treated as a public patient in the bottom half of a two-tier health system where the delays in accessing treatment can actually cut your life short.

Inequality underpins our health service sometimes in unexpected ways. For example, having a medical card can be a passport for chronically ill patients to avail of rehabilitation and therapeutic services. As a result, private patients suffering chronic long term illnesses often lose out when they do not have a medical card.

So, how do we ensure absolute equality for all patients? We need to eliminate differences between public patient and private patient. As one hospital consultant has said, "We need to ensure that a doctor is blind to a patient in the sense that income and insurance status is irrelevant and only their sickness matters."

Under the new government plans, income and insurance will be the determinants of which hospital the patient will attend. Co-location will divide rather than integrate the system. Let's be clear that co-located hospitals are "for-profit" hospitals. These are not private hospitals in the old, voluntary hospital sense. These are investor owned, for-profit hospitals. Their loyalty is to their shareholders.

There is an inherent cost involved, not just in tax breaks to these developers but also in the loss of up to €100 million per year to public hospitals. The Department of Finance, in its own memo dated October 2006, expressed its concerns about this policy in terms of financial cost, the loss of trained staff, the increase in private insurance premia and the failure to assess the land value issue.

Currently, every Irish citizen is entitled to free hospital care, subject in some cases to a small daily charge. Consultants' salaries and other costs are payable by the state. Yet half the population opts to pay by means of private health insurance for obvious reasons.

The patient who can pay will skip the queue and get access to assessment and treatment almost immediately. This "medical apartheid" actually encourages discrimination.

Patients without insurance or other means to pay must wait until a consultant is free to see them and then must wait for necessary facilities (beds, diagnostic equipment, and operating theatre time) to become available. The patient who can pay will skip the queue and get access to assessment and treatment almost immediately. This "medical apartheid" actually encourages discrimination. Consultants on a salary have no incentive to treat more public patients, but can boost their earnings if more people go private. Similarly, hospitals on fixed (and often inadequate) public sector budgets have no encouragement to take in more non-paying patients, but can charge fees for patients with money or insurance.

Minister Harney's determination to deliver public-only contracts for hospital consultants is only a partial solution and carries with it the seeds of increased division between public and private care. Indeed, Professor Drumm of the HSE expressed his concerns when he said: "We need to be extremely careful that we do not drive to the front gates of our hospitals and find the road left to the nice flowered structure with a fountain in front where those that can afford it go to that structure and someone else goes sheepishly in the other direction towards the HSE hospital."

Yet that is precisely what we are about to get: separate hospitals, separate doctors, separate patients, separate but not necessarily equal. Where a private patient has a choice of consultant, fixed appointments and personal attention, the public patient has no choice, must queue for hours and is more likely to be dealt with by a trainee doctor. The service for private patients is heavily subsidised: fees charged cover only half the true cost, the rest being covered by general exchequer contributions to the public health service in which private practice operates. It is further assisted by a reduction in income tax for all those paying health insurance premiums.

The important result is that, unless we end the parallel payment system, (salaries and budgets for public patients, fees and charges for insured patients), additional government resources for the health system cannot easily solve the overall crisis.

Over the last 20 years, while waiting lists were growing and the economy was doing well, the numbers opting for health insurance rose from 30 per cent of the population in 1982 to 51 per cent in 2007. Without reform, and if we continue with the Harney plan, the cost of insurance will rise. Private patients are to be asked to pay the full economic cost of their care in the co-located private hospital and this means an increase of 40 per cent, at least, in their current private health insurance.

We need a unified and properly funded health service that treats all patients equally based on medical need, not income. We need a first-class standard of medical treatment for all with a single payment structure. The government's approach makes this more difficult but not impossible.

I would like to set out a possible outline of how a universal model could work. Everyone would be enrolled for personal health insurance. Everyone would be able to choose the VHI, Quinn Insurance, Vivas, or any approved new entrants to the market. The state would pay premiums on behalf of those whose incomes fall below a threshold. The category "public patient" or "private patient" would be abolished. In the same way as it is illegal for a GP to treat medical card patients differently to private patients, it will be a legal requirement for hospitals to treat all patients equally.

Today, when a person who is privately insured needs an elective procedure, they have a choice of consultant, and of hospital. When the treatment is given and the procedure carried out, the health insurer pays the doctor and the hospital that actually treated the insured patient – in other words, money follows the patient. This system gives hospitals and doctors a strong incentive to treat patients and to provide them with a high level of care. It also encourages efficiency since both doctor and hospital know that they will only be paid the going rate by the insurance company for what they do. And it means that, on a global level, resources within the health service flow to where the patients actually are, rather than where bureaucratic budgeting systems think they might be.

Ultimately, the solution to providing both a better and fairer health service is to build a universal system of health insurance. This would ensure that everyone in the population has health insurance, and that the principle that "the money follows the patient" would apply across the health service. To develop the outline further the UHI system should have the following features:

Ultimately, the solution to providing both a better and fairer health service is to build a universal system of health insurance.

- Everyone would be obliged to hold health insurance.
- Those who cannot afford to pay for insurance would have their premium paid by the State. Some would have their premium partially subsidised. Others would continue to pay as at present.
- Insurance would cover GP and other services, as well as secondary and tertiary care.
- The State would regulate the minimum package of services which insurers would provide.
- Optional additional insurance could be sold to cover "hotel costs" but there would be a common standard of medical care available to all.
- Community rating would be a central part of the system.
- Everyone would be entitled to the same high quality of patient care.
- Doctors and hospitals would be paid in the same manner for all patients.
- Statutory protection would guarantee access to health care on an equal basis.

The outstanding benefit of this system is that as far as hospitals and GPs are concerned, there would be no difference between rich, middle income and poor patients. No matter how the insurance premium is paid, hospitals and practitioners would charge the same fees for everybody; there would be no public/private distinction between patients, and discrimination would be irrelevant and illegal.

Over the next five years and beyond we need to focus on the patient and the relationship between patient and doctor in hospitals. If we get that right and if we make it fair, we will transform the way health care is delivered. In my view, extending insurance to all is the best way to guarantee the fundamentals of a modern health service, that of quality, fairness and value for money. Other EU countries have recognised this for a long time and even remarkably some states in the US are now adopting a universal health insurance model. I believe it is time that we in Ireland joined them in taking that vital step forward.

Over the next five years and beyond we need to focus on the patient and the relationship between patient and doctor in hospitals. If we get that right and if we make it fair, we will transform the way health care is delivered. In my view, extending insurance to all is the best way to guarantee the fundamentals of a modern health service, that of quality, fairness and value for money.

Prof Orla Hardiman

Consultant Neurologist, Beaumount Hospital

Born in Dublin and educated at Coláiste Íosagáin, UCD (B.Sc. Hons., MB. BCh., BAO (Hons.) and MD 1992). Post-graduate training in Neurology and Neuropathology at St. Laurence's Hosp., Dublin. Chief Resident in Neurology at Harvard Neurology Program 1989. Fellowship training in Neuromuscular Disease at Mass. General Hospital and Harvard Medical School, Boston. Newman Scholar at UCD 1991 and appointed College Lecturer in Physiology 1994. Became a Fellow of Royal College of Physicians in Ireland 2001 and in 2004 the first Irish-based Neurologist of the American Academy of Neurology. She currently holds research grants from the HRB, ALS Association (USA) and Muscular Dystrophy Association (USA). She is the author of numerous research articles and a member of a number of national and international boards and advisory panels. She is known for her advocacy of health service development and is a founding member of the Neurological Alliance of Ireland and Doctors' Alliance for Better Healthcare

We Should Be Cautious about Embracing Privatisation

The problems in our health service have continued despite an overall increase in annual spending over the past seven years. As a result, there is a perception that the disappointing performance is due to bad management, poor regulation of hospital consultants and general waste of resources. The truth is that the long term implications of the draconian cutbacks that took place in the late 1980s, and the under-funding in the 1990s, continue to haunt us.

While reform is clearly required to reflect the changing demographics and evolving health problems of an ageing population, we are endemically inefficient, not because of a "black hole", but because we are working to the limits of our capacity within a system that was designed for a smaller population with different types of health problems.

Our problems have been compounded by the absence of a coherent, clearly defined long-term plan for our health service. Since the 2001 meeting in Ballymascanlon when the then Minister for Finance, Charlie McCreevy, publicly undermined the "Health Strategy, Quality and Fairness" plan, the trajectory of health policy has been unclear. The "Hanley" recommendations were quietly shelved after the 2002 election. Some of the "cost saving" aspects of the Hanley plan

> Our problems have been compounded by the absence of a coherent, clearly defined long-term plan for our health service.

are currently being implemented in the North East where the smaller hospitals are being downgraded. However, the necessary funding for concomitant expansion of larger regional centres has not been forthcoming and the net effect has been a decline in services in the region.

The subsequent devolution in 2005 of the operational elements of health away from the Department of Health and directly to the HSE added to the confusion, particularly as the HSE, comprising a combination of the former regional Health Boards and other bodies, is still evolving and currently comprises an opaque and labyrinthine bureaucracy. Add to this the public service employment ceiling which effectively prohibits new recruitment within the sector, despite a desperate need for more front line staff, and we have the all the ingredients for a first-class crisis.

And yet, it must be stated categorically that the overall quality of clinical service within the public health system is of a very high standard. But the experience of an Irish citizen who is trying to access appropriate care in a timely fashion within the public health system leaves a lot to be desired. People are genuinely angry about long delays and overcrowding in A&E, long waiting lists for hospital out patient appointments and the virtual impossibility of accessing beds for elective hospital admissions. They read the newspapers and are told that public hospitals are dangerous places. There is a perception that hospital consultants are lining their pockets and engaging in restrictive practices to protect their private practice.

So it is not really surprising that health care professionals, working under tremendous pressure at the frontline of an often hostile population, continue to feel misunderstood, disconnected and alienated from the management process which they feel should be supporting them.

Nor is it not really surprising that under these circumstances there has been a serious loss of confidence in the public health sector in Ireland. There is a widely held misconception that the two tiered system in health benefits those who can afford to pay. While it is true that private health insurance can speed up access to services, there is a belief that the quality of clinical care within the public system is inferior to the private sector.

The private sector (now known as the "independent sector") is marketed as being cleaner, more efficient, more "user friendly" and more accessible to those who can afford to pay. The hotel facilities are better in the smaller private hospitals when compared to the large public institutions. But there is really no evidence that the private sector can deliver superior clinical care.

And while there is considerable international evidence to sug-

And yet, it must be stated categorically that the overall quality of clinical service within the public health system is of a very high standard. But the experience of an Irish citizen who is trying to access appropriate care in a timely fashion within the public health system leaves a lot to be desired.

gest that the quality of clinical care is better in public facilities, the loss of confidence and breakdown of trust within the public sector is now extremely serious. Moreover, attempts by clinical professionals (particularly hospital consultants) to emphasise the need to protect the quality of clinical care within the public sector are often seen as "vested interests".

This combination of loss of confidence within the public sector, coupled with the breakdown of trust between senior health professionals and health managers has had an important and little discussed impact on how we will deliver health care in the future. Excluding health professionals from the management process means that qualitative metrics that depend on clinical experience are at grave risk of being cut out of the healthcare equation. We seem to be entering an era of "managerialism" in which the touchstone is "value for money", and where cost containment is one of the primary objectives.

This gradual shift in emphasis from a clinical metric to a financial "value for money" metric is reflected in the view that the HSE is taking in its role in delivering care. Rather than a health care provider, the HSE now views itself as a purchaser of healthcare. While purchasing will primarily take place within the public sector, there is nothing to stop services that were traditionally funded directly by the HSE being franchised out to the private sector, if the price is right. This includes the franchising of home care, services to private agencies, the leasing of beds for public patients in private nursing homes, the purchasing of cervical smear testing from overseas laboratories and the invitation of consortia to co-locate on public hospital property.

Rather than a health care provider, the HSE now views itself as a purchaser of healthcare.

It might be added that the existence of a ceiling in public sector employment can now become a justifiable mechanism by which the HSE can purchase services from the private sector. There is an obvious benefit from a financial and operational perspective, as the HSE can avoid taking on the added risks and burdens of cost of extra public sector salaries. In this scenario, there appears to be little appetite to establish a metric around clinical excellence, because healthcare has become a "commodity" that can be bought and sold, and the HSE is in the business of buying. And if the service looks like it provides value for money, it should be purchased.

But let me stop here for a moment to pose an important question. While the financial benefits of the current trajectory may be obvious, I wonder whether we as a society have really adequately considered and debated the implications of this approach. Where is the White Paper that outlines the risks and benefits of what is essentially a privatisation of the health service? Have we really identified what we believe constitutes value for money? For example, if the HSE becomes a purchaser of services, who will provide the quality assurance, and who ultimately will be accountable if things go wrong? Permit me to backtrack slightly.

We must first look at terms like "benefit" and "value for money". What exactly is being "purchased" for example? Let me start with a simple example-surgery. Operations are very easy things to measure, as are any procedures. They have a beginning, a middle and an end. We can look at the number of people on waiting lists, look at the number of operations done and calculate the "efficiency" of the service by measuring the numbers of people who are waiting for operations, the numbers of procedures done, the length of stay in hospital and the costs. It seems easy.

But it is actually a very incomplete measure of a health service for reasons that I will explain. And the experience of the National Treatment Purchase Fund would suggest that purchasing operations for public patients from the private sector is a very costly business

Why are waiting lists for operations a poor measure of a health service? Well, most people think that going to hospital means having an operation. But it may surprise you to find that 80 per cent of people admitted through A&E have a condition that does not require an operation and 70 per cent of all public hospital admissions are for non-surgical problems. The majority of these people have a condition that must be managed, but that cannot be cured. They end up in hospital because they experience an acute worsening of their long-term illness. They get a bit better with treatment and go home again.

What constitutes "value for money" when the bulk of your budget is spent managing a chronic disease? Is it patient satisfaction?

So the question is – how should you measure the outcome for these sorts of patients? What constitutes "value for money" when the bulk of your budget is spent managing a chronic disease? Is it patient satisfaction? Although an important and often neglected measure within the public sector, it is not the only one, and in a more scientific environment it is a notoriously unreliable measure!

Is it the number of relapses or exacerbations or complications that require hospitalisations each year? Is it the length of stay in hospital? It might surprise you to find that 40 per cent of bed days in Irish hospitals are taken up by only 5 per cent of patients. Most people who go into Irish hospitals stay there for a much shorter time than they would have for the same condition 10 years ago. So by these criteria, the Irish public sector is performing very well from an efficiency perspective. But how reliable a measure is this of overall hospital efficiency? Maybe we are sending people home too early. Maybe some of these people would be better managed at home if we had the resources (but remember, we have an employment ceiling for public sector, so we can't employ staff in the public sector to manage people at home. Hence the purchase by the HSE of expensive private initiatives like "Hospital in the Home").

Another way to measure the overall impact of healthcare would be to look at outcomes at a population level – like the numbers of reported cancers (through the National Cancer Registry), or the number of deaths from a specific condition like heart disease or stroke. We can attempt to modify our health system to cater for these if the figures look like they are too high. This is the basis upon which we have built our National Cancer Strategy and our National Cardiovascular Strategy. These public population-based interventions are working well, but it is difficult to use population-based datasets to fine-tune the provision of specific services, particularly at hospital level and we still need metrics to measure how these people are faring when they are managed on a day to day basis. Besides, we don't really have adequate data on the frequency of most conditions, as collection of clinical material is limited by the Data Protection Act, which requires that informed consent is obtained from all patients whose details are collected.

So, I think that at present we have two major problems in determining how we make sure we are getting value for money in our health system. Firstly, we don't really know what the denominator is for any condition within our health service. And secondly, we don't really have a clear set of clinical outcome measures that determine the effectiveness of our "investment". So how can we then establish whether the public sector is being efficient or not?

And, from the perspective of the beleaguered public health system, if the HSE is mandated to purchase services and the principal aim is to provide "value for money" with minimal financial risk, what chance has the public sector in competing with the private sector for finite public funds, when there is a general assumption that the public sector is already inefficient and embargoed from further expansion, and yet there are no measures to prove this?

Starved of the necessary funding for development because an increasing number of services are being bought from the private sector with public funds, the public sector will inevitably deteriorate. Services that are not provided by the private sector will remain within the public domain, but these will suffer because of insufficient investment and the quality of care, which remains of high standard at present, will surely decline.

And now let us look at the private sector. It is true that private medicine plays an important role in the Irish health care system, albeit not the one that was originally envisaged when the VHI was set up some 50 years ago. Private healthcare works well if you need an uncomplicated operation that is not an emergency. But private medicine, in its current format in Ireland, is just too small to be effective in managing complex diseases like most cancers and many types of

> **Services that are not provided by the private sector will remain within the public domain, but these will suffer because of insufficient investment and the quality of care, which remains of high standard at present, will surely decline.**

surgery. These are expensive conditions that require large teams of experienced professionals, and it is just not economically viable for the private sector to engage with them. Private healthcare is generally risk-averse, and will either avoid complex chronic disease, or will charge a significant premium to manage it. Private healthcare is also unlikely to provide 24 hour emergency cover unless provided with major financial incentives, which will of course drive up costs. And private health care at present in Ireland is not really subjected to any form of formal clinical audit or public accountability.

The recent introduction of the concept of profit into Irish healthcare risks distorting the primary objective of clinical excellence, and ultimately this has a negative impact on quality of care. Profit is a new element in Irish healthcare. And we ignore this at our peril. This is because outcomes in a "for-profit" environment are measured both in terms of a pre-defined clinical outcome from which a profit can be generated. The juxtaposing of a financial incentive with a qualitative metric like clinical outcome cannot but generate a conflict which has a clear potential to put the quality of patient care at risk. So at the very least, we should be cautious about embracing a process of privatisation that involves profit within the Irish health system.

Profit is a new element in Irish healthcare. And we ignore this at our peril.

So, what are the main caveats? Firstly, there is the worry that public funds will be used to purchase "for-profit" private health care instead of building capacity with the public sector. There is the additional worry that public hospitals will no longer be permitted to treat private patients, and will lose income upon which they depend for their survival. Hospitals are currently permitted to bill the private sector for private patients, albeit at a reduced rate. Shutting down this source of funding will have very serious implications for the large teaching hospitals.

Secondly, there is incontrovertible evidence that the introduction of "for-profit" health care will increase costs for users. Not only will private patients, through their third party providers, be required to pay the full economic cost of private care, but the costs of care in the private sector will include a profit margin, accounting and administration charges, marketing charges, billing charges and charges to support the legal fees of the for-profit institution.

And while this may reflect a policy of a low-tax environment (to shift the cost from the public purse to the private individual) it is likely that over time, a scenario similar to that in the US will prevail, in which those without health insurance are inadequately treated, and those with insurance will pay exorbitantly high premiums for care that, at best, will be equivalent to the current level of care in the public sector and, at worst, much inferior.

In the absence of clearly defined processes of accountability, the introduction of "for-profit" healthcare runs the risk of forcing a general decline in the quality of care. This is because the qualitative metric is devalued in a for-profit environment. Clinical management is dictated by inflexible algorithms based on a rigid return of investment analysis that is vigorously enforced by third party providers. I speak from bitter experience, having worked in the United States under Managed Care in the early 1990s.

We know that the current structures for audit and clinical governance are poor across the public sector, but this has been recognised and a programme of reform is underway. No such process is currently required within the private sector and, even more worrying, the HSE does not seem to recognise that the quality control of services it purchases from the private sector is part of its remit. The track record of HSE purchasing from the private sector has been poor in terms of both ensuring quality and value for money. We need to look no further than the scandal of private nursing homes.

Now, while I have grave concerns about the privatisation of the public health service in Ireland, I believe that there is an important role for private health care in Ireland. Irish people want to have a choice, but I believe that the private sector must be allowed to grow in the context of a robust and well-developed public system. Taking money out of the public health system to attract and support the private sector carries substantial risks for our citizens.

And with hindsight, perhaps it might have been better to have the debate about privatisation before the legislation was enacted, rather than afterwards.

But this is not an ideological argument. I believe that everybody wants an equitable quality-driven health service. I believe that our new Government and the current Minister for Health are motivated by what they see as the most pragmatic approach to a complicated and seemingly intractable problem. I believe that, if we are going to become efficient, we must have accurate ways of measuring this. I believe that we must work hard within both the public and private sectors to establish meaningful outcome measures for clinical activity so that "value for money" can be more accurately measured.

But we must not lose sight of the bigger picture. The vast bulk of health care must continue to be delivered by the public sector. The ideal should be that access to such care is based on clinical need and not on ability to pay. Increasing the ease of access to GPs and increasing the scope of activities within primary care is an important reform that is already being introduced by the HSE.

The HSE itself must also be streamlined and transparent in its operations. It is not good enough that it should act solely as a purchaser of services, be it in the public or private sector. The HSE must

But we must not lose sight of the bigger picture. The vast bulk of health care must continue to be delivered by the public sector. The ideal should be that access to such care is based on clinical need and not on ability to pay.

The HSE itself must also be streamlined and transparent in its operations. It is not good enough that it should act solely as a purchaser of services, be it in the public or private sector.

be accountable for the quality of what is purchased. But qualitative metrics require clinical expertise and the HSE must engage with health care professionals and patient advocates to develop appropriate measures.

And finally, there are two imperatives with respect to the new co-located hospitals. First, the funding stream for public hospitals should not be jeopardised. There will not be a "one for one" transfer from public to private beds, and the majority of costly and complex clinical work will continue to take place in the public hospital. And second, contractual negotiations with the private sector must focus on the key elements of quality of clinical care, equity of access, and, above all, clinical accountability.

Brian Hayes TD

Fine Gael Spokesperson on Health and Children

Born in Dublin and educated at St. Joseph's College, Ballinasloe, Maynooth College (BA) and TCD (HdipEd). Formerly secondary school teacher and National Youth and Education Officer Fine Gael, first elected to Dáil Éireann in 1997. Served in Seanad Éireann 1995-7 and as FG Seanad leader 2002-7. Re-elected to Dáil for Dublin South-West in May 2007.

No Thorough Analysis of Co-location

On any objective basis, Gordon Brown has made a good start in taking over from Tony Blair. A fresh cabinet with lots of new faces allied with a clear intent to change the way cabinet decisions are made in Britain, has helped to change the fortunes of his party, at least in the short term. What Prime Minister Brown has had to say about parliamentary accountability is very interesting. He has instructed ministers not to bypass parliament and to involve themselves in proper parliamentary consultation on all major issues. Statements on Government policy are to be made in Parliament where they can be scrutinised and questioned. Parliament itself is to be given new powers, effectively keeping a check on the power of the executive.

All of this is in marked contrast to the state of our own parliamentary democracy. Under recent Governments, the Dáil has become a rubber stamp. Major public policy positions are now announced at press conferences with Ministers issuing great tablets of wisdom as the Dáil is bypassed and ignored. When a member of the Dáil, either opposition or Government deputy, attempts to raise the latest announcement they are told that they are out of order. I have noticed in recent years that the more controversial announcements are normally left to when the Dáil is in recess. Unfortunately, decision making in our state is now the sole preserve of the executive as the Dáil is treated as an inconvenient debating chamber unable, and sometimes unwilling, to scrutinise the full impact of major public policy positions. What, I hear you ask, has this got to do with the health service and our plans for the future?

In fact, it has everything to do with the quality of decision making in Ireland and the considerable need for Dáil consultation and approval. Decentralisation, electronic voting, co-location, are all examples of a form of decision making which I believe is fundamentally flawed. Each of these decisions is characterised by a high level of self confidence in the capacity of one person to take bold decisive steps.

> Under recent Governments, the Dáil has become a rubber stamp. Major public policy positions are now announced at press conferences with Ministers issuing great tablets of wisdom as the Dáil is bypassed and ignored.

And, of course, once a decision of this nature is taken the decision itelf becomes sacrosanct. The personal and political ego of the decision taker becomes inextricably linked with the decision itself. The subsequent debate is all about defending the decision. After the blood transfusion scandal, after the medical negligence cases, after PPARS, after the nursing home saga one might have expected the Government and its ministers to reflect on their own decision making procedures.

So let us look at the decision to co-locate private hospitals on public hospital grounds. I think all of us will agree that co-location is a major health policy issue, possibly the most significant policy initiative in our hospital system ever. Co-location was obviously going to arouse debate and controversy which it certainly has. Above all, I would argue very strongly that co-location is not a simple matter; it raises very complex issues. It deserved a decision making process commensurate with the complexity of the issue. The aggressive manner in which co-location is being pursued reminds me very much of a driver exceeding the speed limit in a dense fog. I believe co-location warranted the following steps.

First, there should have been a Green Paper setting forward the Government's proposal. This should have been followed by a structured public debate where all interested parties would be asked to contribute. A full financial cost/benefit analysis should have been undertaken. This should have involved the Department of Finance, the Department of Health and the HSE. It is inexcusable that the only value for money study of co-location was delivered to the Dept of Health just a few weeks ago. That's two years after the decision was taken. This study has not yet been made available to the Dáil or to the public. There has been no publication of any internal discussion documents on co-location which may have been carried out by any government department or other government agency. We do not know if any such studies exist.

It is also clear that the Minister of Health never asked the HSE for its formal opinion on co-location. Does anyone seriously believe this is the way to make good decisions in the area of health policy? Indeed the Chief Executive of the HSE, Professor Drumm, is on the record as saying that he believes no additional acute hospital beds are required. Yet, he and the HSE are obliged to oversee the process of bringing almost 1,000 new beds into the system. The whole process should have concluded with a White Paper, followed by specific legislation and an appropriate supervisory mechanism. None of this was done.

Any objective analysis of the co-location decision would have to admit that the decision was taken in a knowledge vacuum. The deci-

It is also clear that the Minister of Health never asked the HSE for its formal opinion on co-location. Does anyone seriously believe this is the way to make good decisions in the area of health policy?

sion was not taken on a thorough analysis of the pros and cons of the case. The decision was based on an emotional attachment to a particular view of health care provision. Even the argument that it will deliver beds quicker doesn't stand up to scrutiny. The best estimate for delivery is 2011, six years after the decision was made-hardly a world record in terms of delivery!

Moving from the decision itself, I now want to examine the implementation of that decision. The implementation of the decision is also clouded in secrecy. I want to put down a marker here. There must be no secret deals on public lands; there must be no secret deals with taxpayers' money. This Government has already shown a liking for secret deals. Speaking in the Dáil on June 26 on a Fine Gael motion opposing co-location, the Minister said: "All details in respect of each site, including the financing will be a matter of public information". I intend to hold the minister to that commitment. There must be no hiding behind the politically useful formula that some contracts are "commercial sensitive".

I want to put down a marker here. There must be no secret deals on public lands; there must be no secret deals with taxpayers' money.

The public are entitled to know the full details surrounding the valuation and leasing of each site. The public are entitled to know the full details of the contract between the private developers and the HSE. The public are entitled to know the details of the service level contracts which will be put in place between the private operator and the HSE. They are entitled to know the insurance liabilities, if any, arising for these private hospitals. They are entitled to know the supervision and inspection regime which will be put in place. The beneficial owners of each consortium should also be available to public scrutiny as should information regarding their right to sell their interest to third parties in the years ahead.

The unregulated rapid expansion of private, for-profit medicine carries huge risk for the future. Yet we plough ahead regardless. I seriously doubt that the Irish public supports this radical shift in policy. In fact, a majority of TDs elected to this the 30th Dáil had during and before the recent election campaign, stated positions against co-location. And still, the decision remains despite the fact that there is no popular mandate for such a policy. It's not democracy as we know it.

Where major public policy issues are at stake, I believe the decision making process itself should be a coherent, rational process. That process should involve politicians, public service, professional and other interested parties and the wider public in a well-structured debate and consideration of the proposal. This was not done in the case of the National Children's Hospital. This was not done in the case of co-location and this is not being done as regards the re-organisation of hospital services in the North East and the Mid West regions.

I believe the quality of the decision making process and the quality of the implementation process will themselves have a profound impact on the success or otherwise of any policy initiative. Taking major policy decisions in isolation and subsequently developing the arguments in favour of the decision dramatically increases the risk of creating a mess.

The A&E crisis, MRSA, waiting lists, the number of patients on trollies and the consultant's contract are all headline grabbing issues which take up so much time in the analysis of our health service. Health was the big issue in the context of the recent election campaign. It was raised on the majority of doorsteps and, from polling data, it topped the list of voters' concerns. While voters said they were concerned about the health service, I am very doubtful that the issue determined voters' choice of party or candidate at a critical moment in the election campaign.

When I was asked the question, what are the priorities for the next five years in terms of health policy, I believe the single most important issue is prevention and how we can, through primary health care and public health policy, change attitudes and behavior. We need to do more as a society to prevent people from going to hospital and living healthier lives in the choices that they make in terms of diet, exercise and lifestyles.

The problems connected with alcohol abuse have dramatic and real consequences for the ability of the Irish healthcare system to deliver an effective service.

I believe that this country is in denial when it comes to the issue of alcohol abuse. The problems connected with alcohol abuse have dramatic and real consequences for the ability of the Irish healthcare system to deliver an effective service. In our debate on healthcare, frequently the issue of alcohol is a taboo subject and its costs to the health care budget and to life outcomes are ignored.

Our prosperity in recent years has been matched by a dramatic increase in the consumption of alcohol in all age groups and in all social classes in this country. I think President Mary McAleese was correct some months ago when she spoke about "the embedded cultural attitude" to alcohol within this country. I believe that attitude must be countered and turned around if we are going to create a healthier society and a more efficient health care system.

It is reckoned that every weekend in A&E departments all over the country between 70 per cent and 80 per cent of admissions are alcohol related. Clearly, this is putting considerable pressure on acute care as nurses and doctors have to work in sometimes appalling circumstances. But look at the knock on effects of this in terms of anti social behavior, sexual assaults, unwanted pregnancies, domestic violence, child neglect, sexually transmitted disease, absenteeism, road deaths, to name but a few. We are paying a high price for our tolerance of a drinking culture that is now out of control.

In 2004, the Strategic Taskforce on Alcohol conducted an in-depth analysis of the cost to the state in terms of alcohol-related problems. It concluded, and it was a conservative estimate, that the state picks up a bill of €3 billion a year, just to deal with many alcohol-related problems. The cost to the health service was estimated to be half a billion euro.

The report noted that Ireland has the highest level of binge drinkers, with 58 per cent of all drinking sessions involving men ending up as binge sessions and 30 per cent for women. It states that alcohol-related mortality has increased. In fact in Ireland, between 1992 and 2002, over 14,000 people died from the following five main alcohol leading causes:

- Cancers related to alcohol such as mouth and liver cancer,

- Alcohol chronic conditions such as alcohol abuse,

- Chronic liver disease and cirrhosis,

- Alcohol acute conditions such as alcohol poisoning, and

- Suicide.

Furthermore, alcohol is estimated to be involved in 40 per cent of road deaths, 30 per cent of road accidents and 37 per cent of all drownings. The Report, and I would remind you we are talking about 2004, estimated that nearly €6 billion of personal income per year is spent on alcohol in Ireland. That represents on average just short of €2,000 spent per year on alcohol for every person in this country over the age of 15 years.

I believe it is time that we reappraised our attitude to alcohol in Ireland, and crucially, politicians must show some leadership on the issue. It is my view that a total ban on drinks advertising and promotion should now be considered, as a clear signal that we are serious about changing public attitudes and ultimately personal behavior. I believe that this action would help in turning the tide towards responsible drinking and thereby relieve the constant burden that is being placed on our health services. To date, politicians have refused to confront the advertising and promotional juggernaut of the drinks industry, which represents €65 million annually. This was seen when the Government refused to introduce an outright ban on the promotion of alcohol in sports involving persons under 18 years of age. A voluntary code was put in its place.

This money is not being spent for the good of nation. RTÉ and all media outlets in this country depend upon the drinks industry in terms of selling space and advertising products. This will be a difficult issue to confront, at every level of Irish society, because vast sums of money are spent in promoting drink. It will be particularly difficult for sporting groups at a national and local level, because

... the state picks up a bill of €3 billion a year, just to deal with many alcohol-related problems. The cost to the health service was estimated to be half a billion euro.

There is, however, something unnatural and crass about sporting bodies having to go cap in hand to the drinks industry for funds, when the activities they are promoting are the counter opposite to the world of excessive or binge drinking.

sponsorship of sport by the drinks industry represents such a rich vein of funding for many organisations. There is, however, something unnatural and crass about sporting bodies having to go cap in hand to the drinks industry for funds, when the activities they are promoting are the counter opposite to the world of excessive or binge drinking. The millions poured into sport by the drinks industry has a pay-off; otherwise there would be no investment.

I agree with the conclusions reached by the Department of Health's report on the impact of alcohol advertising on teenagers in Ireland, published in 2001. The Report's authors concluded that the "selling" aspects of alcoholic advertisements are all to do with linking alcohol to positive images of desirable lifestyles.

The World Health Organisation has said that alcohol represents a major public health problem globally. It certainly represents a problem in this country. We have shown that when strong action is taken against drink driving, with the introduction of random breath testing for instance, that behavior does change. We need to change attitudes to drink as a key public health issue and a good start would be banning the advertising and promotion of alcohol.

Michael Scanlan

Secretary-General, Department of Health and Children

Born in Dublin and educated at Templeogue College, Dublin. Executive Officer, civil service 1973. Dept. of Public Service 1979-93, Secretary to the Gleeson Report on public sector pay 1993, Secretary to the Buckley Report on public sector pay and conditions 1998, Assistant Secretary-General Dept. of Finance 2000-5 and appointed Secretary-General Dept. of Health and Children in 2005.

Extra Investment in the Health Service is Not the Panacea

Any discussion about health service reform has to start and end with people – the people who use the health service, the people who work in the health service and the people who pay for the health service. It is essential, in developing and implementing the reform programme, that we always retain a strong patient/client focus. We also need to recognise that, despite the developments in technology and drugs, health services are essentially delivered by the people who work in the health sector. Finally, we need to recognise that resources are finite, regardless of how a health system is funded. We all have an interest in ensuring these resources are used to best effect.

> ... we need to recognise that resources are finite, regardless of how a health system is funded.

I propose, in this paper, to say something about what we should expect from our health service or, expressed another way, what performance indicators we should set for the health service. I will then discuss briefly a few key drivers of the health reform programme.

A Focus on Inputs is No Longer Acceptable

Much of the public debate about health tends to focus on inputs – the need for extra funding, beds, consultants, nurses, etc. It was probably legitimate at one time to measure success by reference to the scale of extra investment secured for health. For many years, the economy did not generate the wealth required to support significant investment in our public services. As the economy started to grow and the resources invested in public services were increased, there was probably an expectation that all would be well. We now know that substantial extra investment is not the panacea.

The National and Economic Social Council (NESC) has suggested that Ireland could make much better use of the existing resources being devoted to health and concluded that "we need to rely more on the improved use of resources to make the case for additional resources, rather than the other way around".

Measuring Outputs is Better...

More recently, we have tried, with some success, to shift the focus to outputs. A focus on measurable outputs helps to demonstrate what the HSE is delivering in return for the funding being provided by taxpayers. It starts to address the perception that health spending is a "black hole". The HSE's annual Service Plan and the annual Output Statements that each Minister now has to provide to the Oireachtas should help to improve the quantum and quality of the output data.

... But is Not Enough

However, measuring outputs alone fails to capture other important issues such as quality, timeliness and consistency. We need to focus on outcomes such as life expectancy, five-year cancer survival rates and numbers of older people living independently at home.

Safe and effective care is also good value care – poor quality leads to complications and the need for additional care, which raises costs substantially. International evidence suggests that good hospital management, for example, usually results in efficient use of resources and high quality patient care.

We need to identify and address geographic inconsistencies in access to services, differences in hospital admission rates and length of hospital stay, variations in clinical practices and in morbidity and mortality. One of the most significant issues facing cancer services, for example, is the variation in survival rates within Ireland . On the other hand, there are many examples of good practice in service design and delivery around the country and the reform programme offers the scope to spread these system-wide.

We need to define what we expect from our health services. If we want to debate how our health service is performing, we first need to say what we expect our health services to deliver.

We need to define what we expect from our health services. If we want to debate how our health service is performing, we first need to say what we expect our health services to deliver. I want to offer you one possible performance framework. I have kept it short and used only a limited number of objectives in order to give a clearer sense of the key priorities under each heading.

An Overall Performance Framework

I would suggest that the first objective should be: "To keep people healthy". A core aim of health policy should be to improve the health and well-being of the population of Ireland. This would encompass issues such as:

- Increasing healthy behaviours/lifestyles;
- A focus on prevention and early detection;
- Reducing health inequalities and, in particular, improving the health status of vulnerable groups; and
- Providing children with a healthy start to life and helping older people, persons with disabilities and people affected by mental illness to live as independently as possible.

A second objective should be "To provide the health care people need". A core function of the heath services has to be the provision of services to those in need of them, with a focus on timeliness, geographic location and equity. This would encompass issues such as:

A core function of the heath services has to be the provision of services to those in need of them, with a focus on timeliness, geographic location and equity.

- Access to emergency care without delay;
- Shorter waiting times;
- Providing services as close to patients as possible; and
- Fair access to services.

A third objective should be "To deliver high quality services". The services provided have to be safe, consistent and effective. This would encompass issues such as:

- Providing care in the right setting;
- Integrated service delivery;
- High quality clinical treatment; and
- Consistency of treatment/care and outcomes.

Finally, the fourth objective should be "To get best value from health system resources". Our health system, like health systems world-wide, is faced with the need to deliver better value for the resources made available. This would encompass issues such as:

- Strong corporate and clinical governance;
- Sound resource and financial management;
- Skilled motivated staff working in an innovative environment,
- Sustainability.

Clearly, this is only one way of expressing what we expect from our health services. Nor would I claim any credit for it. You will see that it is very similar to the four national goals outlined in the 2001 Health Strategy and that it is consistent with the HSE's Transformation Pro-gramme. However, I offer it as a reasonable starting point for an in-formed debate about what the health reform programme needs to deliver.

Priority Drivers of Reform

The health reform programme represents an enormous undertaking. It involves one quarter of all Government expenditure, over 100,000 staff and the delivery of a huge range of different services for very large numbers of people from one end of the country to the other. It has to be rolled out while simultaneously maintaining and developing services. What then should we focus on to drive the reform programme? Clearly, there are many elements to choose from but I have selected five, as follows:

1. The importance of information;
2. Chronic disease management;
3. Patient empowerment;
4. Changes in work practices and behaviours; and
5. Building credibility and confidence.

Information

Although much of the focus on health reform in recent years has been on structural reform, I would suggest that information is even more important than structures. All health care systems depend upon, and indeed run on, good information. Good information is essential to drive improvements in safety, efficiency, quality, effectiveness and sustainability, and to evaluate the performance of the health system.

> **Although much of the focus on health reform in recent years has been on structural reform, I would suggest that information is even more important than structures.**

The most effective and reliable means of collecting health information is as a by-product of actual service delivery, rather than as an optional extra. The focus has to be on patient services and helping the professionals providing those services. One of the critical shortcomings of modern health care is the lack of a consistent ability to get critical clinical information to the doctor or health professional at the point of care.

We don't have to wait for perfect information. Nothing will drive improvements in information faster than making existing information widely available. Making even relatively basic information available stimulates improvements in quality and efficiency. One only has to look at the hygiene audits and the measurement of waiting times in Emergency (A&E) Departments to see the power of information collection, dissemination and publication.

We need to harness the potential of ICT enabled health care. The technology is possibly the easiest piece of this: two of the more important elements are information governance and standards. Work on a Health Information Bill is underway in the Department and HIQA will have a lead role in developing information standards. We will also need to work with the HSE to ensure that information planning is integrated with overall health service planning and delivery.

Chronic Disease Management

In Ireland, as in other countries, acute hospital care gets all the publicity even though chronic conditions account for most of the cost. The international evidence is that approximately three-quarters of health-care spending is related to chronic diseases. In the UK, patients with chronic illness or complications account for some 80 per cent of GP consultations and use over 60 per cent of hospital bed days. Almost 60 per cent of the disease burden in Europe is accounted for by seven leading risk factors: high blood pressure, tobacco, alcohol, high blood cholesterol, over-weight, low fruit and vegetable intake, and physical inactivity. In addition, there are strong interrelationships between physical and mental health with both related through common determinants such as poor housing, poor nutrition or poor education, or common risk factors such as alcohol.

A recently adopted World Health Organisation strategy for chronic disease recommended that countries adopt an integrated strategy which includes population level, health promotion/disease prevention and targeted chronic disease management programmes that focus on individuals at high risk. Leading EU countries are now following this approach and the WHO are working with a small number of Member States, including Ireland, to set out the components of an integrated chronic disease policy. The Department is currently developing a chronic disease policy framework which will focus on the full cycle of care and on maximising self-care and minimising admissions to acute hospitals.

Patient Empowerment

Empowered patients often experience better health outcomes at lower costs to the health system. Effective patient/user empowerment would see individuals taking co-responsibility for their health outcomes; would provide an appropriate counter-balance to the views of health care providers in the planning and development of services; would help to identify unmet needs; would increase understanding of local health issues and identify new approaches to tackling them; and would help to quality assure our services.

There are many ways in which patients and the public are already involved in policy development, and in service planning and delivery. We have consumer panels, community workers, advocacy groups, social partnership structures, regional forums and complaints

Almost 60 per cent of the disease burden in Europe is accounted for by seven leading risk factors: high blood pressure, tobacco, alcohol, high blood cholesterol, over-weight, low fruit and vegetable intake, and physical inactivity. In addition, there are strong inter-relationships between physical and mental health with both related through common determinants such as poor housing, poor nutrition or poor education, or common risk factors such as alcohol.

procedures, to name just a few. However, more needs to be achieved before we can say that our services are truly person-centred. The Department is currently reviewing, with the HSE, how to enhance the effectiveness of the health services' engagement with the public.

Changes in Work Practices and Behaviours

Securing changes in health service employees' working regimes, skill mix and behaviours is a crucial part of the reform programme. Effective chronic disease management programmes will require good business processes such as care protocols and data collection, analysis and feed-back systems. It will also require an environment which helps GPs and other professionals to change and trusts them to do so.

The provision of timely and high quality clinical care will require consultants working in teams and within a medical hierarchy to deliver care personally to patients over an extended working day. It will also require the appointment of extra hospital and community-based consultants as well as consultant leadership of, and participation in, the reform programme.

The settlement terms in the recent dispute with nurses envisage the development of a different role for nurses which would deliver significant added-value to the health service. They present an opportunity to address issues such as more cost-effective and appropriate skill mix, nurse staffing ratios, enhanced duties, and more efficient rosters in a way which would provide an expanded role for nursing and a much better configuration and deployment of our nursing resources.

We need to build confidence in the health service among the public, at political level, in the media and among our staff. Constant criticism of the health service can affect staff morale and, ultimately, impact on the quality of patient care provided.

Building Credibility and Confidence

We need to build confidence in the health service among the public, at political level, in the media and among our staff. Constant criticism of the health service can affect staff morale and, ultimately, impact on the quality of patient care provided. While it is necessary and appropriate to question and challenge the reform process, it is essential also to recognise and acknowledge the progress being made.

Very often those working in the health service seem to highlight deficiencies in their part of the service in the expectation that this is the best way of securing extra funding and staff. Private organisations do the opposite – they talk up their service to build a positive image which will attract more customers. We are working with the HSE to develop an approach to investment which rewards innovation and success rather than loud cries for more of the same.

I believe that people working in the health service want to be part of a high-performing organisation and want to take pride in their work. The reform programme offers a unique opportunity to harness that good will and to combine the local knowledge of those at the front line, who know what changes are required to deliver better services, with the overall strategic approach which the HSE can bring to bear as a single national delivery agency.

The best way of building confidence in our health service is to deliver results. Operational management of the health system should concentrate on short-term deliverable changes which are consistent with overall policy. There is a need to tell people what they can expect to see incrementally over time, to focus on what has to happen to get us there and to deliver demonstrable changes. This would build trust and, thereby, engagement in the reform process. Small changes, delivered over short time horizons, which are consistent with the overall reform objectives would be a very powerful way of creating the necessary confidence. Put another way, we should reach for the low-hanging fruit instead of trying to boil the ocean!

The best way of building confidence in our health service is to deliver results.

We Are Not Alone

Health systems around the world are facing similar challenges to us – rising costs, demographic pressures, an increased burden of disease, expensive new technologies and treatments. Worldwide quality is poor or inconsistent and access in many countries is inadequate. Other health systems recognise they cannot continue with a "more of the same" approach given demographic and disease prevalence trends.

Eamon Ó Cuív TD, Minister for
Community, Rural and Gaeltacht Affairs

Donal Connell, Chief Executive, An Post

Catherine Buckley, National
President, Macra na Feirme

Chapter 11

Developing Life in Rural Ireland

To Develop Life in Rural Ireland You Need People
EAMON Ó CUÍV TD
Minister for Community, Rural and Gaeltacht Affairs

An Post – Part of the Solution, Not Part of the Problem
DONAL CONNELL
Chief Executive, An Post

Voluntary and Community Organisations Are Essential
CATHERINE BUCKLEY
National President, Macra na Feirme

Eamon Ó Cuív TD

Minister for Community, Rural and Gaeltacht Affairs

Born in Dublin and educated at Oatlands College, Mount Merrion and UCD (B.Sc.). Formerly Gaeltacht Co-op manager, first elected to Dáil Éireann 1992. Member of Seanad Éireann 1989-92. Minister of State for Arts, Heritage, Gaeltacht and the Islands 1997-2001 and Minister of State for Agriculture, Food and Rural Dev. 2001-2. Appointed Minister for Community, Rural and Gaeltacht Affairs in 2002 and reappointed to this portfolio following the election of May 2007. Member of Galway Co. Council 1991-7

To Develop Life in Rural Ireland
You Need People

As a Government Minister, I am, to my knowledge, the only Minister of Rural Development in the European Union who is not also a Minister of Agriculture and this shows that the Irish Government believes:

1. That both rural development and agriculture and fisheries are so significant that two separate Cabinet Ministers should have responsibilities for these important issues and

2. That rural development, though complementary, is a separate issue from the industry of agriculture.

Looking at the principal policy parameters within which Government operates, there is a clear mission to develop rural communities.

Looking at the principal policy parameters within which Government operates, there is a clear mission to develop rural communities. At European Union level, one of the main objectives in supporting rural development as set out in Article 4.1 (c) of the 2005 Rural Development Regulation is: "improving the quality of life in rural areas and encouraging diversification of the rural economy." At home, the Government's own White Paper on Rural Development sets out as a key part of its Future Vision and Policy Agenda that:

> The Government is committed to ensuring the economic and social well-being of rural communities, to providing the conditions for a meaningful and fulfilling life for all people living in rural areas and to striving to achieve a rural Ireland in which there will be vibrant sustainable communities...

According to the new Programme for Government, "Vibrant rural communities are vital to the future of our nation." This is the clear policy framework within which this Government and I as Minister must operate.

To explain how my own views on rural and agriculture development developed over the years and my journey to the firm belief in the importance of both, I would like to give you a very short synopsis of my own background. I was born, brought up and educated in the city of Dublin, as were both my parents and one grandparent. Three of my grandparents came to Dublin in the late nineteenth century and none of them pursued careers related to agriculture.

However, having completed university and having an interest in the Irish language which is mainly spoken as a community language on the west coast of Ireland, at the age of 23 I became a Farmers' Co-Op Manager in a small community co-operative. The initial idea of the co-operative was to develop and improve farming services, particularly through the intensive fattening of hill lambs. During its early years – I was the first employee – the co-operative very much focused on agriculture. However, very quickly, two issues changed fundamentally, not only the direction of the co-operative but also the direction of the local community. One was the difficulty, in an area of very poor marginal land, of an agricultural co-op becoming viable and the second was the realisation, very early on, that no matter what investment took place in agriculture, it would in no way sustain the local population and that what was needed was economic diversification of the rural economy and the creation of off-farm jobs. I am glad to say that through the efforts of the co-operative, there are now 200 industrial jobs in the region and that the population decline has at last been stemmed. Agriculture, although still important to the local economy, is no longer its mainstay and the vibrancy of the community is very much linked around a multifunctional, multidimensional economy.

> Agriculture, although still important to the local economy, is no longer its mainstay and the vibrancy of the community is very much linked around a multi-functional, multi-dimensional economy.

Having seen the dramatic effect that such an approach had on a small rural community and seeing this as an incubator or experimental plot, I came to the conclusion that the only possible long-term approach to rural development and halting the rural decline which is pervasive throughout both the developed and developing world, was to develop diverse, multi-sectoral, local, rural economies. Such local rural economies should have a mixture of both local enterprise and access to public jobs. A sensible and well-delivered policy of decentralisation of public jobs has a key role to play in developing rural life and releasing the congestion strains on our main urban areas.

There was recently a headline in the Irish newspapers which said that, for the first time ever, more than half of the world's population live in cities. It said that the people were continuing to flee the countryside into our cities. I think we have to ask ourselves the question as to whether this is socially and economically a good thing or whether the maintenance of balanced population structures and population stability would not be more desirable. The Irish Government certainly believes this is so, as does the European Union, which has been increasingly putting emphasis on spending in the general rural economy. Some people will say that these policies are built on a kind of idealistic view of green fields and frugal living and that such a policy is economic madness. I believe, however, that there are very cogent arguments which show that the maintenance of rural populations and ensuring that the growth of cities is not at the expense of rural communities not only makes economic sense, but also makes social sense. As the Minister with responsibility for urban deprivation as well as rural development, my Department has a bird's eye view of the challenges facing different communities in Ireland. From what I can ascertain, the pattern in Ireland is replicated in many other developed countries.

The reasons why the Irish Government believes that rural development is an important engine for ensuring the balanced development of our country are as follows:

It makes no sense, in economic terms, to have rural areas with a wide range of services including schools, health centres, social facilities etc. which are under-utilised due to population migration and, at the same time, have rapidly growing cities that cannot cope in terms of the provision of these very same services because of their burgeoning population.

1. It makes no sense, in economic terms, to have rural areas with a wide range of services including schools, health centres, social facilities etc. which are under-utilised due to population migration and, at the same time, have rapidly growing cities that cannot cope in terms of the provision of these very same services because of their burgeoning population.

2. Examination of deprivation levels in Ireland show that while the richest communities in the country are urban communities, it is also true to say that the 46 most deprived communities in Ireland are also all urban communities. No rural area in the country has either the social, economic or quality-of-life deprivation issues that are experienced in our most deprived urban communities.

3. It is well established that children from rural Ireland, irrespective of their parents' education attainments, have on average, a much better chance of attaining third level education than children in urban Ireland. When one compares the average across all socio-economic groups in rural Ireland with those in deprived areas of urban Ireland, you get even more startling results with, in most cases, between 50 per cent and 75 per cent of rural children going to third level education and with as few as 1 per cent and 2 per cent of the children in the more deprived urban communities getting the same opportunity.

4. It is the Irish experience that given the job opportunities, many people wish to live in rural communities, particularly when they come to settle down and rear families and that a large number of people feel that the quality of life afforded is better than that available in urban areas. Our policy in Government is to afford this real choice to as many people as possible.

Having accepted the desirability of rural development, the next questions that obviously arise are:

- What policy measures should be pursued to achieve the objective? and

- Have policies to date been adequate to the purpose?

Amongst the focused measures that we in Government have pursued to achieve the rural development objective have been the work of our CLÁR Programme tackling physical and social infrastructural disadvantage, the Sustainable Rural Housing Guidelines, Decentralisation, rural proofing of Government policy, the LEADER and rural development programmes, the Rural Transport Initiative, and the Rural Social Scheme. To achieve the objective of developing rural life we need also the recognition by all organs of state of their role in ensuring that the democratic will of the people as expressed through their Government is achieved. I believe that the extent to which policies are adequate can largely be measured by examining population statistics and standards of living. Obviously, Government and EU policy is achieving its goal if rural populations and standards of living are rising. Similarly, policy is failing if decline continues.

The issue of population is at the very core of developing life in rural Ireland because it is easier to provide services and to stimulate diversification of the rural economy when you have a stable or growing population. This is something about which our planners have to become more sensible. I am not questioning the professional integrity of our planners, but I have to question the mindset within which they operate. Some planners can only see a hierarchy of cities, towns, hubs and gateways while ignoring the holistic approach of Government policy and the National Spatial Strategy's commitments to rural communities. Let's be clear about this; when we talk of rural Ireland, we are referring to dispersed rural communities, not cities, major towns, hubs or gateways.

Our society itself strongly recognises another hierarchy of place – that of townland, parish, county and province, but planners consistently ignore this hierarchy. It is a brave or foolhardy person in rural Ireland who would ignore the attachment to this hierarchy of place. There are a lot of Sligo people who could tell us a lot about what attachment to place meant when their county recently won their first Connacht championship in thirty-two years. There are also many Limerick and Tipperary rugby supporters who can tell you what loyalty to the province of Munster or even the Munster hurling championship means to them. It is our belief that, in terms of Government priorities, these two spatial hierarchies can live in an uneasy equilibrium.

The Gaelic Athletic Association in particular, throughout rural Ireland, is a leading example of how deeply a sense of place runs in

Some planners can only see a hierarchy of cities, towns, hubs and gateways while ignoring the holistic approach of Government policy and the National Spatial Strategy's commitments to rural communities.

our rural communities. Driven by a community and voluntary commitment to getting the better of the neighbouring parish or county, and sometimes even province, the GAA has a large number of signed-up members and a well-dispersed network of playing and social facilities. The GAA has an estimated 800,000 members, with some 415,000 playing members at all levels. Its 2002 Strategic Review estimated that the GAA itself had, on a voluntary basis, invested the then equivalent of over €2.6 billion in playing facilities, pavilions and social facilities, North and South, over the previous 50 years. This is a striking example of what attachment to your own area means in rural Ireland in terms of population and economic impact.

The Gaelic games and culture, fostered on a daily basis by the GAA, is part of our living rural heritage. Amidst the important debate about preserving the heritage of our countryside and the value of its traditions, music and culture, the point is often missed that without our people, these cease to exist. For traditional music and dance to survive in a rural area, it needs a new generation to renew it and to pass it on. This goes to the heart and soul of what European Union policy and Government policy sets out to deliver in terms of developing community and economic well-being in rural Ireland. This is at the core of why developing sustainable rural populations is one of the Government's priorities over the next five years.

In summary then, drawing the main strands of the clear and rational rural policy objectives and the binding ties of rural Ireland together, the main point is that if you want to develop life in rural Ireland, you need people there. Therefore, you need houses, jobs, facilities and a social life. In Ireland, the situation is that a large number of rural areas are now in a period of rapid growth but these are mainly peri-urban areas within 30 or 40 miles of the major cities and towns. The population in the rural areas outside the influence of major cities and towns is still stagnant or in many cases, in decline and, until this is reversed, our policies will not have achieved their goals. As you know, this year, we commemorate the Flight of the Earls. It took Ireland a long time to recover from that drain of human resources. Now, we enjoy previously unparalleled opportunities. With the human, economic and technological resources that we have at our disposal, surely we have the wherewithal to develop vibrant rural communities, rather than drain rural Ireland of its lifeblood?

The population in the rural areas outside the influence of major cities and towns is still stagnant or in many cases, in decline, and until this is reversed, our policies will not have achieved their goals.

Donal Connell

Chief Executive, An Post

Began his career in the former Dept. of Post and Telegraphs where his father also worked. An engineer by profession, has held several senior management positions in Unitrode Ireland, 3Com Ireland and Maxtor Ireland where he was General Manager before taking up his present position in August 2006. He is Chairman of the Institute of Technology, Blanchardstown and of An Post National Lottery Co.

An Post – Part of the Solution, Not Part of the Problem

As a national service provider with a long and proud tradition of public service, we have a strong interest in what happens in rural as well as urban areas. We are currently dealing with the issue of the provision of services under our Universal Service Obligation, the equally significant issue of European Union-led liberalisation of postal services and the ever-present matter of meeting important commercial imperatives. And each of these is as relevant to our activity in the urban arena as it is in the rural environment.

I'd like to start by painting a brief picture of demographic trends, using preliminary data from the Central Statistics Offices's 2006 census. This underscores in a very sharp way what most people know intuitively, which is, that for many years there has been an inexorable move away from rural areas to urban areas, even allowing for a strong underlying growth in the population.

Today, Ireland's population stands at 4.2 million, an increase of some 8 per cent over a four-year period and up a full 50 per cent on its 1961 low point of 2.8 million. Many factors have influenced this, with variations in the natural increase being at times increased or off-set by net migration patterns. However, what is most pertinent to our discussion today is the switch which has occurred, between urban and rural populations. Back in 1926, when the population was 3 million, two-thirds of us lived in rural areas and one third in urban areas – defined as towns with a population of 1,500 people or more.

By 1966, with almost exactly the same population of 3 million, the split was half and half – 1.5 million in rural areas and the same number in urban areas. Against the background of a sharply growing population, today the number of rural dwellers has increased slightly in absolute terms to 1.67 million. But over the same period, the number of people living in the country's 170 urban areas has grown to 2.57

This underscores in a very sharp way what most people know intuitively, which is, that for many years there has been an inexorable move away from rural areas to urban areas ...

million, now accounting for 61 per cent of the total.

Interestingly, I think, this trend towards increasing urbanisation is most evident in the towns rather than the cities. The combined population of towns with a population of 10,000 or more is now over 600,000. Smaller towns, with a population of between 1,500 and 10,000 increased in population over the last four years alone by 13.9 per cent – well in excess of the growth in the national average of 8.2 per cent.

This trend, the movement from rural to urban living, has been reflected in our own statistics. In the years 2000 and 2001, 93 contractor-operated offices closed down. Since then, a further 151 contractor-operated offices have closed and a further 271 have been converted into postal agencies.

Overall, nine of the 26 counties have lost at least 30 per cent of their contractor-operated offices since the beginning of 2002, the greatest declines being recorded in Leitrim, down 41 per cent, and Cavan, Sligo and Westmeath, each down 40 per cent. The reality is that these closures have not been planned or structured on our part. They are a response by our contractors to the enormous difficulties they have faced in terms of changing demographics, trends in consumption patterns and consumer behaviour. Increased use of cars to access large centres for shopping has taken its toll on villages and rural communities throughout Ireland and An Post is by no means the only service provider to experience this.

When a contractor decides not to renew a contract we will do everything in our power to replace them in the same location, but the reality is that there has to be sufficient local business for it to be an attractive proposition to another business person.

It should be remembered that the An Post network is based on a model which has been in existence for some 200 years. It was set up in the 1700s in the only way that a diffuse postal service could be run economically when horses were the main mode of transport. With a more evenly distributed population giving their business locally, and with contractors and agents not solely reliant on postal business for their livelihoods, the system worked to everyone's satisfaction for many years.

But, as we all know, times have changed. Our legacy, even allowing for the many closures which have occurred over recent years, is still a network of 1,362 outlets. Just to put that into a broader perspective, that compares with Spar's 300 outlets nationwide and AIB's 280. It makes An Post by far the largest retailer in the country.

And here's another way of looking at that statistic and another cause for thought. That figure of 1,300 outlets represents one outlet for every 3,000 adult men, women and children in the State. That's one of the lowest ratios by far throughout Europe. In Spain, for ex-

That figure of 1,300 outlets represents one outlet for every 3,000 adult men, women and children in the State. That's one of the lowest ratios by far throughout Europe.

ample, the ratio is 12,000 to 1 - four times that of Ireland and figures for the main developed countries such as France, Germany and the UK are much higher again.

Now I'm not saying that this is a good thing or a bad thing, per se. But one thing is certain; the ad hoc way in which the network has changed in recent years has not been conducive to the efficient running of the business and is downright confusing and somewhat disheartening for the local communities we serve. That is why we will be embarking on a detailed review of our network later this year. This review will be focused on identifying the optimum configuration, taking account of the needs of all our users. For our customers' sakes and in the interests of sustainability, we want to adopt the best model of service provision for the future.

I'm delighted to say that An Post is still held in high regard by local communities throughout Ireland. There is a special trust based, I firmly believe, on a mutual respect built up over many, many years. As Chief Executive of the company, I am fully aware that this level of trust is one of the most important assets that we have. We fulfil a range of needs in the community. Many of these go well beyond our service mandate and reflect the character and integrity of our employees as individuals. This important connection with the community is something we respect and value.

In our mainstream activities we are a core provider of Social Welfare payments, we provide money transfer and bill payments services and a host of others, including savings and other personal banking services, both directly and in an agency capacity. Recently, we have taken the big step of launching a new service, Postbank. This exciting joint venture, undertaken in partnership with a genuine leader in the European financial services industry, Fortis, reflects our commitment and determination to remain a strong force in the rural as well as the growing urban communities. This joint venture has been designed to bring something truly fresh, some genuine innovation, to a personal banking sector cluttered with "me too" offerings and which, to be blunt about it, are viewed with suspicion by the public at large.

We know that people want straightforward and transparent banking services. They want to be assured that they are getting good value for money and they want to deal with people they know and trust. And, I'm delighted to say, we are in an excellent position to meet those needs. I think it should be recognised that this initiative will help us achieve a number of objectives. It should help us to earn revenues which will strengthen An Post's financial position – and that's important for us. An important part of my job is to look after the bottom line, to make sure that we can pay our way and stay in business. If I don't do that no one else will and I make no apologies

> We fulfil a range of needs in the community. Many of these go well beyond our service mandate and reflect the character and integrity of our employees as individuals.

for stating the obvious.

But Postbank does more than this, much more than this, from a strategic point of view. It will increase, and is increasing, footfall and therefore business transactions throughout our network. Every Post Office in the country has a part to play in Postbank. Obviously we are not going to open the equivalent of AIB's 280 branches in each and every one of our 1,300 offices, but every outlet will be in a position to participate in the provision of Postbank services and to earn revenue from it and a large number of outlets will be providing a comprehensive range of those services.

That means, most importantly, that our customers will be able to do business with Postbank in many more locations and often at more convenient times than with any of the traditional banks. What's more, because our products are deliberately straightforward and un-complicated, they will appeal, indeed we know they are already appealing, to a range of people who would not traditionally have considered opening a bank account. I'm sorry if all this feels as if it has a touch of sales spiel to it, but I do firmly believe that Postbank represents an important lifeline not just to An Post as a company but also to the many communities we serve nationally.

The Universal Service Obligation, or USO, is a core part of our structure. It's the requirement that we provide a five day delivery service to all parts of the country.

Over the past couple of years An Post has done very well, I'm pleased to say. Just four short years ago, our Board had to sanction a Strategic Recovery Plan with the specific aim of restoring the company to financial stability. Last year, for the third year in a row, we were able to report profits. At an operational level the profit was €14.7 million. That was a particularly creditable performance given that we lost more than €30 million on the Reserved part of the Universal Service Obligation. The Universal Service Obligation, or USO, is a core part of our structure. It's the requirement that we provide a five day delivery service to all parts of the country. In that well known phrase, "It's part of what we are".

During the year we processed up to 3.5 million items of mail each day, a figure which rose to 8 million a day over the Christmas period. This was made possible by increased automation which enables us to sort automatically right down to route level – a major improvement in efficiency and productivity. Furthermore, this growth in the core mails business was achieved despite the fact that 62 per cent of mail revenue was earned in sectors open to competition. But full liberali-sation of the market looms and we are under no illusions about the threat that this poses to us.

Recently, we have been informed that liberalisation in respect of what are termed "reserved areas", which was due to happen in 2009, has been deferred. An additional two year transition period has also been granted to new EU member states and those with "remote topography and numerous islands". This recognises the scale of the difficulty for postal operators in ensuring the viability of the Universal Service Obligation in a fully liberalised market. But it is only a postponement of what is to come and we need to spend the time we've been given doing some hard head scratching on the difficult issues of how the loss-making USO can be financed fairly between all the parties in a liberalised market designed to stimulate competition.

In many respects, you could see it as not unlike the issue of "community rating" in the health insurance market – except our issues are actually much more complex! They involve many different sets of costs, one for collection and one for distribution, parcels as well as letters, and domestic versus international. Then there are other issues such as whether someone on Clare Island sending a letter 30 miles should be paying more for their service than someone sending a letter from Ballsbridge to Raheny, because the costs of providing that service are higher. It is going to require the wisdom of Solomon to sort this issue out, but sorted it must be.

In the UK, they are now looking hard at the possibility of a "zonal pricing", charging different prices depending on the distance between point of posting and point of delivery. That's because full liberalisation there created unexpected problems. Many new entrants to the market took the opportunity to insert massive volumes of ready sorted mail into the UK Post Office delivery system, downstream of the large central processing hubs, creating serious financial strains. These are the sort of issues we really cannot afford to get wrong here.

But against this background we are not sitting idly by, awaiting an outcome, I can assure you. We are, at heart, optimistic, with a belief that being proactive and open to fresh ideas is the best way to ensure we can meet our obligations to the communities we serve. Recently, for example, we commissioned some detailed research into the specific needs and wishes of vulnerable communities. This involved two well-qualified researchers engaging directly with a wide range of organisations representing these communities to identify the barriers experienced by them in accessing An Post's services and to find out how we could better provide services to them in the future.

As you know poverty, and exclusion continue to be realities for a significant number of Irish people. Even though the numbers living in relative poverty have dropped, the number living in consistent poverty has increased. One-parent families and people living alone, especially older people in rural areas, represent a disproportionately high figure of the total. It is perhaps not surprising, given what we know anecdotally on this subject, to discover from the latest census that the highest average ages of population, at over 38 years, are to be found in Roscommon and Leitrim, against an average of under 33

> Then there are other issues such as whether someone on Clare Island sending a letter 30 miles should be paying more for their service than someone sending a letter from Ballsbridge to Raheny, because the costs of providing that service are higher.

years in Dublin Fingal and a national average of 35.6 years.

Our enquiry into vulnerable communities included ethnic and racial minorities, single parents, the travelling community, the elderly, people with disabilities and people living in isolation. We were welcomed by the various representative bodies we approached and we got some extremely useful feedback which will enable us to input these to the review I mentioned earlier and to improve our services to them in a variety of ways.

Communication – of what we offer, of how we operate and how best we can be used – is an important area of opportunity. We were particularly gratified, I should add, at the broadly positive consensus which emerged on the quality of our services, which are seen as friendly, accessible and non-intimidating.

One important thing to emerge is that for vulnerable communities "equitable access" to our services is not so much about the number of post offices as it is about gaining access to them – in other words, it's about better transport. After all, a post office located a mile away is just as remote as one 20 miles away if you have no means of getting there.

The Rural Transport Initiative managed by Pobal has developed a model of rural transport that is tailored to meet the needs of these communities, collecting people at their doors and bringing them to shops, the bank, post offices and health centres. Last year it provided almost one million journeys. It works extraordinarily well, providing opportunities for social interaction on the journey as well as for doing what's needed in such establishments. Apart altogether from the surprising scale of this initiative, a measure of the indirect benefit of this interaction was further identified in the South West of Ireland where public health nurses have seen a decrease in the use of anti-depressant medication by those older people using the transport initiative to access their post offices, health centres and shops.

There may very well be scope for a partnership arrangement to be developed between An Post and the Rural Transport Initiative, obviously subject to the provision of appropriate funding. In Switzerland, for example, the post office runs an extremely successful and popular rural bus service, and there are other examples around the world. In other countries, including the UK, they've taken an alternative approach of bringing the post office to the people with mobile post offices serving local communities, in much the same way as mobile libraries here.

All of these ideas are worthy of consideration and at An Post we are keen to be involved because in addressing the issues of rural communities and the problems of rural isolation, we are determined to be part of the solution, not part of the problem.

> One important thing to emerge is that for vulnerable communities "equitable access" to our services is not so much about the number of post offices as it is about gaining access to them – in other words, it's about better transport.

Catherine Buckley

National President, Macra na Feirme

Born in Co. Cork. Comes from a farming background and is a certified public accountant by profession. A member of the Macroom Macra na Feirme club in Muskerry for over ten years, she was the organisation's national treasurer 2004-2006 and served as chairperson of Macra's national competitions committee in 2006. In March 2007, she was elected unopposed to the position of National President – the first woman to hold the office. Macra na Feirme has over 8,000 members in 300 clubs throughout the country and puts emphasis on social interaction and participation.

Voluntary and Community Organisations Are Essential

Macra na Feirme advocates and strongly supports rural development – rural development that puts people, especially farmers and young people, first. As we look at the future of life in rural Ireland, I think it is important that we recognise that our plans must revolve around a range of activities, economic and social, that will enable citizens to support themselves and their communities in the long-term, and through changing circumstances. Paramount to this is the ability to ensure a good quality of life.

Modern life progresses and adapts. Information technology, primarily telecommunications and computers, is part of the change. However, telecommunications and other forms of information technology do not offer a magic solution for rural development. The process of rural development is more complex than that.

The essentials components of rural development can be classified into three categories:

The first category is investment in **Human Capital**. This means providing education, employment, housing, healthcare, transport and general amenities for the residents of all rural communities. People are the only important resource – all else depends on their thoughts and actions. Traditionally, the farmer has been the backbone of all rural communities. Farming and the continuation of the family farm must be supported and encouraged by government. Whatever new rural initiatives are introduced, the fact that farming is a business enterprise must be remembered and such initiatives must contribute to the continuation of farming in the future.

Last autumn, when the European agricultural ministers met, at the heart of the European Model of Agriculture which they discussed was multi-functionality. This means that, together with competitive food, fibre and energy production, farming also delivers other services for society as a whole. These services include safeguarding viable rural societies and infrastructures, balanced regional development and rural employment, maintenance of rural landscapes, protection of the environment and high standards of animal welfare and food safety. These services reflect the concerns of consumers and taxpayers. Farmers provide these multi-functional services for the benefit of society as a whole, which often incur additional costs without a compensating market return.

The second essential category is investment in the **Physical Infrastructure** necessary for economic development – water, power, transportation and telecommunications. The telecommunications infrastructure is important today because of the dramatic changes in what is possible and because failure to change may leave rural communities at a serious competitive disadvantage. Nevertheless, we must not forget that telecommunications are only one element of essential infrastructure. An adequate supply of clean water, electricity and transportation networks are also essential.

In my inauguration speech in May of this year, I called for support for the concept of "working from home " – particularly e-working. I asked all the political parties to facilitate employees working from home through "e-working" – that is, electronic working. I believe this concept has a huge role to play in the development of life in rural Ireland. Work-life balance has been a buzz-phrase for a few years now but the concept should not be discounted. It is widely accepted that working from home can bring huge benefits, helping workers to organise their time more efficiently, work more effectively and reduce the stress of commuting. Studies have also shown that by offering employees a flexible working environment such as the option to work part-time from the home, productivity and employee retention levels are increased while costs can be reduced.

Giving people the opportunity to work from home would also be an effective way of allowing local people in rural areas the chance to work in the areas where they are living, providing them with more time to become involved in community life.If more people were facilitated in this way it would reduce the number of commuters on our roads, improve peoples' family life and would also mean that less people are wasting hours and hours per week stuck in their cars, increasing carbon emissions and having a detrimental impact on the environment.

Many employers and employees may not be aware of the fact that equipment provided to an employee by their employer is not assessed for tax as a benefit-in-kind so long as it is used primarily for

It is widely accepted that working from home can bring huge benefits, helping workers to organise their time more efficiently, work more effectively and reduce the stress of commuting.

business. An employer can also provide expenses to cover costs such as heating and light, without the employee being taxed.

Employers are often reluctant to provide the opportunity for employees to work from home rather than from the traditional desk in the office. I'm sure an tUasal Ó Cuív and his colleagues will look at ways to encourage more employers to provide this option to employees. The various departments of government could and should lead the way, not just by decentralisation but by encouraging e-working. For this to happen, however, it's vital that we get leadership in this area from our politicians. Obviously there are infrastructural barriers, such as the lack of broadband. ComReg's report for the first quarter of 2007 to the end of March, estimates that there are around 450,000 residential sector broadband subscriptions in Ireland - this equates to just 30 per cent of all households. Addressing these issues would be a key part of the strategy to develop life in rural Ireland.

The third essential category, and probably the most difficult, is our **Social Organisations** – the ways in which we collectively relate to each other. Social pressures are strong, particularly in small rural communities, and changes necessary for rural development require local leadership.

In November 2006, the taskforce on active citizenship published their report. In it they identified some of society's trends in today's Ireland, trends which are affecting the communities in which we live. The report outlined two definitions of what is an active citizen. Firstly, one relating to involvement in a voluntary activity and the other to wider civic, political and social participation. The report outlined how many saw voluntary and community organisations as the "backbone" of active citizenship, providing opportunities for civic engagement and volunteering. According to the report, this is delivered through voluntary and community groups' abilities to achieve trust, cohesion and confidence in ways that governments cannot.

As a voluntary organisation, operating particularly in rural Ireland, Macra Na Feirme has huge concerns about the social changes happening in many communities. While we've seen increased prosperity in Ireland in recent years, many people are now also faced with the increased pressures that comes hand-in-hand with modern living. Long hours at work, ever increasing commuting time and family and other commitments mean that people are spending less and less time involved in community-based activities. All too often we hear people saying that they don't even know their own neighbours. Research has shown that there are countless positive benefits to interacting with those who live close to us, but an unfortunate fact of life in modern Ireland is that we are just not doing this.

Last year, Macra na Feirme successfully started the initiative

> The report outlined how many saw voluntary and community organisations as the "backbone" of active citizenship, providing opportunities for civic engagement and volunteering.

known as "Know Your Neighbour". The 2007 Know Your Neighbour Weekend was successfully run in mid-July. Over the past number of weeks, we have been inundated with requests for organisers' packs as people from every corner of Ireland prepare to have an activity happening in their area. Macra hopes that as people embrace this initiative, it will continue to be a step to taking an active interest in participating in all aspects of their community. With ever increasing demand on peoples' time and continuous talk about work-life balance, there is an onus on us to foster a sense of volunteerism.

Fifty-eight per cent of people volunteer because they are asked. We must encourage people to volunteer and once they do, we need to support them through leadership training and skills development.

Fifty-eight per cent of people volunteer because they are asked. We must encourage people to volunteer and once they do, we need to support them through leadership training and skills development. The corporate sector have a huge role to play in this-under corporate responsibilities, communities can tap into a range of resources that could be made available particularly through local enterprise.

Young people in particular need to learn about volunteerism and being active in their community. Such attitudes developed at an early age will remain with them for life and help develop our communities in years to come. Let's not forget these are the leaders of the future. There can be no democracy without participation and, therefore, it is vital for the health and depth of our democracy to have greater youth participation and active citizenship.

A bemused Maurice Regan

Brian Cowen makes time for local radio

Dick Roche TD, Minister of State for European Affairs

Ruairí Quinn TD, Former Leader of the
Labour Party

Prof Brigid Laffan, Principal of the College
of Human Sciences, UCD

Chapter 12

Reinforcing the European Union

The Reform Treaty Will Serve Europe's Citizens
Dick Roche TD
Minister of State for European Affairs

The European Union Must Move Decisively Ahead
Ruairí Quinn TD
Former Leader of the Labour Party

Legitimising the EU and Its Policies is a Core Challenge
Prof Brigid Laffan
Principal of the College of Human Sciences, UCD

Dick Roche TD

Minister of State for European Affairs

Born in Wexford and educated at Wexford CBS, UCD (BComm., DPA, MPA). Formerly civil servant and university lecturer, he was first elected to Dáil Éireann in 1987. Member of Seanad Éireann 1992-3 and 1993-7. Appointed Minister of State for Europe at Dept. of Foreign Affairs 2002. Minister for the Environment, Heritage and Local Govt. 2004-7. Appointed Minister of State with responsibility for European Affairs following election of May 2007. Has served on numerous Oireachtas committees including chairing Joint Committee on State Sponsored Bodies 1989-92.

The Reform Treaty Will Serve Europe's Citizens

Europe has been remarkably successful over the past five decades but it cannot hope to be anything like as successful in the future if it tries to deal with its contemporary challenges with systems and structures put in place to serve a Union of six member states. This is the reality that informs the Unions current reform efforts.

We are entering the final stretch of an extended effort to reform the Union to enable it to cope with the challenges of a 27-member Union. In the coming months, member states will set about agreeing a new Reform Treaty. This will serve to enhance the efficiency and effectiveness of the Union. But it must do so in a way that will bridge the gap between Union and citizen.

The proposed Reform Treaty is still a mystery to many. This is hardly surprising when its final shape is not yet decided.

The proposed Reform Treaty is still a mystery to many. This is hardly surprising when its final shape is not yet decided. There is, however, no need to regard the Reform Treaty as a stranger. It is, after all, a very close relative of the draft Constitutional Treaty that came into being during Ireland's 2004 EU Presidency. The seeds of our present work were sown in the groundbreaking discussions that took place at the European Convention, and the ensuing Intergovernmental Conference (IGC), which concluded during the 2004 Irish Presidency.

The Convention on the Future of Europe

The Convention represented a remarkable and positive break from the past. It was a unique collaboration between representatives of governments, national parliaments and the European Parliament. It was open. It was unlike anything Europe had seen since the Messina Conference.

The draft Constitutional Treaty of 2004 drew its inspiration from the energy and ideas that flowed through the Convention. Because of this, the draft Constitutional Treaty reflected the views of a far wider spectrum of European opinion than had been the case with past reforms. Most importantly, the Constitutional Treaty was driven not by the views of the powerful, the bigger member states, but by a consensus of participants that demanded they be treated as equals. This latter point is of particular importance in Ireland where we all too often see ourselves being at the receiving end of decisions "made in Brussels" than as participants in the decision making process. Nothing could have been further from that image insofar as the convention is concerned. The smaller member states – through the Friends of the Community Method Group of which Ireland was a founder – played in many ways the most coherent role in the Convention – far more coherent than many of the largest member states. That reality is closely reflected in the outcome of the Conventions deliberations.

The focus of the Convention, which was reflected in the draft Constitutional Treaty, was:

- To produce a new Treaty which would serve to bring Europe closer to its citizens,
- To enable Europe to play a positive role on the international stage, and
- To put in place arrangements that would allow the Union to function effectively with its greatly increased membership.

Europe's Reform Process is Now Reactivated

Given the merits of the Constitutional Treaty, it is a pity that ratification of the draft Constitutional Treaty by all 27 member states did not prove possible. The negative referendum results in France and the Netherlands meant that the Treaty could not be ratified in its original form. The results also made it necessary for the Union to reflect on how the essence of the Treaty could be salvaged and how the Union could move forward. That process of reflection has taken all of two years – rather too long in my view – to produce the results achieved at last month's European Council.

Last month's European Council set out a very detailed mandate for an Intergovernmental Council (IGC). Key decisions have been made concerning the shape of the future Reform Treaty. Ireland's approach in discussions leading up to the European Council was to preserve as much as possible of what we had achieved in 2004. We recognised that some changes would have to be made but were anxious that they would be minimised. That has been achieved to a very large degree. The great bulk of the original Constitutional Treaty

Ireland's approach in discussions leading up to the European Council was to preserve as much as possible of what we had achieved in 2004.

will be retained. The reform package will be implemented in what is now being referred to as 'the traditional method' – adjusting existing Treaties. Personally, I would have preferred to keep the Constitutional Treaty in its original form, albeit in a slimmer edition, but I am a political realist and recognise that some remodelling of the text was inevitable.

The IGC mandate will ensure that the Reform Treaty will retain the balance between the interests of large and small member states, one of the great victories of coherent collaboration between small and medium states in the Convention. It will simplify the Union's decision-making arrangements. It will also make clear distinctions between national and EU-level responsibilities. In a positive new feature, it will give an enhanced role to national parliaments in scrutinising draft EU measures. I strongly welcome this move which I feel will strengthen the Union's democratic standing as national parliaments and the democratically elected European Parliament combine to vet EU legislation.

The new Treaty will finally resolve such contentious issues as the composition of the Commission and the voting arrangements in Council. The fact that all member states, large and small, will enjoy absolute equality in their entitlement to nominate members of the Commission is a real gain for the smaller countries. This was a battle hard fought and won in the Convention where, on occasions, President Giscard seemed taken aback when confronted with the view that the equality of member states small and large was an essential element for the Union's future.

The new voting arrangements, under which laws can only be passed with support from more than half of the member states and almost two-thirds of the Union's population, will ensure that Europe will only do things that enjoy genuine, widespread support.

The new voting arrangements, under which laws can only be passed with support from more than half of the member states and almost two-thirds of the Union's population, will ensure that Europe will only do things that enjoy genuine, widespread support. The Reform Treaty will also set out sensible, workable arrangements in the areas of justice and home affairs, an area where Ireland has still some decisions to make, and in common foreign and security policy. While the title of "Foreign Minister" has been dropped, the new High Representative on foreign affairs and security policy will play a crucial role in bringing greater coherence to the Union's external actions.

I would like to speak briefly about the Charter of Fundamental Rights. Discussion of the Charter at the European Convention was, for me, the most heartening part of my work there. It has attracted particular interest in Ireland and I am glad to say that it enjoys broad support across the political spectrum.

The Charter captures all that is best about the Union. It encapsulates the principles that have brought civilised peace. The various titles of the articles will illustrate this point. The Charter speaks of

Human Dignity, of Freedoms, of Equality, of Solidarity, of Citizens' Rights and of Justice. More than any other aspect of the Treaty, I believe the Charter will resonate with the Irish people and with people right across Europe. It speaks to the heart. It is infinitely more uplifting and in tune with the views of the majority of Europe's citizens than so much of the prosaic language that flows from the Union and its institutions. While the text of the Charter will not appear in the Treaty itself, something I regret, the Charter's legal status is being explicitly confirmed.

I am aware that some confusion may have arisen regarding Ireland's position on the Charter. I want to be very clear on this and to avoid any ambiguity. Let me say plainly that the Government strongly supports the Charter. We have not sought and will not be seeking any opt-out.

Next Steps

Our immediate priority must now be to finalise the text of the Treaty. The Portuguese Presidency has set a deadline of mid-October to reach a political agreement on the Treaty text. Though ambitious, I believe that this is an achievable goal. It is all the more achievable given the detail of the mandate that has been agreed by the European Council. The next important business is, of course, the delicate issue of ratification. A target for the ratification process has been set. The target is to bring the Treaty into force in time for the election of a new European Parliament in June 2009. The actual method of ratification is of course a matter for each individual member state operating within its own constitutional arrangements. Ireland will hold a referendum on the Reform Treaty next summer.

Listening to Citizens

European political leaders frequently protest that the citizens of the Union are its greatest asset. That is a noble sentiment and of course it is true. Oddly, the Union's greatest weakness is the failure of the institutions to connect with the people they serve.

During Ireland's Presidency, arising from our experience with Nice, I launched the Communicating Europe Initiative.

There is an unfortunate, even arrogant, presumption that the European Union is a good thing and that this fact is so self-evident that it must never be challenged. That frame of mind needs to change. Europe and its institutions would learn valuable lessons from listening more attentively to the concerns and frustrations of the citizens and indeed to the points made by critics. Listening is an essential part of

> Oddly, the Union's greatest weakness is the failure of the institutions to connect with the people they serve.

communication. That reality is sometimes lost sight of in Europe.

In the coming debate on the Reform Treaty, those of us who believe that an effective European Union remains vital to the collective well-being of Europeans need to make our voice heard but we must first learn to listen. We must learn from the lessons of the past and avoid a repeat of the first Nice Referendum when the real issues were sidelined, reasonable concerns were left unanswered and misinformation flourished.

I hope that next year's referendum campaign will be conducted in an atmosphere of factual debate and reasoned argument. We should discuss all aspects of the Treaty with candour and honesty; we must listen and when we have listened answer the questions and concerns that are raised.

Reform Treaty Is More Evolution Than Revolution

On the matter of candour and honesty, we need to see the Reform Treaty for what it is rather than for what it is not! It is the next stage in the EU's evolution, reflecting the collective wisdom of the member states about how the Union ought to be run and what it ought to do. It is not a document that aims to transform the Union in any radical way. It does not represent any kind of massive leap forward for Europe. It is not a blueprint for an EU super-state. In short, it is what it says on the box – a reform Treaty aimed at making Europe work better in all of our interests. Referring to it as a "constitution" was probably a mistake. It suggested that the document was more than it actually was. The title Reform Treaty while more prosaic is closer to the reality. The Reform Treaty will enable the Union to do more of what it has done so successfully this past 50 years – serve Europe's citizens.

The record of the Union is impressive. A war-torn Europe has been transformed into a place of peace and prosperity, envied by other parts of the world. A vast single market has been created which has provided, to some significant degree, the basis for Ireland's current prosperity. The Euro is now the currency of 13 EU countries. That will rise to 15 from January of next year. We work together in ways that are unprecedented, but yet our distinctive cultures and traditions continue to flourish. There are nearly twice as many member states today as there were prior to 2004. These are huge achievements and we need this process to continue in the challenging years ahead.

An expansion that we have just been through, and the possibility of future expansion, requires an improved institutional framework. We need new ways of working if the Union is to function as effectively as it needs to do. That is why we need the Reform Treaty.

It is not a document that aims to transform the Union in any radical way. It does not represent any kind of massive leap forward for Europe. It is not a blueprint for an EU super-state. In short, it is what it says on the box – a reform Treaty aimed at making Europe work better in all of our interests.

Other Challenges Facing Europe

The successful conclusion of the Treaty reform process will mark a fresh beginning for Europe. It will give us the opportunity and the impetus to make progress across the range of issues facing our continent in a changing world. After the fall of the Berlin Wall, former German Chancellor Willy Brandt famously said: "Now, what belongs together is growing together". Those words resonate as strongly now as they did when first uttered.

Europe faces many challenges in addition to the challenge of establishing a Reform Treaty:

- The challenge of creating jobs;
- Protecting incomes;
- Improving competitiveness;
- Leading the international fight against Climate Change;
- Helping to bring peace and security to the rest of Europe and to the wider world.

In an increasingly competitive global economic environment, our Europe's prosperity cannot be taken for granted.

We, the member states of the EU, need to work together to build a strong, dynamic and knowledge-intensive economy. The Lisbon Strategy, adopted by the Union in 2000 to meet this challenge, is now showing positive results. Europe's economy is now on the move after a decade of comparative doldrums.

Securing Europe's future energy supply and tackling climate change are clear priorities. We also face the dangers of organised crime, of human trafficking, international terrorism and the trade in illicit drugs. As these threats multiply, we need a cross-border framework within which we can act effectively against such menaces.

The challenges that we now face do not respect national boundaries, and no single state can tackle them alone. They demand a multilateral response and a strong, effective institutional framework. They require a European Union which is forward-looking, focussed on dealing with the challenges of the future and free from the institutional introspection that has dogged us for much of the recent past. They require a Europe that is in harmony with the citizens.

Celebration of 50 Years

The vision which inspired pioneers like Monnet, Schuman and Adenauer, was one born of the horrors of the first half of the twentieth century. That period saw the devastation of two World Wars. It is important that we recall the past and remind ourselves why the Eu-

> The challenges that we now face do not respect national boundaries, and no single state can tackle them alone. They demand a multilateral response and a strong, effective institutional framework. They require a European Union which is forward-looking, focussed on dealing with the challenges of the future and free from the institutional introspection that has dogged us for much of the recent past.

ropean project has been, and remains, so important to us.

Bearing in mind the desolation and ruin which faced that first generation of post-war European leaders, the successes of the European Union are all the more impressive. The very notion of a war between member states of the Union has become unthinkable. Respect for democracy, human rights and the rule of law is the foundation of civic life across the continent. Our peoples enjoy an unparalleled prosperity and quality of life. We are the world's largest provider of overseas development aid, delivering almost €50 billion each year to more than 150 countries. The continent has been united in a way that would have been unimaginable a generation ago.

Conclusion

This New Ireland looks to its future in Europe with confidence. It is important for ourselves that we continue to play a positive role at the heart of the new European Union and that we play that role with commitment and enthusiasm. With the unity of purpose, which has always been part of the European ideal, Ireland will continue to work with our partners to ensure that Europe in the coming decades will expand on the legacy of the past fifty years. The Reform Treaty will facilitate Europe's future success. Uniquely, we the citizens of Ireland will be asked to consent individually to the Treaty and to allow Europe to take the next vital steps forward. I hope our answer will be positive.

With the unity of purpose, which has always been part of the European ideal, Ireland will continue to work with our partners to ensure that Europe in the coming decades will expand on the legacy of the past fifty years

Ruairí Quinn TD

Former Leader of the Labour Party

Born in Dublin and educated at Blackrock College, UCD (B. Arch) Athens Centre of Ekistics (HCE). Formerly architect and town planner, first elected to Dáil Éireann for Dublin South-East in 1977. Minister of State at the Dept. of the Environment 1982-3, Minister for Labour 1983-7, Minister for the Public Service 1986-7, Minister for Enterprise and Employment 1993-4, Minister for Finance 1994-7. Deputy leader of the Labour Party 1989-97, he was elected leader in November 1997 and stood down in Aug. 2002. In 2005, published his memoirs, Straight Left: A Journey in Politics.

The European Union Must Move Decisively Ahead

Since the collapse of the Berlin Wall in 1989, and the subsequent re-union of the continent of Europe, the European Union has been pre-occupied with enlargement. Despite whatever else was happening in the rest of the world, the institutional changes necessary to cope with a larger and more complex union were always on the agenda, irrespective of the issues of the day. The Amsterdam Treaty 1997 was followed by the Nice Treaty 2001. Subsequently, the convention to draft a new Constitutional Treaty was launched with the commitment to provide for an inclusive form of dialogue so that the public would be engaged. The openness and transparency of the process, it was agreed, would attract widespread public interest, participation and support. The outcome of that convention was successfully converted into a draft Constitutional Treaty and agreed, under an Irish Presidency, of the Inter Governmental Conference in 2004.

Nine months later, despite all its preparation, it was rejected by the French and Dutch electors in two referenda. Notwithstanding its current ratification by eighteen member states, the test of unanimity was not passed and so the grandiosely named Constitutional Treaty was quietly buried. In its place, the German Presidency, in the first half of 2007, has successfully proposed a reformed Treaty which will retain most of the institutional and decision making mechanisms of the old draft Treaty. It is the intention of the new Portuguese Presidency to proceed, rapidly, with a compact Inter-Governmental Conference whose task would be to produce a draft Treaty modelled closely on the compromise wording produced by the German Presidency.

The timetable envisaged is to have this project completed by the end of 2007. The next year will be given over to the process of ratifi-

> Despite whatever else was happening in the rest of the world, the institutional changes necessary to cope with a larger and more complex union were always on the agenda ...

cation in all 27 member states with the intention that it should start to come into effect from January 1st 2009. This will be in time for the European Parliament elections of June 2009 and the formation of the new Commission at the end of 2009. It is not yet clear if all of the institutional changes will start immediately, such as the reduced size of the Commission to fifteen members or the creation of a President of Europe with a two and a half year term of office. But the mood clearly is to get on with it and put this whole chapter of institutional reform and internal change behind the European Union – a truly continental Union.

New Member States

The enlargement of ten more member states in 2004 with the addition of two more in 2006 completed the bulk of the expansion of the European Union envisaged by the collapse of communism in Europe in the early 1990s. It has taken Europe twenty years to get to where we are now. While the process has been remarkably successful, let us now hope that the period of introspection and institutional restructuring is virtually at an end.

Making Progress

The next five years must see the European Union moving decisively ahead, equipped with the new machinery of institutional reform and clear decision making.

The next five years must see the European Union moving decisively ahead, equipped with the new machinery of institutional reform and clear decision making. Ireland must play its role in encouraging the national leaders within Europe and also the national parliaments to re-engage with the real issues that concern European citizens.

If there is one message from the European citizens, over the past few years, particularly here in Ireland, through for example the Forum on Europe, it is that the prolonged debate on institutional reform is boring and does not engage the excitement of the European citizen.

A New Momentum

Let's turn then to an issue which does. Every European citizen is aware of energy and climate change. There is no need to develop the new programmes of communication on this matter. The domestic heating bills, the increased cost of petrol and the changing weather patterns are daily realities that confront us all. More significantly, they do not respect national boundaries. Their impact reveals the inability of national governments to act decisively on their own. Eric Hobsbawm in his recent book, Globalisation, Democracy and Terrorism, describes how the impact of globalisation is undermining the citizen's faith in their national governments to take effective measures to protect them. This was, after all, he reminds us, one of the historic tasks which were cited as the justification for the establishment of the nation state in the first place. The instruments and implementation used to establish the nation state in the first instance were frontier posts, border controls, customs and tariffs, separate currencies, separate market laws and national armies.

Today we have got rid of most of these within the European Union. But now, if they were to be reintroduced, would they protect us from rising petrol prices, the insecurity of gas supplies or erratic weather patterns producing heat waves or flooding across the continent? Our parents could see the sense in pooling together the raw materials of war with the establishment of the European Coal and Steel Community 1950. Our children are demanding action on energy and climate change so as to confront the future.

New Instruments of Action

When the new reform Treaty is ratified and brought into operation, as I believe it must be, our member state governments will have new and effective machinery to take important decisions together on behalf of us all. I believe that the Irish government must, for example, make energy and climate change a national and European priority for the next five years.

A Common Energy Policy

Why is it that we have pooled responsibility within the European Union for our national trade policy? Because Ireland negotiating with China in the World Trade Organisation does not have the same clout as the European Union negotiating on behalf of 27 member states and a population of 450 million people representing the richest domestic market in the world.

Why has our Common Agriculture Policy survived for so long? Because the alternative of national policies was inferior for both the consumer and the farmer. Even with the many changes which are occurring, as a result of globalisation and WTO policies, no serious political force in Europe is campaigning for the re-nationalisation of agriculture policy in today's globalised world.

The process of integration continues. We are completing our internal markets, not just for goods but for services as well. Thirteen member states share a single currency, the euro. A number of developed member states such as Denmark and Sweden have their curren-

Why is it that we have pooled responsibility within the European Union for our national trade policy? Because Ireland negotiating with China in the World Trade Organisation does not have the same clout as the European Union negotiating on behalf of 27 member states
...

cies pegged to the Euro. As a condition of their membership, all new member states will be required to join the euro when their national economies qualify to participate. There are many more examples of integration that affect our daily lives in so many different ways which time prevents me from referring to here. However, there is one major item that is studiously avoided.

The Elephant in the Room

This obvious exception to the march of market integration which I have summarised above is energy. Europe has made very poor progress in this area. Whether it is energy efficiency, the inter-connection of our energy grids, standards of building insulation, the development of renewables or the consolidation of security of supply, progress has been patchy and behind schedule.

This obvious exception to the march of market integration which I have summarised above is energy. Europe has made very poor progress in this area. Whether it is energy efficiency, the inter-connection of our energy grids, standards of building insulation, the development of renewables or the consolidation of security of supply, progress has been patchy and behind schedule. The big failure underpinning all the others is, in my view, the absence of a single market across the European Union. Indeed we should be looking at the European economic area so as to include countries like Norway and Switzerland as well as the existing 27 member states.

Energy is a complex and highly specialised subject at one level but its basics are very clear and easily understood by all of us. With oil now over $70 a barrel compared to $20 some five years ago, the days of cheap fuel from that source are over.

The large European dependence on Russian national gas is dominated by issues of security of supply. Moscow's treatment of the Ukraine last year and President Putin's recent behaviour towards foreign energy companies operating within Russia should leave no one in any doubt about the future. We have entered a new era where 'pipeline' diplomacy has replaced its 19th century predecessor 'gunboat' diplomacy. Sweetheart deals such as the Russian-German pipeline along the Baltic Sea bypassing Poland cannot be reliable. Besides, such bilateral action has a hard historical resonance for the Poles when they think of the consequences of the Molotov-Ribbentrop Pact.

Lessons from the Past

Do we have to relearn all the lessons of destructive trade barriers and custom tariff wars of the past? Have we forgotten Black Wednesday, September 1992, and the destructive roller coaster of currency competition and currency speculation? Those turbulent financial years made nonsense of sensible macro economic management, prudent investment and national income policies.

The public understood, against this background of currency turbulence, the consequences of political inaction or indeed the maintenance of national pride. Politicians like Helmut Kohl or Francois Mitterrand could seize the moment of the collapse of Communism to persuade their people, respectively, to convert the DM into the Euro single currency in return for a united Germany anchored firmly within the framework of the European Union.

Do we know enough already or must we have another crisis before decisive action is taken? Against the background of all the evidence, both international and national, what is holding back our elected leaders, governments and parliaments? I believe that the public are already ahead of them and I know our children are already ahead of us.

What to Do Now

The priority now for the new Irish government must be to advance the energy agenda on all fronts – local, national and European. Enhanced building insulation standards, not just in new construction but in existing housing stock would be a start. And by that I mean significantly going beyond the existing minimum standards recommended at European Union level. But our public buildings, including schools and hospitals, must be included in this expanded nationwide programme.

The full interconnection of the Irish electricity grid with our near neighbours must be advanced and speeded up so as to maximise the gains that can be had from such a connection. This should be part of a European wide effective integration of the continental electricity grid. Why can't Norwegian hydro power heat Spanish homes in the winter while Greek solar panels could provide the electricity necessary for air conditioning in Poland during its torrid summers?

Conclusion

Energy is but one issue that is a reality for all of the citizens of Europe. But it is not the only one. The majority of our European policy initiatives must be to incorporate those common sense concerns into an agenda for action which the public understand and support. Furthermore, they know instinctively that the nation state, acting on its own, cannot solve the problem. No matter how large France is or how insular Ireland is, neither country's government can begin to successfully confront these issues acting nationally. That was also the conclusion which led to the Coal and Steel Community in 1950. The ratification of the Reform Treaty will give all of the member states and the institutions of the European Union the necessary decision making powers to get on with the job.

> The full interconnection of the Irish electricity grid with our near neighbours must be advanced and speeded up so as to maximise the gains that can be had from such a connection. This should be part of a European wide effective integration of the continental electricity grid. Why can't Norwegian hydro power heat Spanish homes in the winter while Greek solar panels could provide the electricity necessary for air conditioning in Poland during its torrid summers?

Prof Brigid Laffan

Principal of the College of Human Sciences, UCD

Born in Caherciveen, Co. Kerry. Educated at Presentation Convent, Caherciveen, Univ. of Limerick (BCS), TCD (PhD) and the College of Europe in Bruges (Diplome de Hautes Etudes Européennes). Jean Monnet Professor of European Politics, UCD 1991-2004. Was the founding Director of the Dublin European Institute in UCD in 1999. She was appointed Principal of the College of Human Sciences UCD in 2004. She is a member of the Research Council of the European University in Florence, the National Economic & Social Council (NESC) and the Irish Govt.'s Asia Strategy Group. She is author of Integration and Co-operation in Europe *(1992),* The Finances of the Union *(1997) and has published extensively on the dynamic of European integration.*

Legitimising the EU and Its Policies is a Core Challenge

Challenges to the European Union

The 25-year-period 1985 to 2010 is a critical phase of European integration characterised by a step-change in the political, economic and social scope of the Union. Beginning with the single market project, deepened by the establishment of the euro and the enlargement of the structural funds, the economic and regulatory reach of the Union expanded significantly and made the Union a more important actor in and for the member states. Deepening of the scope of integration was accompanied by the most dramatic widening of the Union in its history. The collapse of the Cold War order in Europe brought enlargement to the top of the Union agenda for the 1990s and the first decade of the twenty-first century. The enlargement to 25 states in 2004 and 27 in 2007 fundamentally altered the geographical reach of the Union and transformed the scale of the Union. The two interacting processes of deepening and widening took place against the backdrop of changing dynamics in the wider world. The rise of China and India introduced new forces to global geo-economics and 9/11 altered the security challenges facing the world. From 1985 onwards, the Union engaged in a process of treaty change in an effort to build the constitutional and institutional framework to cope with the pressures of market creation, global competitiveness, enlargement and the expectation that Europe would play an increasing role in the world. The Reform Treaty is the latest and perhaps the last in this

The collapse of the Cold War order in Europe brought enlargement to the top of the Union agenda for the 1990s and the first decade of the twenty-first century. The enlargement to 25 states in 2004 and 27 in 2007 fundamentally altered the geographical reach of the Union and transformed the scale of the Union.

phase of constitution-building in the Union. The reason why much political and official time has been invested in treaty change over the last 25 years is that, in the Union, what the EU does is always bound up with how it does its business. Because the end goal of integration has not and cannot be agreed, the member States opted for further negotiations about how it should develop. The political energies and costs associated with treaty change have been rising, and it could well be that the Reform Treaty will mark the end of a 25 year process of treaty making in the Union.

Among the many challenges facing the European Union, I would like to draw attention to three ties and tensions that have run through integration from the outset. These are (1) the ties and tensions between states and markets, (2) the ties and tensions between the EU as a problem solving entity and a polity and (3) the ties but also tensions between Europe and the outside world.

1: States and Markets

From the outset, the EU was designed to act as a force of economic liberalisation by creating a market that eliminated the barriers to trade and other economic activities among the member states. The limits of market creation were evident in the early 1980s as barriers continue to impede economic performance in Europe. The single market signalled a step change in the scope and ambition of market creation and, although it is a continuing process, market creation was largely completed for goods and services. The single market was underpinned by the euro in those countries that opted to join. Market integration in the Union was always accompanied by side-payments and compensatory measures, notably the CAP, the social fund and the later structural funds.

The Union faces renewed challenges concerning the balance between states and markets or public and private power. The rise of China, India and enlargement to the east have introduced new competitiveness pressures to the European economy. The Lisbon process, launched in 2000, was designed to promote economic reform in Europe. Its impact and outputs have been mixed. The old debates between those states committed to liberalisation and those who want Europe to act as a buffer vis a vis globalisation have re-emerged. President Sarkozy used the opportunity of the treaty discussions to signal France's interest in deploying the EU as a buffer against globalisation. His desire to weaken the reference to competitiveness in the Reform Treaty may well be an exercise in symbolic politics or it may signal the beginning of a political drive to limit market creation in the EU. The services directive was widely seen as a contributing

Because the end goal of integration has not and cannot be agreed, the member States opted for further negotiations about how it should develop. The political energies and costs associated with treaty change have been rising, and it could well be that the Reform Treaty will mark the end of a 25 year process of treaty making in the Union.

factor to the "no" vote in the French referendum. The discussion on the balance between states and markets relates also to a discussion on Social Europe and the role of the EU in the social sphere. The diversity of levels of economic wealth and the diversity of domestic welfare systems militates against a strong role of the EU in the social sphere. To date, it has been limited to social regulation, a number of budgetary instruments and the wider impact of integration on fiscal systems in the member states. It is likely that the role of the Union will remain predominantly in the sphere of social regulation but the issues of taxation will, in the longer term, also have a major impact on domestic welfare systems.

2: Problem Solving and Polity

The French and Dutch "no" votes to the Constitutional Treaty are but the most recent manifestations of a changing dynamic in European public opinion about integration. Legitimising the EU and its policy range is a core challenge for the Union. There is extensive academic debate about the democratic deficit and politicisation in and of the EU but little agreement about what should be done.

The EU was and continues to be driven by a strong functional dynamic, responding to issues (for example food safety) as they arise on the agenda either at global, EU or domestic level. EU policies, programmes and instruments are moulded by the problems that they are designed to address. The EU was and continues to act as a problem solving arena for its member states. However, the expansion in the reach and salience of integration has meant that the EU has moved well beyond a problem solving entity and is now a polity or political system, however distinctive, in its own right. Treaty change, enlargement, the expansion in the scope and reach of European regulation and the continuing debate about the "Future of Europe" have politicised integration in the member states. There is far more contention about "Europe" than ever before and resistance to further integration from a variety of political forces. The French and Dutch "no" votes to the Constitutional Treaty are but the most recent manifestations of a changing dynamic in European public opinion about integration. Legitimising the EU and its policy range is a core challenge for the Union. There is extensive academic debate about the democratic deficit and politicisation in and of the EU but little agreement about what should be done.

3: Europe and the Wider World

Global geopolitics and geo-economics have played a central role in the dynamic of the EU from the outset. The role of the US, the Cold War and the end of the period of European imperialism were fundamental to the establishment and evolution of the Union. However, the boundaries between the EU and the outside world and the pressures of globalisation have reinforced the impact of the Union's external environment on its development. There is considerable pressure on the EU to become a more strategic actor in the international environment, to project its power and to attempt to influence external events. The relationship with Russia, the Middle East, Trans-Atlantic relations, Africa, China and the other emerging economic powers in Asia are crucial to the future of the Union. The boundaries of the Union and the relationship between the EU and its external environment are mediated by the politics of enlargement and the question of Europe's borders. Given that this phase of globalisation is not Eurocentric or driven by Europe, the states of the EU face the challenge of mediating with global forces and rapidly changing geo-politics and geo-economics. The what to do about Russia, Turkey, Trans-Atlantic relations, the Middle East, Africa, and the emerging markets are all pressing. The member states differ in their preferences and policies in relation to many of these issues but "European" discussion is required concerning the global trajectory of this small continent.

Ireland in its European and Global Context

This year marks 35 years of Ireland's membership of the EU. Ireland as a member state in 2007 is a very different state, society and economy to the relatively poor and peripheral state that joined in 1973. Then, membership of the EU was a project for Ireland's future and a framework for economic and social modernisation. It was also a framework for Ireland's relations with the wider world and for managing the dynamics of British-Irish relations and communal conflict in Northern Ireland. The transformation of Ireland from small peripheral and poorer state in the EU into a "model" was highlighted by the success of the Presidency in 2004, particularly the accession of 10 new states and agreement on the Constitutional Treaty. Ireland had come of age as a member of the Union. The Programme for Government states that "The EU was a key catalyst in Ireland's economic and social transformation" (Programme for Government, 2007, 46) and there is a commitment to engaging with the EU in a manner that makes Ireland and the Union stronger. What are the key priorities for the next five years?

> The transformation of Ireland from small peripheral and poorer state in the EU into a "model" was highlighted by the success of the Presidency in 2004, particularly the accession of 10 new states and agreement on the Constitutional Treaty. Ireland had come of age as a member of the Union.

1. **An effectively functioning Union**: Ireland like all small states has an interest in ensuring that the EU continues to function in a manner that enables it respond to the challenges it faces. Following the failure of the Constitutional Treaty, the completion of the IGC and subsequent ratification by the member states is a priority. Although considerable agreement was reached at the June 2007 Brussels Summit, there are difficulties remaining among the member states. That said, the Union cannot afford a long-drawn out discussion of issues that have been rehearsed many times be-

fore. The subsequent ratification challenge in the member states including Ireland should not be underestimated. Following the French and Dutch "no's", a referendum will require considerable political commitment from the Government to ensure that the electorate is au fait with the broad parameters of the treaty and its meaning to Ireland. The campaign must be more like Nice II rather than Nice I.

2. **Effective Engagement by Ireland in the Union**: The expansion of the Union to 27 states and the consequent transformation in scale makes it more difficult for all small states to ensure voice and presence. Managing scale is now an imperative for all states in the Union. Bilateral relations have become more important as has tracking dossiers as they are prepared in the Commission. By the time a proposal comes fully formed from the Commission into the Council, it is too late. Ireland's management of European business at home must be the subject of periodic review both in terms of substance and process.

3. **Maintaining Domestic Headroom and Identifying Priorities**: Only if 1 and 2 are achieved, will it be possible to track European developments in a way that allows Irish preferences to be promoted and, where necessary, protected. Ireland, as a net contributor, should champion the new member states because economic catch-up in East Central Europe is good for that part of the continent and for the Union. The further reform of the budget is a major issue on the Union's agenda. Here, the challenge facing Ireland is to move beyond its position as a key member of the CAP supporters' club. Managing the dossier on fiscal policy, particularly corporation policy, will prove difficult as tax competition is regarded in many member states as a challenge to national exchequers and welfare systems.

> Ireland, as a net contributor, should champion the new member states because economic catch-up in East Central Europe is good for that part of the continent and for the Union. The further reform of the budget is a major issue on the Union's agenda.

4. **Addressing the Triple Lock**: The triple lock requires a decision by the Irish Government, Oireachtas and a UN resolution before the state will commit troops to peacekeeping or conflict resolution situations. The latter provision is a major problem if a member or members of the Security Council block resolutions. In relation to Macedonia, a Chinese veto prevented agreement on a resolution and hence the Chinese effectively had the last say on the deployment of Irish troops. The law should be amended to allow for a situation where a UN resolution is impossible. The existence of the triple lock also impacts adversely on Ireland's engagement with the Nordic Battle Group. A motion in favour of Irish involvement with the Nordic battle group was passed by the Dáil in April 2007. However, the other members of the group will only assign periph-

eral and limited duties to Irish troops because of the uncertainty caused by the triple lock. This is a great disservice to the Irish Defence forces and the experience they have gained in a myriad of peacekeeping operations.

5. **Ireland beyond Europe**: The Union is an important framework for Ireland's engagement with the world but not the only one. Ireland is now well placed to project itself as a small but significant player in global geopolitics and geo-economics. Ireland's relations with the emerging markets in Asia and Latin America require sustained attention. The commitment to quadruple Irish Aid by 2012 is a major commitment to addressing inequality and problems of development in Africa and elsewhere. Ireland needs to gear up its intellectual capital and instruments to ensure that the increase in aid expenditure actually makes a difference. Ireland's experience of conflict management and conflict resolution provides us with considerable experience that is in short supply in the wider world. The commitment to making conflict resolution a major component of Irish foreign policy is to be welcomed. It brings a distinctiveness to Irish foreign policy.

6. **Interrogating Ireland's Recent Experience**: Traditionally interest in Ireland and things Irish was the result of the development of modern Irish nationalism, the cultural revival of the late 19th century, the foundation of the state and the richness of Irish literature. Irish Studies focused on history and literature by and large. What makes Ireland interesting today? Ireland is a laboratory of rapid economic, technological, social and cultural change. The transition from poor and peripheral to wealthy was rapid. So, too, was the transition from a country of emigration to immigration, from high unemployment to very low levels of unemployment. This has been matched by the increasing urbanisation, the transformation of rural Ireland and the extensive development of fringe areas between the urban and rural. Ireland over the last 15 years has experienced a very intensive process of globalisation. This experience needs to be understood not only from an Irish perspective but is of more general interest as states and societies throughout the world grapple with the dynamics of internationalisation.

Ireland's experience of conflict management and conflict resolution provides us with considerable experience that is in short supply in the wider world. The commitment to making conflict resolution a major component of Irish foreign policy is to be welcomed. It brings a distinctiveness to Irish foreign policy.

The Four Donegal Tenors

A thoughtful Brian Friel at one of the sessions